Y0-CUW-556

Discovery
Writing to Learn

Bruce H. Leland
Western Illinois University

*With the staff of the
WIU Writing Program*

 **KENDALL/HUNT PUBLISHING COMPANY**
2460 Kerper Boulevard   P.O. Box 539   Dubuque, Iowa 52004-0539

Illustrations by Jennie C. Trias, Dan Baldwin & Sulah Robinson

Copyright © 1990 by Kendall/Hunt Publishing Company

ISBN 0-8403-5985-3

All rights reserved. No part of this publication may be reproduced, stored in a retrieval system, or transmitted, in any form or by any means, electronic, mechanical, photocopying, recording, or otherwise, without the prior written permission of the copyright owner.

Printed in the United States of America
10 9 8 7 6 5 4 3 2 1

Contents

List of Readings, v
Acknowledgments, vii
Introduction, ix

Chapter One	**DISCOVERING WRITING**	**1**
	Attitudes and expectations	
Chapter Two	**THE COMPUTER AS A WRITING TOOL**	**9**
	Using WordPerfect	
Chapter Three	**WRITING TO DISCOVER**	**29**
	The writing processes	
Chapter Four	**DISCOVERING EXPERIENCE**	**41**
	Using writing to discover patterns and significances in experience	
Chapter Five	**DISCOVERING AMBIGUITY**	**61**
	Writing a meditation	
Chapter Six	**DISCOVERING DIVERSITY**	**81**
	Recording another person's experience	
Chapter Seven	**DISCOVERING INFORMATION**	**111**
	Finding and reporting information	

Chapter Eight	**INTERLUDE: WRITING ESSAY EXAMS** 149
	Techniques for tests
Chapter Nine	**DISCOVERING VALUES** 155
	Using writing to explore ethical issues
Chapter Ten	**DISCOVERING WRITING AGAIN** 191
	Exploring discoveries about writing and the writing process
Appendix One:	*Thirty-Seven Things to Write About in a Journal* 193
Appendix Two:	*More on the Writing Process* 197
Appendix Three:	*Additional Writing Assignments* 207
Appendix Four:	*Guides for Groups* 211
Appendix Five:	*Advanced WordPerfect Commands* 217
Appendix Six:	*Additional Readings* 227

Index, 271

List of Readings

Baker, Russell, "The Wonders of Writing on a Computer" **235**
Bambara, Toni Cade, "The Lesson" **178**
Charters, Brian, "Form and Content" **3**
Clemons, Rick, "The Western Illinois University Library" **128**
Cording, Sue, "August 28—A Meditation" **68**
Cosby, Bill, "Turn That Crap Down" **228**
Courter, Jim, "It's All in the Jeans" **240**
Courter, Jim, "Opening the Tap" **6**
Crouse, Darby, "Theatre at Its Best" **120**
Donley, Gregory, "A Visit from my Grandfather" **48**
Eberle, Judy, "To Spank or Not to Spank: A Question for Everyone Who Likes Kids" **124**
Etter, Dave, "Postcard to Florida" **144**
Fay, Steve, "The Drought Grapes" **263**
Frost, Robert, "The Road Not Taken" **176**
Fulghum, Robert, "Mushrooms" **268**
Gould, Stephen Jay, "Darwin's Delay" **138**
Habib, Siraj, "It Doesn't Only Happen in America" **105**
Hallwas, John, "The Return of the Hero" **172**
Harlan, Mary, "41 Phone Book Names, Benicia, California" **82**
Jackson, David, "The Grate" **230**
Jacobus, Kris, "Begin at the Beginning" **18**
Jow, Ebrima A., "The School Day" **255**
Larkin, Phillip, "Church Going" **66**
Larkin, Phillip, "Reasons for Attendance" **65**
Leonard, John, "Nausea in the Afternoon" **261**
Lopez, Rose, "Promoting Hispanic Culture" **114**
Mairs, Nancy, "On Being a Cripple" **242**
Manon, Carshon, "Blackie's Death" **44**
Mayhew, Henry, "I'm Used to It" **85**
Meredith, Diana, "Covering Campus Tragedy" **259**
Murray, Toss, "A Writing Process" **33**

Norton, Kay, "Holiday Shoplifting Carries Big Price Tag" **115**
Singer, Peter, "About Ethics" **158**
Sudgen, Faye, "Table Talk" **238**
Terkel, Studs, "The Mason: Carl Murray Bates" **89**
Terkel, Studs, "Telephone Operator: Heather Lamb" **94**
Terkel, Studs, "Gravedigger: Elmer Ruiz" **99**
Toth, Susan Allen, "Christmas Vacation" **51**
Villanueva, Yolanda, "What's Important" **4**
Walker, Alice, "Brothers and Sisters" **231**
White, E. B., "Once More to the Lake" **70**
Zinsser, William, "Gutenberg Was Through" **10**

Acknowledgments

Instead of either a self-congratulatory preface or an introductory essay addressed to teachers, an expression of thanks is the only suitable beginning. The preparation of this text has been a collaborative project of the WIU Writing Program. Many faculty members, teaching assistants, and students have made significant contributions, sometimes without realizing it. I am deeply grateful to them all. I want to take advantage of the opportunity I have here to recognize and thank several of the people who have contributed most actively to the project. First, I need to offer particular thanks to David Jackson, who served an undergraduate internship as my editorial assistant; to Jennie Trias for her illustrations and Dan Baldwin for his diagrams; to Ann Robinson for her cover painting; and to Kris Jacobus and Rick Clemons, who contributed portions of the text. In addition, Judi Hardin and Mitzae Mullins provided invaluable assistance by typing, copy-editing, tracking permissions, and cheering me on.

I would also like to acknowledge the work of the English Department's Writing Committee, whose members over the past two years have included Carl Bean, Judy Brown, Kathleen Brown-Johnson, Jane Claspy, Steve Fay, Teri Faulkner, Kris Jacobus, Joan Livingston-Webber, Sue Mayer, Ann Robinson, and Randy Smith. These committee members assisted with curriculum design, participated in brainstorming sessions, suggested readings and exercises, and responded to drafts of chapters. This project would have been impossible without their help and support. Others who offered suggestions and advice include Noel Berkey, Toni Boyd, Jim Courter, Linda Eicken, D. J. Faries, David Haney, Jerry Hansen, Iris Keller, Victor Kemper, Hallie Lemon, Barbara Myers, Sean O'Donnell, and Ron Walker. To those I may have omitted from this list, my apologies. Only partial amends can be provided by repeating my thanks to the entire English department for their help and their support.

Thanks are also due to the students in my writing classes, whose responses and advice helped me to refine many of the exercises included here, as well as to all of the students who gave me permission to reproduce their essays in the text. Thanks, too, to Eileen Leland, who provided encouragement and support throughout the writing process.

Finally, I must acknowledge the continued influence that countless teachers, colleagues, theorists, practitioners, and authors have had on this text. In particular, the work of Donald Murray, Ken Macrorie, James Kinneavy, William Perry, Janice N. Hays, Rise B. Axelrod and Charles R. Cooper, Kenneth Bruffee, Elizabeth Cowan Neeld, Patrick Hartwell, Donald Stewart, and Dorothy U. Seyler has had an identifiable influence. To them, and to others whose influence is so pervasive that it is no longer recognized, my thanks.

Bruce H. Leland
Macomb, Illinois

Introduction

There are a great many textbooks available for use in college composition courses, and dozens of new books are published each year. Why, then, did the faculty at WIU feel the need to compose their own text?

When we designed English 180 we examined the published texts and discovered that almost all were directed to an inappropriate audience: They were written for composition teachers rather than composition students. They gave logical, teachable order to the insights about writing that we teachers had already discovered, but they did not give readers the opportunity to discover the writing process for themselves.

That seemed an important error. We wanted less a book of rules or advice, and more of a text which invited the active participation of the readers. So we adopted the alternative of writing our own book for the new course. Beginning with the course description and drawing on several theories of how writing works, we worked together to develop course materials. The resulting text is, therefore, a collaborative effort, with contributions from many members of WIU's writing staff. In addition, students in the English department, both graduates and undergraduates, as well as several freshman composition students have made major contributions. The names of some of these collaborators are noted in the acknowledgements. Ultimately, however, one person took on the primary authorial responsibilities, and at this point that authorial voice (the "I" you will encounter throughout this book) will take over.

The Uses of This Book

I want first of all to let you know what you can expect. As a student in English 180 you will be invited to make your own discoveries about writing, using this text as your guide. Most significantly, you will have opportunity to discover the way writing works *for you*. You will find your own writing process for yourself, and then (I hope) learn ways to make that process more effective. Furthermore, you will have a chance to discover how your writing process can help you to clarify what you already know and then to discover new ideas. The specific writing exercises, which form the heart of the text, are designed to lead you to these discoveries.

The exercises include assignments which explore your memories and lead to the discovery of the meanings you construct from experience. You'll also examine the meanings that other people have developed from their different experience. Other assignments will invite you to reach conclusions after considering an ambiguous issue and to make discoveries about your personal values. The text will also help you discover ways that you can use writing in college classes to help you learn.

Contained within the text is a selection of essays. These essays will invite you to think about your own experience and they may also stimulate some discussion. A significant part of your reading for the course, however, will be the writing that you and the rest of the class will produce. You will write on a number of subjects this semester, and much of your writing will be read by other members of the class. As you discover what you know about yourself and about others, you will have a chance to share these discoveries with others and, in the process, discover how writing can best work for you.

Envoi

Reading a book about writing in order to learn how to write is sort of like reading a book about cars in order to learn how to drive. To be sure, a book can give you some useful information. In fact, most driver's education courses do have a textbook. But no one expects to be able to read a book and then get into a car and drive. (This comparison between learning to write and learning to drive is one that I will return to from time to time. If it seems more useful for you, you can substitute learning to play the piano or learning to play tennis.)

We learn how to drive (or play the piano or play tennis) by doing it, not by reading about it. So you should be suspicious of any book that tells you it will teach you how to write—including this one. The best any book can do is try to offer some direction, provide some information, and inspire you to give it a try. Any learning that you do will come not from the text, but from your practice and from your interaction with your teacher and other students in the class.

In other words, you are active participants in the learning process this semester. You will be asked to write frequently, revise often, participate in class discussion, work in small groups, and record your growing insights. And so let's begin:

Chapter **1**

Discovering Writing

I

Let's start with a writing assignment. Take about a half an hour to write your response to this question:

> What is more important in writing: what you have to say or the way that you say it?

Feel free to draw on your own past experience with reading and writing, both in school and out, as well as what you've been told by teachers. Try to illustrate your answer with some specific examples.

II

Since you're taking a writing course, I thought it would be best to start by writing. You'll be doing a lot of that throughout the semester. I also wanted to give you an opportunity right at the start to discover what you already know about the subject of the course.

As you wrote this first assignment I hope you discovered that you, in fact, do know quite a bit about writing. At the very least you have some ideas or opinions or attitudes about what's important in a piece of writing. These ideas have probably been accumulating ever since the first time a teacher or a parent asked you to write a sentence, or a story, or a letter; maybe since the first time someone read you a story.

Till now you may not have paid much attention to this accumulation of knowledge and attitudes. Most of us, most of the time, approach writing as a job to be done, not a subject to think about. In many ways it's like driving a car. Usually we just do it. For example, when there's a left turn ahead, the hand moves almost automatically to the signal lever. Faced with a broken lever, however, we have to become self-conscious about what we're doing and work to recall the appropriate hand signals. Alternatively, when we're trying to learn a new technique (like driving a stick shift), we can again discover that it helps to remember what we already know in order to apply it to the new situation.

This semester you'll be asked to explore some of your current insights into the act of writing. That self-awareness will help you appreciate your accomplishments, deal with any problems that need to be fixed, and apply your knowledge to new situations. I'm hoping that as you come to better understand what you do and what you know, you'll be able to become more proficient and confident as a writer.

Notice that I've put a lot of emphasis on *your* ideas and attitudes, not mine, and not your teacher's. Of course your teacher and I both have our own ideas, and from time to time we'll share them with you. But we won't be giving you a lot of our own rules. Most "right answers" about writing skills are not dictated by higher authorities. Rather, they start first in each writer's personal experience; then as one writer shares those experiences with others, some consensus may begin to emerge. What "right answers" we have about writing have grown from agreements reached by groups of writers bringing their own ideas and expectations together to discover what they value in common. Your class is one such group of writers, and you can begin now to take the first step toward discovering consensus.

III

Here are the essays that two WIU freshman wrote on the first day of class in response to the question about form and content:

Form and Content
Brian Charters

When it comes down to it, what you have to say and how you say it are both vital parts of an essay or speech. Your topic should be one that the audience can be interested in, though if it's not, you can still make the audience become interested. In that case how you express yourself is of the utmost importance.

For example, if you have a topic like "How to Breed Corn" and your audience is a group of businessmen from Chicago, you are going to have to make the speech successful by being lively and dramatic. You will need to use the language the audience is familiar with, explain your points in business terms, and relate your topic as much as possible to their profession.

On the other hand, you could talk about something that a certain group wants to know about, such as a presentation to a group of reporters about what the president is doing, and still make it dull by being simplistic, quiet, or uninterested.

When preparing for communication (either written or oral) you should always spend some time choosing a topic and collecting all the facts. However, most of the time should be spent on putting it together, choosing words and phrases your audience knows, using interesting and understandable examples, and creating a clear order for your ideas.

Once back in tenth grade I was gathering facts on nuclear reactors for a speech. A lot of the words I was going to use named parts of these machines which a majority of my audience had never head of. So, as I was putting this paper together, I realized much more of my own input was going to be needed to keep my audience interested. I made out clear definitions of all the technical words and gave them to my audience. I worked to make it as easy to understand as I could, while still keeping it as dramatic as possible. After everything was over and done, I got an "A" on the paper, and according to my peers the speech was a great success.

Reprinted with permission of the author.

What's Important
Yolanda Villanueva

What you have to say may be important to you, but is it interesting enough to keep your audience's attention? If listeners are not interested in the topic being discussed, they tend to quickly lose attention. In order to keep our listeners interested, we, as speakers, have to find new ways to keep our audience's attention. This is why I, when speaking, tend to add a little of myself to my speech.

For instance, at freshman orientation, we were all asked the same questions: our name, where we were from, our year at Western. If I were to simply say, "My name is Yolanda, I'm from Burbank, and I'm a freshman," people might respond with "Big deal." Or else "Where the heck is Burbank?" Or maybe "Yo . . . Yop . . . What did she say?"

Perhaps it would be easier to keep my audience's attention by saying exactly where Burbank is, or giving them some background about the town. Or if you have an unusual name, like I do, you could repeat it, or make a joke about it, or explain its origin. For example, maybe your mom named you after she saw a particular movie—like my mom did. She named me after the character Yolanda in her favorite movie, *The Wise Indian Princess*.

In my opinion, in order to keep your audience's attention, the manner in which you say something and what you have to say are equally important, in both speaking and writing.

Your next task is to try to find out what agreement you can reach with other writers about the things that are important in writing. I think this quest for consensus can be accomplished most effectively if you work with three or four classmates in small groups. You can explain your answer to the initial question to the others in the group. Then together you can explore the ideas you have in common with one another or with the two essays you just read. Note, at the same time, the ways that you differ. Your group will certainly disagree about some points and your individual conclusions will remain your own; nevertheless there will be several points on which you can all

Reprinted with permission of the author.

agree. Keep track of these. They're important. You'll be working all semester to add to this list of consensus points (a page of your journal may be a good place for this list).

IV

Journal? What journal? Read on.

On Keeping a Journal

A journal is part of the basic equipment of many professional writers. Poets often carry notebooks in which they can write down ideas, images, even pleasant-sounding phrases as they occur to them. William Butler Yeats used a journal to write out prose versions of his poems, which he could then work through to turn into poetry line by line. Another example is Gwendolyn Brooks, who, in one of her recent visits to Western, described the importance of her journal for

her work. Novelists and playwrights also use journals, often to record plot ideas and write down bits of conversation they overhear. And essayists, such as Henry David Thoreau, have used ideas collected in journals as the basis for their essays.

Creating a sourcebook for future writing is one important purpose for keeping a journal. Even if a particular journal entry isn't of immediate use, it stays there, available whenever it might be needed. With a journal you need never face the despair of knowing the brilliant idea you had yesterday (or last month) is lost forever. Further, the journal allows you to explore those ideas in a non-threatening setting. No one is going to argue with you. No one will laugh if your exploration leads to a dead end. No one will sneer if you sound naive or inexperienced.

But perhaps you don't, at the moment, plan any future writing beyond what this course will require. No matter. Your journal will still be important. Some of the ideas you will explore there will likely be attempts to make sense of your experience. Quite apart from any value as a source for writing, a journal is extremely valuable as a way to make connections, to struggle with fears and doubts, to discover recurring patterns of behavior, or to face unresolved issues from the past. It is a way to use writing to discover truths about ourselves.

And, finally, it is a way, in this class, to keep track of your growth as a writer. You can record initial ideas for paper assignments, difficulties (and successes) you encounter while writing, feelings about completed assignments, techniques learned as a result of a particular writing experience, or reactions to your instructor's comments.

Here, now, is another perspective, a short essay by Jim Courter, who is a free-lance author as well as a writing instructor at Western:

Opening the Tap

Jim Courter

Why keep a journal? Before you answer, "Because the teacher says I have to," or "Because it's part of my grade," consider this.

Reprinted with permission of the author.

Journal writing, properly approached, releases something, gives you access to a source inside you that you may not know exists. It's a little like turning on a faucet, an everyday occurrence we all take for granted. But did you ever consider that water is coming through pipes in your house which are fed by lines coming in from the street which ultimately lead back to the water tower? And that tower draws on some greater source, *out there* somewhere, a river or a lake or a reservoir, which in turn—who knows—may ultimately connect up to the great watery continuum that covers three-quarters of the globe?

In the case of journaling, though, you are able, in that fine phrase of Dorthea Brande's, "to hitch your unconscious mind to your writing arm," to tap your deep self, a source in its way more rich and diverse and powerful and teeming than all the oceans and seas combined.

And what is the value of that? You might as well ask what value your dreams have. All *they* do is keep you sane by venting things that would otherwise build up inside of you and either explode or poison your system.

So go ahead—open the tap, let it flow. You'll be healthier for it in ways that have nothing to do with grades.

You can begin your journal with the list of ideas your group reached consensus on. And while you're at it, you might note your reaction to the experience of working in the group. How did you go about solving the problem you were given? How did you negotiate to reach agreement? How did the members of the group get along with one another? Do you remember the names of the people in your group?

From time to time in the remaining chapters of this text I'll make suggestions for journal entries, and your instructor will no doubt make additional journal assignments. But the primary source of ideas for journal writing is within you, or, if you need some extra inspiration, in Appendix One of this text. You'll notice, by the way, that I have made liberal use of appendices as repositories for ideas, information, and readings which would otherwise clutter the text. Use them.

V

After that interlude, it's time to write again:

> Drawing on your class discussion and the points the group reached agreement on, as well as on your experience and your thinking, what do you believe is more important in a piece of writing: what you have to say or the way that you say it?

If it were clear in my mind, I should have no incentive or need to write about it. . . . We do not write in order to be understood; we write in order to understand.

C. Day Lewis

Chapter **2**

The Computer as a Writing Tool

I

Chapter Three will pick up on the work you just completed in Chapter One. In that chapter, however, you'll be asked to produce a piece of writing on the computer. So before we go on, we'll pause to practice some techniques for writing with a computer.

For some of you this will be a familiar activity; for others it will be a challenge you've been looking forward to; and for quite a few it will be about as welcome as major surgery. So I've decided to start this chapter with an essay by William Zinsser. Actually, it's the first part of his book, *Writing With a Word Processor,* in which he explains how he overcame his doubts about computers. I recommend the whole book, but here I'm just reproducing the part about his initial resistance. If you're feeling fearful about this part of the course, the essay may prove reassuring. Otherwise, just enjoy it.

Excerpts from WRITING WITH A WORD PROCESSOR by William Zinsser. Copyright © 1983 by the author. Reprinted by permission of Harper & Row, Publishers, Inc.

Gutenberg was Through
William Zinsser

1.

I first realized that the act of writing was about to enter a new era five years ago when I went to see an editor at *The New York Times*. As I was ushered through the vast city room I felt that I had strayed into the wrong office. The place was clean and carpeted and quiet. As I passed long rows of desks I saw that almost every desk had its own computer terminal and its own solemn occupant—a man or a woman typing at the computer keyboard or reading what was on the terminal screen. I saw no typewriters, no paper, no mess. It was a cool and sterile environment; the drones at their machines could have been processing insurance claims or tracking a spacecraft in orbit. What they didn't look like were newspaper people, and what the place didn't look like was a newspaper office.

I knew how a newspaper office should look and sound and smell—I worked in one for thirteen years. The paper was the *New York Herald Tribune,* and its city room, wide as a city block, was dirty and disheveled. Reporters wrote on ancient typewriters that filled the air with clatter; copy editors labored on coffee-stained desks over what the reporters had written. Crumpled balls of paper littered the floor and filled the wastebaskets—failed efforts to write a good lead or a decent sentence. The walls were grimy—every few years they were painted over in a less restful shade of eye-rest green—and the atmosphere was hazy with the smoke of cigarettes and cigars. At the very center the city editor, a giant named L. L. Engelking, bellowed his displeasure with the day's work, his voice a rumbling volcano in our lives. I thought it was the most beautiful place in the world.

I had always wanted to be a newspaperman, and the *Herald Tribune* was the newspaper I wanted to be a man on. As a boy I had been reared on the *"Trib,"* and its Bodoni Bold headlines and beautiful makeup fixed themselves early in my mind as exactly how a newspaper should present itself to the world. The same mixture of craftsmanship and warmth ran through the writing. A *Herald Tribune* story always had some extra dimension of humor or humanity, or surprise, or graceful execution, that didn't turn up in other papers. The people who put this paper together obviously worked with care and loved the work. My dream was to be one of them.

As a teen-ager I wrote for the school newspaper and learned to set type at the local shop where the paper was printed. The afternoons I spent there were some of the happiest of my boyhood. I loved the smell of the ink and the clacking of the linotype machines. I liked being part of a physical process that took what I wrote and converted it into type and locked it in a frame and put it on a press and printed it for anybody to read. One Christmas I asked my parents for a printing press—a wish that they must have regretted granting, for it was installed in the attic, directly over their room, and the house shook at night with irregular thumps as I fed paper into the press and pulled its huge handle down. I bought books on type and studied the different typefaces, learning how type cutters and printers over the centuries had shaped the letters to achieve legibility and a certain emotional weight.

At college I was editor of a campus magazine, and I hung around the university press where it was composed and printed. I was hooked on a tradition. Even when I left college during World War II to enlist in the army I didn't escape the process of getting the day's events validated on paper. Colonel McCloskey, finding a captive writer (and a mere sergeant) in his midst, took no chance that his feats of command might go unrecorded. He commanded me to write the company history, and, sitting in a wintry tent in Italy with an old typewriter and a lot of paper, I did.

After the war when I went looking for a job I inevitably went looking at the *Herald Tribune,* and when I heard George Cornish, the managing editor, offering to hire me as a beginning reporter at forty-five dollars a week I considered myself as rich as Rockefeller. Well, almost. The paper in those first postwar years was a constellation of journalists at the top of their form. I still remember the routine excellence of the local reporters and foreign correspondents and the elegance of the critics and columnists: Virgil Thomson, Red Smith, Walter Lippmann and many others. It was a paper whose editors coveted good writing. Not only did they publish the best writers; they cultivated good writing in younger members of the staff by showing that they cared. Those older men who made us rewrite what we had written—and rewritten— weren't doing it only for our own good but for the honorableness of the craft. They were custodians of a trust.

Surrounded by veteran reporters, I studied their habits and was struck by their fierce pride. The *Herald Tribune* always had less money and a smaller staff than its august competitor, *The New York Times*. Nevertheless it was an article of faith that one *Trib* reporter could cover a story as well as the three *Times* reporters assigned to the same beat. Nobody exemplified this idea more than Peter Kihss, who was covering the newly established United Nations in New York. He wasn't just a member of the *Trib*'s United Nations bureau; he was the bureau, and every afternoon he came back staggering under heavy reports issued by the UN's burgeoning agencies and committees. He then sat down at his ancient typewriter, which he pounded with demonic speed, and wrote two or three articles that put into coherent form everything important that the UN had done that day. He was a man possessed by facts.

Though I didn't know it at the time, those years were the end of an era for the *Herald Tribune*. High costs and various other factors began to erode the paper's quality, and over the next decade the stars gradually left and went elsewhere, correctly sensing that the *Trib*'s sickness of body and soul would be terminal. Some reporters went over to *The New York Times,* including Peter Kihss, whose by-line continued to be a warranty of truth doggedly pursued.

When my own turn came to leave the *Herald Tribune*—I resigned to become a free-lance writer—I also took plenty of baggage along from my apprenticeship with editors and printers whose standards were high. I found that I was never quite satisfied with what I had written; I had a compulsion to rewrite, to polish, to cut, to start over. This meant that I not only did a lot of rewriting; I also did a lot of retyping. At the end of the day my wastebasket was full and my back and shoulders were stiff.

My family quite properly urged me to get an electric typewriter, and I tried one out. It drove me crazy. My touch was far too heavy from all the years of pummeling an Underwood; the electric typewriter, designed for gentler hands, kept putting spaces within the words as well as between the words. M y se nt e nces lo oke d some ething lik e th is, and I spent more time erasing— and swearing—than writing. I also didn't like the typewriter's steady hum; I hate unwanted noise, and I didn't want it as part of the writing process. The job is hard enough in silence.

But during the 1970s I began to realize that everything I knew about printing—the process of getting words on paper—was becoming obsolete. Gutenberg was through. His invention of movable type had changed the world and lasted five hundred years. Now nobody wanted Gutenberg's "hot type." The new thing was "cold type"—type that didn't exist as type at all, but only as an image on film. Magazine writers continued to write on a typewriter, but the person who "set" their articles no longer sat at a linotype machine. He sat at a keyboard that put the words on tape, and the tape somehow got converted into film. The proofs that came back from the printer no longer had the bite of type into paper; they looked like what they were—photographs of type. Something had been lost: the clean edge of letters, the age-old flavor of craft.

But a great deal had also been gained. With actual type eliminated, a whole series of cumbersome and expensive steps was bypassed: setting the type, arranging it in flat pages, and making curved plates from those pages that could be fastened into high-speed rotary presses. Just compose the type on film—call it "photocomposition"—and fasten the film to the presses. Eureka!

Still, I assumed that writers couldn't be plugged into this system. Writers were human—they couldn't be wired like machines. (This is not to say that some writers aren't very peculiarly wired.) And yet—portents were in the air. A few friends who worked for newspapers told me that their papers were "converting to terminals." What could that mean? It seemed to mean that writers could be plugged into the system after all. If typesetting could be done on film (saving the time and cost of setting real type), writing could be done on film (saving the time and cost of having someone retype on film what the reporter had written on paper). Just take the reporter's paper away and sit him down in front of a new kind of computer. Call it a word processor. Process that reporter's words right out of his brain and into an electronic circuit. Eureka again.

This was the new stage that journalism had reached when I went to see the *New York Times* editor in 1978. The paper had just completed a radical conversion of its plant: the editorial rooms had been torn apart to accommodate sophisticated new wiring and equipment. I had heard talk of the chaos that accompanied the change, but I hadn't really pictured what the new city room would look like. Maybe I didn't want to know. Now I knew. As I walked between the long rows of reporters at their silent terminals my journalistic past evaporated.

I asked the *Times* editor how the reporters were adjusting to the new procedure. He said that of course they all hated it at first, especially the older ones. They kicked and screamed and said they could never write on these terminals. But after a few weeks they began to feel comfortable, and now most of them said they never wanted to go back to a typewriter. He said the reporters really liked being able to instantly revise what they wrote, deleting or inserting or moving words and phrases and whole sentences and seeing their work always neat and tidy on the screen. He pointed out that not only were the writers doing their writing on the screen; that was also where the editors were editing all the copy. They summoned the reporters' articles on their screens, making their own changes, as editors will.

I wondered how this would affect the subtle relationship between writers and editors. I thought of all the times when a *Herald Tribune* editor brought over a piece of my copy to discuss changes he had made or wanted to make, and of all the times when I—as an editor or a teacher—had gone over my changes with a young writer or a student. To be apprenticed to a good editor is the best way to learn how to write. What would happen when all the editing was done on film by successive editors? Who would know who had done what? Who would remember what the original copy said? And who would be accountable for what had been changed? Nobody's handwriting—or fingerprints—would survive to tell the tale.

These were questions that I would want to know more about. But for the present I had seen enough of the future, and I started to leave. As I was walking back out of the city room my eye was caught by an unusual sight. In the middle of a row of desks with reporters working at terminals I saw one reporter writing on an old standard typewriter. He was a gray-haired man, obviously near retirement. Just as obviously he had rebelled against learning the new technology and had been granted special dispensation to stick with the venerable tools of his trade. I looked at him with sympathy and with a certain admiration: the last puritan, true to his values. The more I looked, the more familiar he seemed. There was something about the intensity with which he peered through his thick metal-framed glasses at what he was writing, something about the ferocious energy with which he attacked the typewriter keys. I had seen this reporter before.

Then I realized where I had seen him. It was Peter Kihss.

2.

The sight of Pete Kihss lingered with me. I identified with him more than I cared to admit. Just because America's newspapers were forcing their reporters and editors into electronic bondage for production reasons of their own, I as an individual writer didn't have to join the stampede. What set writers apart as individuals was their individuality. I had been getting along fine with my old Underwood, and I wasn't about to change.

But the notion of writers at their word processors started to tug at my consciousness. When I watched "Lou Grant" on television I no longer thought it was odd to see reporters writing at a terminal. And I began to see word processors in magazine layouts and Sunday newspaper sections devoted to home decoration. Designers were tastefully accommodating them in the study, where, only yesterday, nothing vulgar had been allowed to intrude on the quiet elegance of the antique desk, the leather-bound dictionary and the glass paperweight holding down the day's genteel mail.

I also began to hear about real authors writing real books on their own word processors. Jimmy Carter went home to Plains to write his memoirs on a word processor: the first President to go electronic. (If Lincoln had had one for the Gettysburg Address he probably would have deleted "Four score and seven years ago" and made it "87." Thank God he wrote the sonorous phrase by hand and didn't want to erase it.) Suddenly all the magazines were running cover stories about "the computer in your life." In only a few years, we were told, everybody in America would be sitting at the keyboard paying bills, instructing his bank and his broker, heating his home and pool, calculating his calories, playing the horses and presumably programming a satisfying sex life.

Meanwhile the word processor had invaded the American office, welcomed as a miraculous savior by every executive whose business required the same clusters of words to be neatly typed again and again. Law firms, for instance, with their long and lugubrious paragraphs of "boilerplate," could simply store these standardized blocks in the memory of the machine and call them up and insert them wherever they were needed. Architects started using the word processor for specifications, and doctors for medical reports.

It was also a Godsend for all the businesses that depend on correspondence with their customers—mail-order houses, for example, that receive a daily flood of special orders, queries and complaints. Now they could store all the paragraphs that answer all the routine queries (the item is out of stock, there will be a delay of several weeks, the product has been discontinued, we regret the inconvenience), plus the gracious opening and closing paragraphs that thank the customer for writing and for being such a faithful friend.

Clearly the day was not far off when vast numbers of Americans would be writing on word processors—not just "writers," but all the people who had to do any writing to transact the ordinary business of the day. This would be especially true as the nation's secretarial pool continued to dry up. Five years ago it was common for two middle managers to share a secretary; today the ratio is as high as fifteen to one. Good managers can no longer afford to wait for an available secretary to type a memo; they will write their memos on a word processor and transmit them instantly to the company's out-of-town offices, where other managers will read them on a terminal and answer them. Writing on a word processor, in short, would soon become second nature.

All this I began to know objectively. But subjectively it still didn't touch me. Word processors were what happened to somebody else.

Then, one day, my wife said, "You ought to write a book about how to write with a word processor."

"Who?" I said. "Me?"

II

Zinsser went on to learn to write with a word processor, and the rest of his book is the record of his experience. He admits his success at the end, when he reveals that his entire book was, in fact, composed at a computer.

In "Gutenberg Was Through" he notes some of the obvious advantages of word-processing: always having a clean copy to read, not needing to retype, being able to move text and make changes, becoming part of a communication system. Yet in spite of these advantages, he still initially resisted. He would not become converted to this new method until he had mastered it and experienced for himself the advantages (as well as the problems) it offered.

Accordingly, you too will now need to dive in and experience word processing for yourself.

III

The word processing program used at WIU is WordPerfect. If you already know WordPerfect, you'll be busy for the next few classes as a resource person, helping others to learn it. If you already know a different word processing program, you'll find that it's fairly easy to adapt to the new program. And if this is all new to you, hang on, pay close attention to your instructor, read this chapter carefully, practice as much as you can, and ask for help, either from others in the class or from a tutor in the University Writing Center.

(*A note to the WordPerfect pros who will be helping the rest of the class*: Be patient. Don't assume that things that are obvious to you are also obvious to everyone else. Encourage the novices to try things out for themselves. Answer questions, but don't take over the keyboard.)

The following introduction to WordPerfect is written to the novices. It takes you through some essential steps, starting with how to turn on the computer and leading you to the point of entering, saving, and printing your first text. It will be best to read the next few pages while sitting at a computer, following the instructions as they are given. You won't get it by reading about it. You need to do it.

Begin at the Beginning
Kris Jacobus

Booting the Program

With the start-up disk in the top drive (the top slot on the face of the computer), turn the computer and monitor on with the switches located at the back on the right hand side. A prompt (message) will appear on the screen asking for the date, followed by a blinking line, the cursor. This cursor is the position where any text you type will appear. Type in the current date using numbers and dashes (01-22-90), then press the ENTER key. Your screen will then ask the time. Enter the time using colons to separate the hour from the minutes (4:00); do not specify a.m. or p.m. Press the ENTER key. The next prompt will tell you to insert the WordPerfect disk into the top drive (A:) and your data disk into the bottom drive (B:). After both drives are ready, press any key to start (boot) the program. After just a moment you will be looking at a blank screen with a status line across the bottom and a blinking cursor at the top of the screen.

The Status Line

The status line indicates the current document number (Doc), the current page number (Pg), and the line number (Ln) of the cursor. The position indicator (Pos) shows the exact location of the cursor between the margins. Unless you change margin settings, the cursor position will range from the left margin setting of 10 to the right margin setting of 75. Move the cursor with the arrow keys on the right of the keyboard and watch the line and position indicators change.

The Cursor

The cursor moves as you type in text, or when you move it with the arrow keys. It has a number of uses; for example, the cursor can be used to insert text or to write over text. The insert key on the bottom of the numeric pad of keys on the right side of

Reprinted with permission of the author.

the keyboard is a toggle switch. Press the INS (insert) key one time, and the word "typeover" appears on the lower left side of the status line. Press the key again and "typeover" disappears. When the Insert key is toggled to typeover, the cursor will write over existing text, deleting text as you type. When the typeover option is off, the cursor will insert letters (words, sentences, etc.) at the cursor position. The remaining material will be moved ahead and realigned automatically by WordPerfect. This means that you can insert many paragraphs of text at the cursor position and not have to worry about retyping or reformatting the material that follows.

The Function Keys

WordPerfect is driven by a set of function keys (F1, F2, . . . F10) located on the left side of the keyboard. The keys are surrounded by a template to help you remember what each key can do. Since WordPerfect is capable of forty functions, each key must perform four separate functions. The F7 key, for instance, in conjunction with one other key, performs the functions: FOOTNOTE, PRINT, MATH/COLUMNS, EXIT. If the function is colored pink on the template, the CTRL key is held down while the F7 key is pressed once. If the function is colored green on the template, the SHIFT key is held down while the F7 key is pressed. If the function is colored blue, the ALT key is held down while the F7 key is pressed one time. If the function is white, the F7 key alone performs the function. As you can see, the template makes manipulating text easier, much like menus do on some menu-driven word processors. (For an explanation of every function on the keyboard, press the F3 key for HELP.)

Opening a File

To enter information in a file, simply type what you want onto the screen, using the keyboard as if it were a typewriter. The character that you type will appear at the position of the cursor. You need not press the Return (ENTER) key at the end of each line. WordPerfect will automatically align your text between the margins. This feature is called line wrap and is very helpful if you decide that you need to insert or delete any words. The program will realign every line of the paragraph. To end a paragraph,

20   *Discovery: Writing to Learn*

or to skip a line, just press the Return key. A hard return, signified by a triangle on the screen, will end the line each time the document is printed. In order to better understand this information, practice by typing the following material onto your blank screen (see the hints below).

NAME:
HOME ADDRESS:
HOME PHONE:
MACOMB ADDRESS:
MACOMB PHONE:
HOBBIES:
MY EXPECTATIONS FOR THIS CLASS:

Hints: Press the CAPS LOCK key to type in all capital letters. Press the ENTER key after each colon to end the line; then press it again to skip a line. Triangles (hard return symbols) will appear on the screen wherever you press the Return key. If you make a mistake, you can make corrections by using the backspace key (the arrow pointing left on the upper row of keys) to eliminate the errors to the left of the cursor. Retype the correct information. You may also use the DEL key to correct errors; this key deletes text both at the cursor and to the right for as long as the key is pressed. When you have typed in all the information above, save the file.

Saving a File

The way to save what you write onto your data disk is one of the most important techniques to know. Whenever you type text onto the screen, you need to save it. To do this simply press the F10 key and the prompt "Document to be saved:" will appear on the bottom left side of the screen. This is the time to name your document. Right now type the name INFO to name the file you just wrote. File names should be eight letters or fewer and should contain no spaces or special characters (characters such as * & ^ % or $) other than a period. You'll eventually have several files on your disk so be sure to use a name that will help you remember what's in each file you write. (The name INFO should remind you that the file contains information about yourself.)

If you have a file with the same name on the disk already, the computer will ask you if you want to replace the file. If you answer yes to the prompt, the original file will be replaced and lost. The second and subsequent times that you save to the file the same prompt will appear. Take time to ask yourself, "Do I really want to save the file as I have just rewritten it?" If the answer is yes, then type Y to replace the old file. If you want to save the old file, you'll need a new name for the new version.

Remember: Files do not exist on your disk until you have saved them. After saving the file the first time, the name of the file is on the left side of the status line across the bottom of the screen until you exit the file.

Saving the File to Another Disk

If you wish to save the file on another disk, simply remove the first disk from drive B: (the one on the bottom) and replace it with the disk on which you want to copy the file. Press the F10 key, and the file will be saved on the second disk with the same name that you gave it when you saved it the first time. This is an easy way to back up your files. Every file that you have should be copied onto a separate disk and kept in a secure place in order to ensure that the work you have done will not have to be rewritten if a disk should be lost or damaged.

Typing Text

Now that you have practiced saving a file, go back and fill in the appropriate information required in each category of the file INFO. Place the cursor on the hard return symbol after each category and begin typing. Blank spaces may be inserted with the space bar, and blank lines with the Return key. When you are writing the information in each category, do not insert hard returns; just type the information. The word processor will start new lines when it needs to do so in order to stay within margin settings. (WordPerfect is able to reformat text between hard returns. It cannot adjust a line with a hard return in it.) Here are a few tricks for moving the cursor which will let you enter text more efficiently:

Keystrokes	Movement
↑	Move up one line
↓	Move down one line
→	Move right one character
←	Move left one character
Ctrl, →	Move to the beginning of the next word
Ctrl, ←	Move to the beginning of the previous word
Home, ↑	Move up (backward) one screen
Home, ↓	Move down (forward) one screen
Home, →	Move to the end of the line
Home, ←	Move to the beginning of the line
PGUP	Move to the beginning of the previous page
PGDN	Move to the beginning of the next page

Save Often

In order to record the information on disk that you have just typed, the file must be saved again. Save by pressing the F10 key. The message "Document to be Saved: [your file name]" will appear. Press Return. The message "Replace: [your filename] (Y/N) N" will appear. To save you must press the Y key.

Printing the File

The letter A, B, C, or D that appears on the label on the front of your computer becomes important when you want to print a file. That is the letter that must be selected on the silver data switch for your printer, or you cannot print. (Each computer has a unique number, but each computer also has a letter A, B, C, or D assigned to allow four computers to use one printer.) Turn the printer on and check to see that it has enough paper to print your file. Hold down the SHIFT key, and press the F7 key one time. A list of seven choices will be displayed across the bottom of the screen. Press the number 1 key ("Full Text" on the bottom of the screen) one time and the printer should print your file. If the printer does not respond to the number 1 key, check the data switch and the power to the printer before pressing the number 1 key again.

Exiting

You have now created a file, written to it, saved it, and printed it. When you are finished working with a file and have saved your work, you must exit from the file. Press the F7 key. The program will ask you if you want to save the file. There is no need to save the file again unless you have made changes since you last saved it. The program will then ask you if you want to exit WordPerfect. Press N and a blank screen will appear. This is the way you should leave the screen at the end of the class.

The Directory

Your data disk can hold approximately 360,000 characters in as many files as you want to open. In order to keep all these files straight WordPerfect lists your files whenever you press the F5 key followed by the Return key. Be sure to press the F7 key to exit each file before retrieving another. If you do not exit with the F7 key, the file you retrieve will be tacked onto the bottom of the first file you retrieved. If you have multiple copies of a file when you print, you most likely failed to exit one file before retrieving another.

24 *Discovery: Writing to Learn*

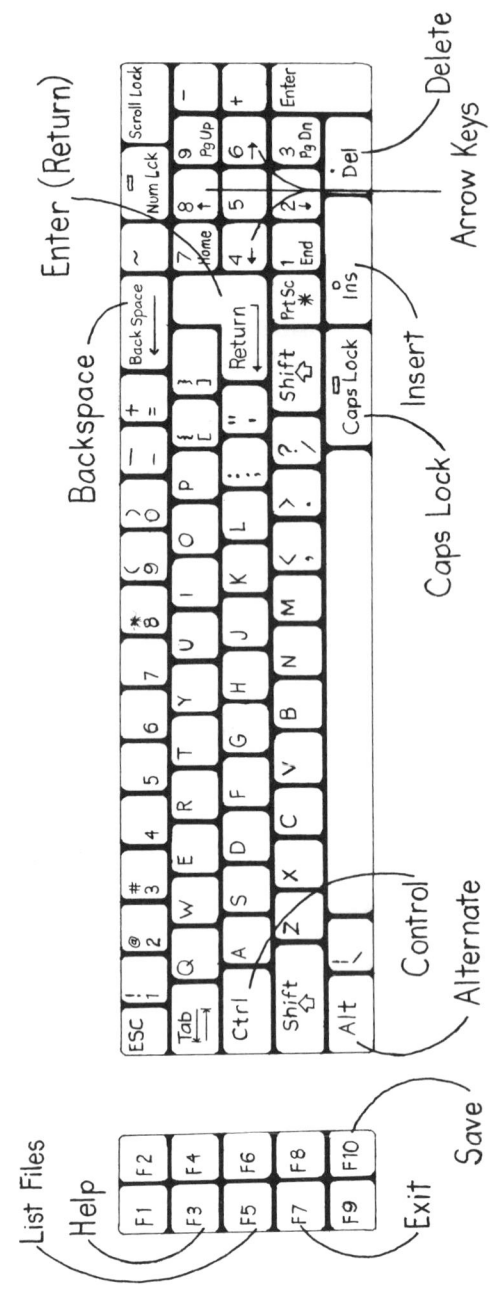

Summary of Commands in Chapter 2

Arrow keys:	move the cursor one space in the specified direction.
Backspace key:	delete text to the left of the cursor.
Caps Lock key:	press to type all text in capital letters.
Delete key:	delete text at the cursor position and to the right.
Function keys (F1–F10):	perform the 40 functions that drive the WordPerfect program.
F3 key:	get help with the commands and functions.
F5 key:	get a directory of the files on your disk.
F7 key:	exit from the file you are working in. Remember to press the F7 key to exit the current file before retrieving another. Failure to exit will merge two separate files into one.
Shift-F7, then #1 key:	print a file while the file is on the screen.
F10:	save a file (files are created when you save the first time). To save the file to another disk, in order to back up the file, replace the original disk with the back up disk and press the F10 key to save.
Insert [Ins] key:	toggle switch allows cursor to insert text or write over text at current position.
Return [Enter] key:	leaves a blank line or forces a line to end before the right margin. Signified by a triangle on the screen.

IV

What you've just worked through is an introduction to a word processing program. It's important to note here that there is a *difference* between word processing and actually using a computer to help you write. Word processing is, after all, merely the means of entering data into a computer, manipulating it, saving it, and printing it. It's a rather mechanical process.

Writing—composing—with a word processor is a more sophisticated process. It involves using all of the features of the computer program as part of your composing process. Moving blocks of text, deleting words and lines, inserting text, making notes, moving easily to any part of a document that needs attention—all of these actions can help make the process more effective. And with practice they can begin to help you discover what you know and what you need to write.

In the meantime, you may feel more comfortable writing out a draft by hand and then entering it into the computer. That's okay. I used this method for quite a while before I weaned myself from my pen (which always seemed to leak ink all over my hand anyway) and started composing at the keyboard. And many writers have chosen to continue to work from handwritten drafts. You should, however, at least experiment with writing an entire paper at the computer sometime during the semester. You may find it an interesting experience.

To work up to that point, you might try using the computer to make journal entries. Your whole journal can, in fact, be written at the computer and stored on a disk. You might use just a single disk file, called "journal," which you add to every day, or you could write each entry in a separate file, naming each with the date you write it.

Don't worry if this act of composing at the computer seems a little unnatural at first. After all, you have to get used to seeing just a few lines of your text at a time, instead of the whole page. And you have to look up toward the monitor to see it at all. Besides that, you're probably not used to creating first drafts at the typewriter, so using a keyboard to compose will feel strange; even people who are very comfortable with a typewriter usually take some time to adjust to the computer keyboard.

What happens, you ask, if I don't know how to type? Fear not. That's one of the beauties of the computer. It's very forgiving. No matter how clumsy you are at the keyboard, no matter how many mistakes you make, all can be corrected. Even the most unskilled typists (and I number myself among them) can produce clean and correct texts. And the more you do it the easier it will become.

With that reassurance, it's time to anticipate what comes next. Chapter Three is going to ask you to explore your current writing process (before we started complicating it with computers). In the meantime, here's a writing exercise that may have some relevance to your experience learning WordPerfect. (Don't, however, use the computer as your subject. You'll have more fun with it if you choose something else.)

> Recreate an experience that you've had (good or bad) with a machine.

If I didn't have writing, I'd be running down the street hurling grenades in people's faces.
Paul Fussell

Chapter 3
Writing to Discover

I

Chapter One invited you to think about what's important in a finished piece of writing. You started a list of important features that you and others in the class could agree on. Now, rather than looking at that finished piece, this chapter will pay attention to the methods, tricks, and rituals you have discovered to help you produce that writing.

Just as in Chapter One, you'll start the consideration of the subject by exploring some ideas in writing. I should, I guess, explain here why I want you to begin this way again. A number of writing experts have noted a close relationship between writing and thinking. They argue that all of us think better (and learn better) when we are actively involved with a subject, and that one of the best ways to become actively involved with an idea is to write about it. In fact, it may have already happened if you learned something about your attitudes toward writing when you wrote the first paper.

How does this happen? There are many different explanations. It might be a good topic for you to explore (in writing, of course, perhaps in your journal) based on your experience. For me, writing leads to learning partly because it makes me put my sometimes unformed ideas into words. That is, I may have some knowledge about my subject, but only by putting it into words can I learn what I know.

The other feature of writing that helps me learn is the need to organize my thoughts into sentences and paragraphs. I'm forced, then, to make connections and see relationships as I put sentences next to one another. And for me, that opportunity to see relationships is central to my learning. Ideas become meaningful when I see them in a pattern of other ideas. In one sense this entire course is a test of this theory. As you explore topics and ideas on paper throughout the semester you should, if the theory works, learn a great deal about them. What's more, if your experience is anything like mine, this preliminary exploring, this learning by writing, can, every once in a while, actually be a lot of fun.

So, to begin learning about the various methods of writing, let's explore what you know already, in writing:

> Recalling your experience with writing (both in and out of school), write a description of the method you use to produce writing.

Here are some questions that may help you get started:

What do you do when you get a writing assignment?
How do you get started?
Do you need to be in a particular environment to write?
Do you need to use a special pencil?
How long do you spend in preparation?
How long do you spend actually writing?
Do you usually use a computer as part of your process?
How much are you likely to change your work once you get it down on paper?

Other questions you need to answer should begin to occur to you as you start writing (that's another way that the act of writing stimulates the thinking process). If possible, try to use some specific examples from your writing experience as you discuss your usual method.

Even if using a computer hasn't been part of your method, you should begin to make use of it with this assignment. If it's easier for you to write first on paper and then enter your work in the computer, that's fine. Or you can try composing on the computer from the beginning. It may seem to take a little longer the first couple of times you do it this way, but trust me. Before long you'll wonder how you ever wrote without a computer!

II

I'm assuming here that you actually stopped and wrote that assignment before you continued reading. If you didn't, please do so, since the next section of the chapter is going to make yet another assignment.

Thanks. Now that you've given some attention to your own method of writing, your next project will be to examine someone else's method. In particular, you're going to interview someone else in the class and write a description of your partner's process. This is an activity that writing researchers often indulge in, studying the methods of specific writers in order to reach some conclusions about all writers. Of course you'll use your own customary routine to produce this paper, but this time I'll make a few suggestions about how to get started.

Step One: Begin by preparing a list of questions that you need to ask if you're going to understand your partner's writing process. Start with the questions I already suggested in Part I of this chapter, then add the ones you asked yourself about your own process. Next, you'll find it helpful to share questions with others in your group—chances are others will have thought of questions you might be able to use. You should have at least a dozen questions before you begin to interview your partner. And one of them should be: how did you write the last paper for this class?

Step Two: Interview your partner, using your prepared questions, but supplementing them with follow-up questions whenever you need more information. Be sure to keep careful notes.

Step Three: As soon as possible after the interview, try to organize your notes into a useful order. It may be best to just start writing. As you write, keep track of anything that you don't know but would like to know. Keep a list of all the additional questions you should ask your partner.

Step Four: Get together with your partner again and ask the new questions. Then use those answers to finish work on your paper in your usual manner.

> Based on your two interviews, your observations, your own experience, and your appropriate analysis, write a description of your partner's usual method for producing writing.

III

Here's my process:

When I'm faced with a writing project, I try to give myself as much time as possible to think about it before I start writing. Sometimes that's just a way to justify procrastination, but the thinking time usually does prove valuable. The writing, once I sit down to do it, goes more smoothly than it does if I don't have a lot of lead time.

Some of that thinking is conscious and deliberate. I'll mull over the subject while driving, or while doing some other routine activity, like cooking or watching the news. Other thinking will happen subconsciously. Part of my mind, knowing the subject I need to write about and the problems I'm going to need to solve, continues to sort through the available material even when I'm not aware of it.

Two other techniques I regularly use at this stage are reading and note-taking. If the subject is one that I don't know enough about, or if I need to take account of other people's ideas and opinions, I'll read as much as I need to. And during this "prewriting" I take notes for myself with ideas for the essay, usually on whatever scraps of paper are available at the moment. (The backs of old envelopes get a lot of use!) Those notes are occasionally in the form of sentences I might use. More often they take the form of lists.

The computer has significantly changed my approach to the writing stage. I used to write out drafts by hand, then struggle through my sometimes illegible pages to revise and edit the work before typing it (a noxious job). When I first learned to use a word processing program, I continued to write drafts in longhand. Then I typed them into the computer for revision. Gradually, I learned to do my composing at the keyboard, which is faster, more efficient, and more fun.

Revision is the other part of the process helped by the computer. When I finish a draft (or more often just a section of a draft), I'll read it on the screen, making corrections and changes. Then I'll print it out. I still find I can revise most successfully by looking at the printed page instead of just the few lines appearing on the monitor.

This revision may involve moving sections of text around (when I wrote the introduction to this book I moved sentences and paragraphs around several times before I got them in the right order). Or I may cut parts that don't fit, or add sentences to sections that seem incomplete. And as I reread, I remain on the lookout for sentence errors and spelling mistakes.

Whenever possible I try to let someone else look at my work as soon as I'm done revising. I've found that just the act of showing someone else my work serves to make me terribly aware of what's wrong and what I need to do next. So the next step is to make those changes I now know I need to make, as well as at least some of those my reader may suggest.

Usually by this time I have run out of time and need to print a final copy, though I may still want to make some last minute revisions and corrections. I've found that finishing a paper doesn't really mean that it's done, but only that deadlines have forced me to stop. Like now.

IV

Now here's the paper that a student who interviewed me wrote about the way I work. You'll notice that he observed some different features of my process, emphasized some more than others, and reached some different conclusions:

A Process of Writing

Toss Murray

Everyone has a technique when it comes to writing a paper, whether they notice it or not. The method used by Bruce Leland has been proven to work for him. He begins with several rituals to get started.

One of his rituals is to write at home during the night. This habit started in his days in high school. He now feels that it gives him the chance to be free of interruptions such as household daytime chores. He prefers to write in his study because this gives him the needed space and isolation to come up with creative ideas. It is also where he keeps his word processor, which has increased his productivity. With the computer, he states, "writing has really become exciting. I write more now, and my writing has improved." On the word processor he can edit out any unwanted

Reprinted with permission of the author.

material, revise, and store material without loss of time. He also appreciates the spell-checker, though he still has occasional use for the dictionary.

While interviewing Bruce Leland I learned that taking breaks can be very important. They keep his brain from "running dry," they prevent the forcing of material, they allow the brain to fill up with data, and last of all they give him a chance to watch his favorite TV programs.

Watching TV while writing a paper initially seemed strange to me, but the way Bruce explained it helped me understand his method. He said, "While writing a paper it helps to have the television on. It gives me the feeling that I'm staying busy." For all that happens during break time, the usual time for his intermission is about ten minutes or less. The reason for keeping breaks short is to avoid mental blocks that disrupt writing.

After a paper is drafted and before finished copy is due, Bruce will show it to a friend or two. He receives criticism from a variety of people, from fellow instructors to students. As I understand it, this is a recommended practice because it allows exposure to different points of view. When Bruce receives advice he always pays close attention and takes everything into consideration. If he decides to change something, it will be in the area of criticism, though he might not take the specific advice the reader offered.

Another strategy Bruce uses is writing under pressure. Knowing he's under pressure helps him to write efficiently in the available amount of time. This brings out immediate ideas and deep concentration. This is a strategy I use too. With consistent procedures and goals to follow he usually comes up with a self- satisfying paper.

Now it's time to stop again and finish the paper on your partner's process before you go on. When you're done, I'd like you to do some self-examination, by means of a few follow-up exercises (perhaps suitable for journal entries):

1. Was it easier to write about your own process or about your partner's process? Why? How did the two papers resemble each other? How did they differ?

2. What did you learn about your own process by writing about it? Was there anything that you regularly do when you write that you hadn't paid much attention to until you had to write about it?
3. What did you learn about your own process by having someone else write about it? Did your partner reach some conclusions about the way you work that you hadn't realized yourself?
4. Did you find any points of agreement, either with your partner or with Toss or with me, that you should add to the "consensus list" in your journal?
5. What ideas did you get from your partner's process that you might want to try out sometime? Are there things your partner does that you know won't work for you? Were your processes more alike than different? Do either of them resemble or differ from the process that Toss and I described?

V

Your answer to that last question is probably to note both some similarities and some differences. I assume that there will be at least something in the process that Toss and I described which resembles your process. In other significant ways it is certainly very different. And the same is probably true when you compared your partner's process with your own. We all have *different* processes that work for us (at least some of the time), but whatever those differences, we each have some things we do before we begin to write a draft, some things we do when drafting, and some things we do after the draft is done. For convenience these three stages are usually called PREWRITING, DRAFTING, and REVISING.

The generalizations that writing experts have made about these three stages can be useful—not to dictate what you *have* to do at each stage, but to suggest some things you might try, especially if one stage or another gives you trouble. This is part of the "advice" I told you I'd be offering. It's still going to be up to you to consider this advice, experiment with it, pick out the parts that suit your needs, and seek ways to make it part of your process. For now I'm going to limit my advice to the first stage, prewriting. The rest will come later.

Prewriting

Prewriting can sometimes be no more elaborate than just thinking, consciously or subconsciously, about the subject you have to write about. This thinking time is probably the most common kind of preparation for most of us. In fact, it would probably be hard *not* to do it. Another useful (and common) way to get started involves talking to other people about the subject as a way of getting some ideas together. Good conversation is almost always a successful stimulus for thinking. Finally, a third common prewriting activity is simply keeping notes of ideas that occur until it's time to actually start writing.

Unfortunately, these basic techniques don't always work. Sometimes the ideas just don't come. You're probably familiar enough with the experience of staring at a blank sheet of paper with an increasingly sick feeling developing in your stomach. When that happens, it's useful to have a few tricks available to help you get started. So here are a couple of suggestions that may help you the next time you're faced with the spector of the blank page.

1. Free-writing: Try just writing. It's that simple. The free-writing exercise calls for getting words, any words, down on paper as quickly as possible without stopping. That's the only rule here: Don't stop. Write continuously for five minutes (make it ten minutes as soon as you get used to it) about whatever's on your mind. Put down anything that comes to mind, and if you run dry, or can't think of what to say next, write about not knowing what to say next. Before long, something will come to you. Don't stop to correct misspelled words. Don't stop to figure out the best sentence structure. Don't stop.

An Exercise

Find your journal. Or, if you've already started keeping your journal on a computer disc, find a piece of paper. Write for five minutes about whatever's on your mind.

This form of free-writing, exploring whatever thoughts or feelings are uppermost in your mind, is a good warm-up exercise. It can get the words flowing before you turn your attention to an assigned paper topic. Or you can use the same free-writing techniques to explore that assigned topic. Done this way, it's usually called LOOPING.

In looping, you should follow the free-writing rules, writing for five or ten minutes without stopping for anything, except this time you should try to focus on the assigned topic. Of course, if you run out of things to say on the topic, or if you get distracted with an intruding idea, go with whatever comes to mind. But don't stop. If you have to, write "I can't think of any more to say," or "Why am I doing this?" or even "This is garbage." Before long an idea will occur to you and you can press on.

At the end of five minutes (or ten), rest your hand a bit, read over what you have written, then do it again. For best results, your second "loop" should build on the best idea that appeared in the first. Then do it a third time, developing the best idea of the second loop, and if you need to, try a fourth. By now you should have discovered an idea that you can develop into a paper. A lot of what you wrote will be thrown out, of course, but that shouldn't be too painful. After all, you didn't spend a whole lot of time on it.

2. Listing. A variation of free-writing is simply to list all the ideas that come to you. It doesn't matter if they're any good or not. Just get them down. As with free-writing, be sure to write your list as quickly as possible. You'll probably find that the more quickly you write the more quickly the ideas will come. Take advantage of the free-association that is certain to occur.

When you're through—that is, when you have listed everything you can think of—you can try to create some order from your list. Cross out the bad ideas, star the really good ones, group them together, draw arrows, arrange them in some appropriate pattern (such as from most important to least important), and add any new ideas that occur to you. Finally, select the most promising items from the list to use as the basis for your essay. (In case you're interested in personal endorsements, this is the prewriting exercise I use most frequently.)

3. Cubing: This method is more complicated, partly because it's more structured. On the other hand, because it's more structured it may be more helpful in some situations. Cubing asks you to quickly consider six aspects of your subject (as in the six sides of a cube). Some of them will seem a little strange for some subjects, but you may find that the strangest questions are the ones that give you the best ideas to write about.

Here are the six sides of the cube:

1. **Describe it.** Use appropriate (or inappropriate) sensory details; explain; define; clarify.
2. **Compare it.** Compare your topic to other things it resembles. If you're feeling energetic at this point, you might make note of the things it differs from.
3. **Associate it.** What does the topic bring to mind, make you think of, make you remember?
4. **Analyze it.** What are its parts? How can it be divided? How is it put together? (If you don't know, make it up.)
5. **Apply it.** What can it be used for? Be imaginative.
6. **Argue for it and against it.** List the advantages, virtues, strengths, good points. Then list everything that's wrong with it.

Two final points about cubing: First, be sure to do it quickly. Spend just enough time with each side of the cube to get your ideas flowing, then move on. And second, realize that only a few ideas you generate here are likely to be of use in the paper you're preparing to write. (There's a good chance that the useful ideas will come from the side of the cube that initially seemed most challenging.) Throw the rest out.

An Exercise

Write about the six "cubing" features of one of the following:
- Latenight with David Letterman
- A problem you've solved
- Diet Pepsi Free
- Computers
- The lounge on your residence hall floor
- Practical jokes
- Chocolate covered cherries

(Cubing is also a good group activity. If you come up with some good responses to any of the questions be sure to share them with the rest of your group.)

These three invention techniques are just a start. There are a great many more available, and you may find one of the alternatives more useful than the three techniques I've suggested here. In fact, you may already have some different techniques of your own. Rather than extend this chapter by including additional suggestions here, I've moved the rest to Appendix Two. Feel free to browse there.

Nothing you write, if you hope to be any good, will ever come out as you hoped.

Lillian Hellman

Chapter **4**

Discovering Experience

I

This chapter and those that follow will each provide a number of specific writing assignments. All of these assignments are designed to let you use writing to discover something about yourself or about some other part of the world. That is, the assignments won't make you prove that you've *already* learned something (as you need to do on most essay examinations). Rather, they are intended to take you through a process of discovery. You'll learn as you write, and your essays, when finished, will take your reader along with you on this journey.

Before we go any further, I'll give you the writing assignment for this chapter. The chapter title is "Discovering Experience," and the assignment is an invitation to remember a specific experience, to re-create it for yourself and for your reader, and to discover, in the process, what it means for you.

Here are four choices for this essay:

> 1. Despite the apparent assumptions of teachers, some of our most important learning experiences happen outside of school. Describe an event which led you to learn something important.

or

> 2. We're usually aware of problems long before we discover solutions to them. Recall a problem that troubled you for a while before you found out how to deal with it (being overweight, learning fractions, being bothered by a bully, resenting a younger sibling). Perhaps your experience will help other people faced with the same problem. Tell the story.

or

> 3. Write about a time when you told the truth, or stuck your neck out for a friend, and it ended up being an inappropriate thing for you to do. What did you learn?

or

> 4. Did Susie Q. Farnsworth tell you to wear your new dress to her tenth birthday party, but when you arrived you found everyone else in shorts and tee shirts? Or did Ronald Bullwinkle tell you that the best way to impress Mary Beth was to act tough and tell her about your deer-hunting experiences, when actually her parents were members of Greenpeace?
>
> Describe a "dirty trick" in which you were the victim. Try to recreate the experience and your feelings at the time. Include a brief reflection on your feelings about the incident in retrospect.

You will first need to decide which of the topics to write about. You may be able to remember experiences which fit all four categories, so you will need to choose the one which will be the most interesting for you to write about. This may be a good opportunity to try out one or more of the invention exercises I discussed in the last chapter. Listing or free-writing may be particularly useful in helping you to explore possible topics, or you might try a computer variation of free-writing called "blind-writing" (see Appendix Two). Or you might use your journal to discuss the possibilities with yourself or to try each topic out before you commit yourself to one. Whatever invention technique you use, be sure to do it rather quickly, just to see what ideas come to mind. Remember, at this point you are the only audience. If a bit of your prewriting doesn't lead anywhere, it doesn't matter. You can easily abandon it and move on to something else.

This preparation will, of course, eventually lead to the choice of a topic for your essay. Once again, that topic should be (of all the possible topics) the one that you find particularly interesting, that you have a lot to say about, that you can get involved in. If you really care about your subject, there is a good chance your reader will be able to care about it too (more on that later).

Your prewriting will also give you a head start in the story you are going to tell. You'll already have a few images, words, phrases, even some sentences that you can use as you begin to write. Even if you didn't take my advice about doing your initial work in writing—that is if you did all your prewriting and topic-choosing in your head—you will still have some words and images floating around. Get them down on paper before they float away.

That "getting down" is an important activity as you proceed to write your draft of your story. Unless your mind works with unusual orderliness, you will probably find your thoughts jumping ahead, recalling one part of the event even as you are trying to describe another. While full attention to the part of the story at hand is certainly desirable, you shouldn't fight the ideas that occur to you out of order. Get them down. Keep a sheet of paper close by to record these randomly occurring ideas. That way, when you get to later parts of the paper, you'll have them available to draw on.

Of course if you've begun composing on the word processor, you can do this recording even more easily. My method is to simply move ahead a couple of lines and record my notes for later, then move back to where I was and continue. For instance, I already have a reminder to myself about my intentions for the end of this chapter. It reads:

> *End of chapter:* Explain the significance of this kind of writing. Opening ourselves to a broader understanding of ourselves. Discovering patterns. Making meaning. Creating our own reality.

I'm not sure yet just how I'll develop the conclusion from those notes. We'll see later. For now, I just want to illustrate my method for keeping ideas from getting away from me. When they occur, I write them down, then come back to them later.

II

As you continue the prewriting and drafting of your essay, we can pause here to look at some examples of essays which deal with meaningful personal experience. Here first is a story by a student about an experience which led to some difficult realizations.

Blackie's Death
Carshon Manon

All of my life I have held the country vet in high esteem. I've read all of James Herriot's books, wondered at the ability of a single person to heal a fighting 2,000 pound bull, cow, pig, or horse. I had always thought that these vets must really love animals a lot to go to all that pain and trouble.

During June of 1987 the startling truth was revealed to me. I borrowed a young untrained, two year old stud from a friend. He was gorgeous, pure black, with a small white star in the center of his forehead. His personality and conformation matched his looks. Perfect.

I had to walk Blackie two miles to get to my house; it was all paved road. As we walked in the ditch, Blackie would sneak bites of the long green grass growing there. For a horse who hadn't been worked with much, he was willing and not too spooky, even when cars raced by us without slowing down.

When we finally reached my house, I put Blackie into a stall and went to catch my mare, Cherokee. I left them alone for a couple of hours and then put them out into the pasture. The two horses played around, ate grass side by side, and raced around the pasture. Things were going fine. My gelding, Chico, was tied out

From Carshon Manon, "Blackie's Death," © 1989 by ELEMENTS. Reprinted by permission.

in the backyard. Since Chico was ignoring the two in the pasture, I went back into the house to watch my soaps.

After an hour or so, I was getting ready to go outside and check the horses when I heard strange noises coming from the direction of the pasture. The first place I went to was where I had tied Chico. He was gone. The frayed rope was all that showed where he had been. I started to look in the neighbors' yards when I heard a lot of pounding hooves. It sounded like the calvary had come to town. I glanced over into my pasture to see three blurs running around. I ran over to see what was wrong.

Chico was chasing Blackie, with Cherokee in hot pursuit. I could hear the hollow thuds as Chico and Blackie kicked at each other. I ran into the pasture just as they were running up towards the front. As they ran past me, I could see the fear in Blackie's eyes; the whites of his eyes were like moons in a dark sky. Chico was close behind Blackie with his big yellow teeth inches away from black, sweat flecked hide. They raced around a tree staked up in the pasture. On their second time around the tree Blackie bucked up his hind end to kick Chico. Oh, my God! Blackie came down on the tree stake. I didn't see anything wrong with him. He took off towards the other end of the pasture, so I thought he couldn't be hurt that bad. I caught Cherokee and Chico and locked them in the barn and ran after Blackie. There he was standing out in the back of the pasture.

When I got to Blackie I could have fainted. The horse in front of me was not the beautiful satiny black animal I had walked to my house this morning. This animal was a pathetic imitation. He stood there with his head hanging down, sides heaving, flecks of foam and dirt on his black hide. Blackie's eyes were all glazed over and half closed, like he was tired and half asleep. Then I noticed something dropping from his back legs. I ran my hand down Blackie's side. It was hot and slimy with sweat and dirt. It was blood dripping from his back legs, and there were yellowish coils starting to fall out a slit in Blackie's underside. I didn't know what to do. I wished I could've been sick. Instead I grabbed Blackie's halter and pulled his head to the side. His body was slowly, slowly, going towards the ground. I counted five blinks before his body hit the ground.

I could hear the sickening gush of intestines as they slid out of Blackie's body.

I ran to the house to have my sister call the vet. I grabbed a bucket of water, a rag, and a horse rug before running back out to Blackie.

Blackie was up and swaying around, dragging a trail of now dirty brown and mud caked intestines. I went to his head to lay him down; his once intelligent and trusting brown eyes were now wide open and all white. I could almost taste the terror he was feeling. As I laid him down, I heard again the sickening gush as more intestines slid from Blackie's body. By now his back legs and stomach were orange with blood.

I picked up some intestines and washed them with water. The were caked with blood, dirt, and leaves. They felt all rubbery and gritty as I washed them. I would wash some and then shove them frantically into the dark cavern of Blackie's body. There seemed to be miles of that soft gooey mess. The more I cleaned and shoved back in, the more there seemed to gush back out at me. My hands, pants, shirt, and face were covered with a paste made from blood, sweat, and my own tears. That's how the vet and my sister found me, trying to put Blackie's insides where they belonged.

The vet was all business. He asked me what I wanted done. I took one look at what used to be a healthy, shimmering, two year old horse and saw a sweat, blood, and dirt covered mass of terrible pain. My voice shook as I told the vet, "Put him to sleep." As Doc Smith went to get the syringe, I put Blackie's head into my lap and stroked his once satiny cheek.

Doc Smith said, "This shot should take effect in about three minutes." As we waited I whispered softly to Blackie, trying to ease the pain as much as possible. My tears dripped to his face and mingled with his sweat.

As the vet and I waited for Blackie to die, I tried to get my feelings in order. Minutes seemed like days. Nothing was happening. The drug wasn't working. Blackie was still alive and in a great deal of pain. Doc Smith came over and kicked Blackie in the chest saying, "Some horses just aren't smart enough to die." "I'll go get my gun." As he stalked back to his truck, I gritted my teeth and kept petting Blackie with my sweat streaked hand.

That's how Blackie's life ended. A once beautiful horse shot by a man who had no feelings for his pain, no compassion for his fight to stay alive. I couldn't watch Doc Smith shoot Blackie; I had already pictured it in my mind a hundred times.

An unfeeling man putting a bullet through the small white star on Blackie's forehead. The terror filled eyes were closing for the last time, the muscles quivering under an orange, mud-caked hide relaxing at last.

I wake up nights reliving Blackie's pain, hating myself for letting this beautiful animal die in such pain. My body jerks awake as once again I hear the shot from the gun. I can almost feel the bullet.

Carshon's comment at the end of the story suggests not only the significance of the experience itself, but also says something about her memory of it. The original event happened some time ago, but, she says, she has relived it in memory many times since then. I want to suggest that this re-living has become an important part of the experience itself. The re-creation of the event in memory, that is, has become a part of the event.

You may be able to remember playing the children's game of Gossip (though you may have had your own name for it). The first person whispers a brief story to the person next to him. Then she retells it to the next person, and so on, till the last person repeats what she heard. Predictably, the final version of the story is much different from the first version.

If memory can't be trusted for the few moments it takes to repeat the story we've just been told, how can we trust it over the long run? We may even play a version of "gossip" with ourselves, in our memory, as we slightly (and naturally) alter our remembered stories each time we tell them to ourselves. In other words, we don't just *remember* experience, we *re-create* it each time we return to it.

Part of that re-creation occurs not only because memory is unreliable, but also because we change. Some of our memories change in significance to reflect the important changes that are occurring in our lives. An event which seemed very important when we were children might look quite trivial when remembered later. Or, conversely, an event which we didn't fully appreciate at the time it occurred might be better understood later in life. In this way Carshon Manon understands her relationship to Blackie, and to the horse's death, differently now than when she first experienced it. Similarly, E. B. White's essay "Once More to the Lake" (in Chapter Five) reveals how past events can be re-interpreted in the light of present-day events. And Gregory

Donley's memory of "A Visit from My Grandfather" offers another memory from childhood which is interpreted in maturity.

A Visit from My Grandfather
Gregory Alan Donley

Easter Sunday of 1973 was a gloomy day at our family's new house in the suburbs of Peoria, Illinois. The entire family had assembled with one exception. My Grandpa Lowell lay in the Intensive Care Unit of St. Francis Medical Center dying of brain cancer.

Three weeks prior to the somber Easter gathering, my mother had taken my brother and me to see my Grandpa Lowell in the hospital. The frail shadow of a man the nurse wheeled out to us was in no way similar to the strong, gentle giant of a man I had loved, admired, and nearly worshiped.

Over the course of his illness Grandpa Lowell had lost fifty pounds or more, and his mottled discolored skin hung off his frame like a poorly fitted suit. His eyes were the vacant, dusty, glass marbles of a stuffed animal. His voice a barely audible, raspy whisper. The words I could hear in that whisper made little sense.

I put my arms around my Grandpa Lowell and held him as tightly as my skinny, eight-year-old arms would allow. I cried silently as I felt the heat of his fever surround me during our embrace. I pulled back far enough to look into my grandfather's face, and in his eyes I could see that some part of him had returned to this broken pathetic shell. In that raspy whisper I heard him say, "I love you, Gregory."

I was my Grandpa Lowell's first grandson. As such he lavished his attention on me. Even after my brother was born we spent a lot of time together. He would take me fishing and for walks in Glen Oak Park, and we would spend Sundays in his living room while he read from one of the hundreds of books he had collected over the years. It was my Grandpa Lowell who told me the folklore and tales of our Irish ancestry. He also told me about members of my family who had died years before I was

Reprinted with permission of the author.

born, in such a way that I felt I was with them in their adventures and trials.

Seeing this great man, a man of compassion and intelligence, reduced to the vegetable-like state traumatized me in such a way that I am still unable to articulate my feelings.

The nurse came that day to wheel my Grandpa Lowell back to his hospital room. After he was gone, I allowed my tears to come. It was then, for the only time in my life, that my mother lied to me.

"Its okay, Greg. Your grandpa has been very sick but he will be better soon." At that time I believed her completely. I had never known my mother to be wrong about anything.

By Easter, as the family moped over mashed potatoes and picked at ham, I knew that my Grandpa Lowell was going to die. No one had told me he was going to die but it was easy to see. I could see it in my father's bloodshot eyes and in the tears that seemed to drip constantly from my mother's eyes. My Grandma Lucille would sit, staring out of the window, not moving or speaking for hours. The Irish tradition of the wake had started early.

At that time my great-grandfather was still alive. After dinner, he took me by the hand and led me to a room where we could be alone to talk.

"Gregory, you know that your Grandpa Lowell loves you very much don't you lad?" It seemed like such a strange question that I didn't know how to answer it at first.

"Yes sir, I do."

"Your Grandpa Lowell is very sick, lad. I know that your mom thinks he is getting better, but it isn't happening."

"Grandpa Lowell is going to die." It wasn't a question but a simple statement of fact.

"That's right, lad. It really isn't so bad. Lowell is the finest man I've ever known and soon his suffering will be over and he will be with God."

I had nothing more to say about it and neither did my great-grandfather. We held each other while the rest of the family dealt with the grief as best they could.

Everyone left around nine o'clock that evening. I kissed my family good night and went to my bedroom. I turned on the light and began to read a book that my Grandpa Lowell had given me.

Around ten o'clock I heard a creak in the hardwood floor of my bedroom. I half turned and saw my Grandpa Lowell standing there. His eyes had their old familiar spark back, and he was the same strong, gentle giant of a man I had always known. There was no fear or concern connected with the experience, only a sense of relief at his apparent recovery.

He sat on the bed, and I heard the springs squeak and saw the mattress sink in under his weight. I felt the bristles of his crew cut hair on my cheek as he hugged me hard. He was smiling from ear to ear.

"I've missed you, Gregory."

"I've missed you too, Grandpa Lowell."

"We're buds to the end, right Gregory?"

"Buds to the end, Grandpa."

"I have to go away now, Gregory, but it's not the end. Remember, it is not the end."

"You're going to heaven to be with God."

"That's right, I'm going to heaven to be with God."

Before I could say anything my Grandpa Lowell faded before my eyes. There seemed to be a presence in the room, a feeling of electricity that filled the air. As the presence began to fade I heard my Grandpa Lowell's distinctive voice say, "Gregory, remember."

I ran downstairs to tell my parents that Grandpa Lowell had been in my room. They told me I was dreaming; the telephone rang, drowning out my protests. It was the hospital calling to tell my mother that Grandpa Lowell died at 10:05 that evening.

I knew then, and I know now, that my Grandpa Lowell did visit my room the night he died. Maybe his will was great enough that he could ease my loss or maybe God was kind enough to let this saintly man say good-bye to his grandson.

Since that day I have know that there is a heaven and a God. My Grandpa Lowell had told me that both existed as an eye-witness.

III

There's a good chance, of course, that you don't have an experience quite as dramatic as either of these. That doesn't mean that your memories can't be turned into effective essays. Ordinary events, like arguing with parents, taking a vacation, starting at a new school, working on a class assignment, going to the hospital, playing with brothers and sisters: all these can be understood as significant events. Garrison Keillor made a career on public radio by telling stories about ordinary events on a show called "A Prairie Home Companion." He later turned some of his stories about everyday occurrences in the town of Lake Woebegon, Minnesota, into several best-selling books. And Keillor is just one of many authors who have achieved success by writing about the ordinary. The following essay, from Susan Allen Toth's book *Ivy Days,* provides one example of the significance of an ordinary event: a trip home from college.

Christmas Vacation
Susan Allen Toth

When the morning of Christmas vacation arrived, with its promise of a noon dismissal, our whole house was in an uproar. Suitcases were piled in the downstairs hall, boots and books jumbled in heaps, coats stacked on living-room chairs for quick get-aways. Taxis, booked weeks in advance, would be waiting outside Seelye Hall for the girls who had tight travel connections. Luckily, I had arranged to share a cab, snatching an offered space from a girl in my History class. A whir of excitement, rare in Lawrence House, filled the halls, as we tacitly abandoned any pretense at Quiet Hours and slammed doors, yelled farewells, laughed and jostled each other down the stairs with our suitcases.

Right after breakfast, those of us who were traveling any distance gathered in the dining room to make our bag lunches. The cooks put out a large glass bowl of peanut butter, another of tuna-fish-and-mayonnaise, and a third of egg salad, next to an institutional-sized loaf of slightly stale white bread. In an even larger bowl were oranges, bananas, and a few shiny red apples. The apples looked so appealing they went fast, as I learned when I quickly snatched the last two. Imagining two impoverished days on trains, I slathered half a dozen sandwiches together. I tried not

From IVY DAYS: MAKING MY WAY OUT EAST by Susan Allen Toth. Copyright © 1984 by Susan Allen Toth. By permission of Little, Brown and Company.

to remind myself I didn't like either egg salad or mayonnaise. For four years, vacation after vacation, Christmas and Easter and summer, the fare on the dining-room table never changed. Peanut butter, tuna fish, egg salad. Telling myself it was free, I always packed twice as much as I could eat. After only a few hours on a warm, crowded train, the egg salad got soggy, the tuna fish smelled funny, the bananas turned brown, and most of all, the sweetish apples were soft and mealy. The smell of apple permeated everything. Even when I tried tinfoil or plastic bags, the apples seemed to tinge every other bit of food. Even today when I think of trains, I still smell the slightly sickening, cidery aroma of softening apples. Yet, seeing those bright red apples in the bowl, year after year, I could never resist them. They signified something about health, vacation, and freedom.

That first Christmas vacation I was too excited to eat right away. When I finally passed the hurdle of changing trains in Springfield, walked down the tunnel to the right track, and found my seat on the New York Central's New England States, I settled back with a great sigh of relief for the overnight trip to Chicago. I watched the changing scenery in a daze of relaxation and happiness. No longer did I need to crane my neck and watch like a tourist for new sights. I had been this way before. The country didn't exactly look familiar, perhaps because I'd passed much of it before during the night, but I didn't care. I didn't need to study the landscape. At one end was Northampton. At the other end was home.

Though I had of course packed my textbooks, I left them in my bag. Somehow Smith seemed to disappear as soon as we left the station in Springfield. I was blissfully alone, able to measure out the miles by watching, daydreaming and dozing between cities. Consulting my timetable, I checked each stop, numbering them like beads, moving them onto another side of an abacus I'd invented. That was Syracuse, Syracuse is gone, no more Syracuse. Now Buffalo, Buffalo in two hours, after Buffalo I'll try to sleep. All that will be left then is Cleveland; after Cleveland, Chicago; and then I'm practically home.

When the hours grew long, I read. Every vacation I packed special paperback books for my train trips, buying them weeks in advance and savoring their possibilities as they lay, untouched, on my shelf. I only chose books I couldn't justify reading otherwise, books that I'd never find in Freshman English or Creative Writing or Introduction to the Novel. One year it was Agatha Christie, another "The Silver Chalice," once—as a senior—"Love without Fear." As if my own emotional state weren't pitched high enough, I plunged deep into those feverish worlds, vibrating to passions that drifted on as endlessly as the miles, pausing now and then to look out the window and muse about romance, sex, mystery. To keep myself company during meals, I continued to read. Through rape, regret, and salvation, I munched absent-mindedly on stale sandwiches, trying to forget the smell of apples. Underneath it all, I always heard the comforting sound of the wheels, carrying me home.

When I reached Chicago, everything speeded up. As soon as I'd left the New York Central, I was back in country that I knew. The few Smith girls I'd recognized on the New England States got off by Chicago, heading to unknown destinations. I went alone to the LaSalle Street Station to catch the Chicago and Northwestern.

Before long we crossed the Mississippi into Iowa. Crawling through the Chicago suburbs, then Rock Island-Moline-Davenport, the train was stuck in urban grime, a harsh industrial landscape that didn't look so different from Cleveland or Buffalo. The Midwest hadn't had much snow that Christmas, and everything seemed grayish-brown and dirty. Looking out the window, I didn't think I had much to celebrate. But soon the wheels of the train sounded more encouraging, as they hurried faster and faster, covering ground with exuberant speed. Now the towns disappeared, and mostly I saw fields, farms, and the gentle curve of an infinite horizon. Smoke and soot evaporated, and the world looked clean again.

I no longer tried to read. During the last hour of the trip, I pulled my wool cap tightly over my ears, buttoned my coat, and stood outside the cars on a swaying metal platform. After two days in stale coaches, the fresh air, cold and crisp, felt wonderful. Below my feet, the deafening sound of metal on metal told me what was happening was real. I blinked and stared, my eyes watering with cold and excitement. Right there, so close I could almost touch them, were silos and fences and snow-sprinkled stubble, grazing black cattle and old-fashioned corncribs and rows of Butler storage bins. I was practically home.

Most of all, I breathed in lungfuls of space, taking huge breaths as if I'd come from a dark submarine into a world of bright skies. In later years, when I sometimes traveled on night trains, I sensed a loneliness about that Midwestern space, as I watched the separate lights of distant farms flutter and disappear in the darkness. But even then, with a sadness I could not explain, I was glad the land stretched so far. Out there, in the country where I belonged, was all the room I felt I would ever need.

Soon we were passing through towns whose basketball teams I had booed, whose cheerleaders I might recognize, whose Presbyterian youth fellowships had attended our synod conferences. I even welcomed the swinging signposts at the tiny stations we whipped past, because they bore names I recognized: Mechanicsville, Belle Plaine, Tama, State Center. As our train meandered through the center of large towns, I saw people on the streets who looked like people in Ames, doing their shopping, driving their cars, or standing at corners. Most of them didn't notice us, and I was aware how removed they were from the excitement I felt. Of course, they couldn't know I was going home. I was glad to see the store signs, Sears, Super Value, Our Own

Hardware; I liked the new developments with their tract ramblers dotting the edges of town; I wanted to wave at an old brick school that looked just like Louise Crawford Elementary, back in Ames.

It was late afternoon when the trained slowed for its arrival in Ames. Hugging myself and stamping my feet, I leaned as far over the platform as I dared to catch my first glimpse of the station. Suddenly I saw them: a huddled group, my best friend, Peggy O'Reilly and five or six others, with my mother standing just to the side. They began waving and screaming as soon as they saw me, and I waved and screamed back. Then the train stopped, I was in the midst of hugs and laughter, registering startled impressions of different haircuts and new winter coats, talking with everyone at once. My mother cleared her throat. "Don't I get a hug too?" she said with a smile. Unlike my friends, she had not run or pushed, so they had reached me first. I felt an awful pang. How long I had anticipated the moment when I would first see her! But she was smiling, and I put my guilt aside.

That moment at the train station, when I plunged into the welcoming circle of my old friends, was the highlight of my Christmas vacation. Happy as I was to pull into our driveway, plop my bags down in my old room, and sink into my chair at the kitchen table, I was somehow more relieved than ecstatic. I wasn't sure why I felt faintly let down. Everything was just as I'd remembered, though perhaps a little more cluttered, just a bit smaller. I noticed a worn spot on the rug and a heap of Mother's magazines on my bookcase. So much had happened to me, so much had changed, I thought, and yet I wasn't sure how I could even begin to explain. I made an effort, told a few stories about Smith that sounded flat out of context, and realized sometime that first evening that I probably couldn't find the words—or the time—to describe what it was like for me out East.

Though I told my mother what I thought she might want to hear, I had less success with my friends. We found we were not nearly as interested in listening to each other as when we'd promised in our letters, "I'll tell you all about it when I see you." When my old friend Christy described the giant papier-mache panda the Pi Phis had built for Northwestern's Homecoming, my mind began to wander. As I tried to evoke our exciting bicycle trip on Mountain Day, Christy interrupted, politely, with a bit of news about the Northwestern marching band. Though

Peggy O'Reilly and I shared details about our college roommates, I think both of us felt surprisingly estranged. After only a few months, our new worlds had swallowed us up.

But we had little time for introspection. Every hour the phone rang, till Mother sighed in exasperation, as if I were thirteen again. People dropped in all through the day, family friends, neighbors, younger friends still in high school. At night the old gang gathered for party after party, mostly informal get-togethers in someone's living room or in the booths of the Rainbow Cafe or at round tables in the Oak Grill. A few of my former boyfriends called for private dates, a movie or ice-skating or just "going out." Somewhere in the midst of all the commotion was Christmas, a short lull, with the usual stockings, turkey dinner, and visiting relatives. On the night of the Christmas Formal, an annual high-school event, three or four of us decided, for a lark, to visit the Great Hall of the Iowa State Union, where it was always held. Once we'd gone to the Christmas Dance as eager participants, nervous, anticipating the night for weeks. Now, dressed in ordinary coats and boots, we shuffled outside the door for a few minutes, watching the new sophomores, juniors, and seniors whirling and dipping inside in the tulles and tuxedos. A few kids recognized us and waved, but we didn't try to go into the hall. Feeling subdued, and old, we left the Union and headed downtown to see if we could spot anyone coming out of the Sportsman's Lounge.

After Christmas, I began to feel scared. The days had gone so quickly. In less than a week, I would have to go down to the train station again, to leave Ames once more and return to Smith. I had done almost none of my backlogged work for midyear exams. My mother said she'd hardly seen me. I had promised Bob we'd go out once more, and Peggy said we still needed to have a good long talk. As I looked ahead to January, I could not imagine surviving the rigors of five three-hour exams. I had never taken any essay test longer than an hour. I was sure I wouldn't know enough to fill all that time and all those bluebooks. I was three weeks behind in Ancient History, four chapters in Geology. I didn't know the French subjunctive, and I'd been conning my way through class discussions about Henry James. What would happen to me?

One night I broke down in front of my mother and cried. I didn't want to go back, I said. She listened sympathetically, her face creased with concern. "Well, I didn't dream you felt this way," she finally said. "You don't have to stay there, you know. Perhaps you should come home and go to Iowa State, or transfer somewhere else at the end of the year." Those did not seem to me like possible solutions. I knew I had to go back. I tried to recover; I didn't want Mother to worry. "No, of course it's not really that bad," I said. "It's a great school. I know that. I wouldn't think of not going back."

Getting on the train on that cold January morning was one of the hardest things I have ever done. Most of my friends had already left, and only my mother, sister, and Peggy came down to the station to see me off. Mother had packed a special lunch bag, with brownies, home-made bread, and an apple she said wouldn't smell. As I hugged my mother good-bye, I wished I had spent more time at home with her. I promised Peggy I would write soon. I knew she hated going back to the convent, and I felt bad for her too. When the train pulled out, I stood on the outside platform, waving, tears welling up, with that recognizable rock in my stomach, until the station had faded from sight. Inside the coach I cried for a while, blowing hard into a handful of Kleenex, hoping no one would notice. I didn't think I could ever be more miserable.

But within a few hours, I began to feel better. I was an old hand at train travel now, and I knew where we were going. After a while I opened my Ancient History book to begin some cramming. It was going to be a long, dull trip, and I might as well make some use of it. I could look forward to Mother's lunch, and maybe tonight I'd eat in the dining car with some money she'd given me. At least I was going to get the exams over with.

When the taxi stopped in front of Lawrence House two days later, I was astonished to find that I felt excited. I hurried up the stairs. When I checked my box, I found some mail waiting. A new calendar had been posted, listing the upcoming foreign films, chapel talks, and lectures. The wooden floors in Lawrence, waxed in our absence, gleamed as bright as they had in September. A fresh linen napkin was rolled in my napkin box. Someone's "New York Times" had been tossed on a chair. I grabbed it, realizing I hadn't seen one for two weeks. On the landing, I studied the week's menus, written in Mrs. Stevens' elegant script, and was pleased to see two of my favorites coming soon, cherry crisp and sticky buns. Upstairs in my hall I saw a sheet of paper tacked to the door of my room. Sophie had written a poem to welcome me back. "I'm here already, so come see me right away," she had penciled on the bottom.

As I read Sophie's poem, I grinned at the funny verses. She had decorated the note with little stick figures. I was so glad she was already here. I dumped my bags in my room, glancing at the furniture to see that nothing had changed. Then I dashed across the hall to see if Sophie and I could go together to Friendly's Ice Cream Parlor for supper. I wanted to have a Big Beef, rare ground sirloin dripping with juice on soppy buttered toast. We didn't have anything quite like that in Ames. Although I didn't want to admit it to Sophie, who knew how homesick I'd been all fall, I was oddly relieved to be back in Lawrence. This, I guessed, was where I belonged now. Somehow, I felt I had come home.

IV

Earlier in this chapter, I encouraged you to use your journal to explore ideas for your essay, just as a way of getting started. I said that it didn't matter if you had some false starts or explored an idea that didn't lead anywhere. After all, for your pre-writing activity, you are the only audience.

When you turn that pre-writing into an essay, however, you will be writing for a wider audience, including at least your instructor, and quite possibly some other class members as well. You will need to write something that will interest other readers, that will engage them, that will make them want to read on, that will make them care. Remember, your instructor and classmates are readers much like you—they will be happier if what they read interests them rather than bores them. I know I said that I wasn't going to give you rules for writing, but I've changed my mind:

A Rule for Writing:

Don't write stuff that will put your reader to sleep.

Most of the time, if you care deeply about your subject, you will have no trouble making your readers care too. Even the most ordinary events will gain significance. On the other hand, there are some techniques you can use which will work to increase your reader's interest even more. A brief analysis of what some effective writers are able to do may help you in your writing. Look again at the three essays in this chapter. Did they succeed in holding your interest? How did you feel as you read each one? Did you enjoy the experience? Which of the three essays was the most interesting?

Having answered those questions, you know what is coming next: WHY? Why did each essay evoke the reaction it did? Why was one more interesting than another? Why did they hold your attention? I suggest that you consider these questions with the members of your group. Talk about your experience of reading the essays. Try to determine what these writers have done to hold your interest, or what they failed to do at the points where they became boring. Make a list of features that create interest. Add it to your Chapter One list in your journal. And, of course, use this list to help to direct your own efforts to appeal to your readers.

(A hint: I hope that at least someone in each group will say something about each of the three authors' use of specific details.)

V

Remember that note to myself I said I had written in order not to forget what I wanted to do at the end of this chapter? It's still here:

> *End of chapter*: explain the significance of it. Open ourselves to a broader understanding of ourselves. Discovering patterns. Making meaning.

The note reminds me (still) that I need to comment on the purpose for writing personal experience essays like this. I hope that's a question you've asked yourself by now. After all, you know perfectly well that you are not going to be asked to produce personal experience essays in chemistry class, or on an accounting exam, or as part of the duties for most after-college jobs. So why do it here?

Just as I hope that you've asked the question about purpose, I hope, too, that you've begun to provide your own answers. (And no, "because an English teacher makes me do it" isn't a particularly good answer.) I find that writing about experience serves at least two purposes, one for the writer and one for the reader. The two are closely connected.

As a writer, I find that the attempt to capture remembered events in a coherent essay (or in a good letter) is a way of creating order. It's a way of reflecting on my past to better understand it, and, subsequently, to better understand myself. This activity works better in writing than in more casual ways of thinking, I believe, because writing forces me to make order. As I put words together into orderly sentences and coherent paragraphs, I am forced to see relationships. And as I try to make connections among the parts of an essay, and lead those parts to a logical and honest conclusion, I can often see some larger patterns emerge.

For me, those patterns are important. Too much of life is chaotic, unexplainable, beyond my control. But if I can see certain patterns in my own experience, in my own behavior, in my own reactions to things, then I can have at least a beginning of understanding.

Similarly, reading the attempts of others to understand their experience, to find their patterns, is also instructive. In the struggle of other writers to tell a story, to discover meaning, to re-create their lives, or to make significant connections, I can recognize something of my own life and my own struggle to understand. Ultimately, I learn from them.

Keep that in mind as your complete your essay. Your reader will be learning something from what you have to say. That doesn't mean you have to be didactic or reach for some kind of obvious moral lesson at the end. Just write carefully and honestly. If your story is told well, your reader will learn from it.

What does a life of total dedication to the truth mean? It means, first of all, a life of continuous and never-ending stringent self-examination.

M. Scott Peck
The Road Less Traveled

Chapter **5**

Discovering Ambiguity

I

The writing project for this chapter is called a meditation. Actually, I wish I could find a different name for it; the word "meditation," for some people, calls up images of incense, chanting, and 60's-types in beads and headbands. For others, it will suggest certain religious practices. For still others, California-style therapy sessions.

In fact, the act of meditation, which involves clearing the mind of distractions, focusing on an object or idea, observing our responses and reactions, and disciplining ourselves, is a useful writing tool. I've described this use of meditation as an invention technique in Appendix Two. But for the purposes of this writing assignment, you won't be asked to engage in any practices that you may find uncomfortable. The "meditation" you will write here represents a specific way of recreating experience, debating an idea with yourself, and reaching a tentative conclusion. In other words, it's a way of organizing your thinking and writing about it. In Chapter Four, you wrote about experience as a chronological narrative. Here you will try a different approach.

The use of the term "meditation" for this type of writing comes from the seventeenth century. That's when John Donne, the poet and clergyman, wrote several essays he called "meditations." His work serves to define the form (which we can also find in essays by Henry David Thoreau and Annie Dillard). Donald Stewart, who teaches writing at Kansas State University, has identified three parts in the structure of the meditation: 1) the composition of the place, 2) the internal colloquy, and 3) the resolution. Here's my explanation of what's included in each of these three parts:

Writing a Meditation

1. *The Composition of the Place.* To begin with, choose a place that has many associations for you. This can be a place you actually visit and observe, or it can be a place that's well fixed in your memory. (Examples: a church, the library, a room in your parents' house, an airport, a swing in the park, a schoolroom, the barn on your grandmother's farm, a graveyard, a locker room.) Keep the place very specific. Don't try to deal with Chicago as your place. Choose one street corner or one room that has meaning for you.

In your first few paragraphs, you should reconstruct this place for your audience. Describe it with appropriate sensory details so that your reader can actually experience the place. Be sure to include details that will lead in some way to part two.

2. *Internal Colloquy.* You chose your particular place because it had significant associations for you. After you have recreated the place for your reader, you can begin to explore these associations. Ask questions. What thoughts, memories, ideas, or issues are suggested by the place? What relation does the place have to your present attitudes and beliefs? What does the place remind you of? What does the place mean to you now? How has the place changed? How have you changed? What does it mean to others? How do you differ from them?

For example: A church may lead me to thoughts of funeral practices. Why do I prefer a funeral in a church to one in a funeral parlor? Or: A room in my parents' basement may remind me of playing there alone, creating my own fantasy world. Why do children create imaginary worlds for themselves? Why did I? How does that activity relate to my adult life now? Or: A visit to a residence hall may remind me of a roommate who left after the third week of school. Why did he leave? What was he missing at school? What qualities do I have (that he didn't) which made it possible for me to survive the first few weeks of the semester? Or: My favorite place in the library is a table on the sixth floor. Whenever I take a break, I wander around the stacks looking at the books. Today I noticed a copy of Miller's play *Death of a Salesman.* I remember how much it affected me the first time I read it. It reminded me of . . . and so on.

3. *The Resolution.* After you have asked questions, made comparisons, examined associations, explored all sides of the issue at hand, you need to bring your meditation to some conclusion. What have you discovered? What have you learned? Where has your exploration led you? You will want to leave the reader with some sense of closure. This conclusion will not be a repetition of some idea you stated at the beginning of the essay. Nor will it be a summary. Rather, it will be a logical resolution to the debate or discussion or exploration you've developed in the essay.

For example: After debating funeral practices I can conclude that I want my funeral to be in a church with the congregation singing "For All the Saints Who From Their Labors Rest." Or, after discussing why my college roommate left school, I may conclude that the values my parents instilled in me may have helped me survive the crisis which made him quit. Or, after remembering the fun of playing in the barn behind my grandmother's house (a place I was forbidden to enter) I might conclude that children need to break the rules their parents set down for them.

Within the three-part structure, you have considerable freedom to choose your subject. Don't rush it. Spend some time in the prewriting stage trying out possibilities. And if your first idea doesn't work out, try another. Here's the assignment:

Go to a special place, in person or in memory. Think through and write a meditation, developing all three parts.

II

The title for this chapter is "Discovering Ambiguity," and as you work on writing the meditation it will help to open yourself to the possibilities of ambiguities in your experiences and ideas. You may have noticed some of these ambiguities creeping into the essay you wrote in the last chapter. You may have noticed, for example, mixed feelings about the practical joke that was played on you. You might have been angry, through at the same time a part of you may have appreciated the attention. Or you may have felt you shouldn't have been quite so truthful with your friend, while still believing firmly in the importance of honesty. In other words, your feelings were ambiguous.

The American Heritage Dictionary defines "ambiguous" as "susceptible of multiple interpretations; doubtful or uncertain." Notice how sterile, how dull, how unambiguous, that last sentence is as a way of introducing the subject of ambiguity. And it certainly doesn't express what *I* want to say about ambiguity. It sounds too negative, like something to be avoided. And although ambiguity is sometimes uncomfortable, and sometimes unwelcomed (as when a teacher writes "ambiguous" next to one of your sentences), it isn't always a bad thing.

In fact, in many contexts, ambiguity is absolutely necessary. And I'm not referring to the use of ambiguity in social situations as a way of avoiding honesty ("That's a new sweater? It's such an *interesting* color!"). I mean, rather, that recognizing ambiguities is, in fact, a way toward honest exploration of experience. Not everything in our experience is easily defined or evaluated. Our emotions are rarely unmixed. Our judgement is sometimes compromised by conflicting beliefs, motives, and opinions. Our encounters with other people are constantly opening new perspectives that we can't always account for.

This is not to say that we should never reach conclusions. Indeed, the meditation paper you are working on calls on you to reach a resolution. Any paper that stops short of reaching a conclusion (at least a tentative one) is likely to disappoint the reader. But you may, along the way, indicate the complexities, the roadblocks, the ambiguities that will modify your conclusion. And the meditation assignment, with its middle "internal colloquy," allows you to do just that. A colloquy, after all, is a dialogue or debate; as you consider the implications of the place you described, you can debate the different sides of the issue with yourself.

An illustration is often the best way to explain a concept. Here is a poem by Philip Larkin, a contemporary British writer, which illustrates the idea of ambiguity. Note also that it is a short meditation, beginning with a place (a British pub or disco) and moving on to consider the writer's relationship to the activity there.

Reasons for Attendance
Philip Larkin

    The trumpet's voice, loud and authoritative,
    Draws me a moment to the lighted glass
    To watch the dancers—all under twenty-five—
    Shifting intently, face to flushed face,
    Solemnly on the beat of happiness.

    —Or so I fancy, sensing the smoke and sweat,
    The wonderful feel of girls. Why be out here?
    But then, why be in there? Sex, yes, but what
    Is sex? Surely, to think the lion's share
    Of happiness is found by couples—sheer

    Inaccuracy, as far as I'm concerned.
    What calls me is that lifted, rough-tongued bell
    (Art if you like) whose individual sound
    Insists I too am individual.
    It speaks; I hear; others may hear as well,

    But not for me, nor I for them; and so
    With happiness. Therefore I stay outside,
    Believing this; and they maul to and fro,
    Believing that; and both are satisfied,
    If no one has misjudged himself. Or lied.

In my reading of the poem, I see Larkin trying at first to simplify his complex reaction to the dancers. He's trying to find an easy way to explain his behavior. Unfortunately, at each point his honesty brings him face to face with the complexity. He is attracted by the happy dancing couples, but he doesn't want to join them. After all, he's by himself, and while he might like to be with a girl, he isn't, so he rationalizes that sex isn't that important anyway. He's an individual. The dancers repel him, as they "maul to and fro." He'd rather be alone, outside, though he is willing to concede that they have

From COLLECTED POEMS by Philip Larkin. Copyright © by the author.

good reasons for being with the group inside. He's happy. They're happy. Unless, of course, he (or they) "misjudged himself. Or lied."

Larkin's shifting back and forth in his reaction to the dancers illustrates the complexity of even the simplest of deeds. His reasons for stopping to look, then for not going in, are complex reflections of his own sense of himself, his knowledge that he is perfectly capable of rationalizing to excuse his behavior, and his suspicion that others behave the same way. It all remains very ambiguous, and is more satisfying, honest, and funny because of the ambiguity.

III

Here are three more meditations: First, another poem by Philip Larkin; then a meditation written by an English teacher at Galva High School; finally, an essay by E. B. White, a well-known American essayist who wrote for the *New Yorker*. I'd like you, first of all, to enjoy them. After that, you might find that a discussion of one or more of them would make a good journal entry.

Church Going
Philip Larkin

> Once I am sure there's nothing going on
> I step inside, letting the door thud shut.
> Another church: matting, seats, and stone,
> And little books; sprawlings of flowers, cut
> For Sunday, brownish now; some brass and stuff
> Up at the holy end; the small neat organ;
> And a tense, musty, unignorable silence,
> Brewed God knows how long. Hatless, I take off
> My cycle-clips in awkward reverence,
>
> Move forward, run my hand around the font.
> From where I stand, the roof looks almost new—
> Cleaned, or restored? Someone would know: I don't.

From COLLECTED POEMS by Philip Larkin. Copyright © by the author.

Mounting the lectern, I peruse a few
Hectoring large-scale verses, and pronounce
"Here endeth" much more loudly than I'd meant.
The echoes snigger briefly. Back at the door
I sign the book, donate an Irish sixpence,
Reflect the place was not worth stopping for.

Yet stop I did: in fact I often do,
And always end much at a loss like this,
Wondering what to look for; wondering too,
When churches fall completely out of use
What we shall turn them into, if we shall keep
A few cathedrals chronically on show,
Their parchment, plate and pyx in locked cases,
And let the rest rent-free to rain and sheep.
Shall we avoid them as unlucky places?

Or, after dark, will dubious women come
To make their children touch a particular stone;
Pick simples for a cancer; or on some
Advised night see walking a dead one?
Power of some sort or other will go on
In games, in riddles, seemingly at random;
But superstition, like belief, must die,
And what remains when disbelief has gone?
Grass, weedy pavement, brambles, buttress, sky,

A shape less recognizable each week,
A purpose more obscure. I wonder who
Will be the last, the very last, to seek
This place for what it was; one of the crew
That tap and jot and know what rood-lofts were?
Some ruin-bibber, randy for antique,
Or Christmas-addict, counting on a whiff
Of gown-and-bands and organ-pipes and myrrh?
Or will he be my representative,

Bored, uninformed, knowing the ghostly silt
Dispersed, yet tending to this cross of ground
Through suburb scrub because it held unspilt
So long and equably what since is found
Only in separation—marriage, and birth,

And death, and thoughts of these—for which was built
This special shell? For, though I've no idea
What this accoutred frowsty barn is worth,
It pleases me to stand in silence here;

A serious house on serious earth it is,
In whose blent air all our compulsions meet,
Are recognized, and robed as destinies.
And that much never can be obsolete,
Since someone will forever be surprising
A hunger in himself to be more serious,
And gravitating with it to this ground,
Which, he once heard, was proper to grow wise in,
If only that so many dead lie round.

August 28th—A Meditation
Sue Cording

My key turns in the lock, and the door open into the room revealing the familiar twenty-five blue and tan student desks and the large gray metal teacher's desk in the rear. The floor tiles are glossy with a fresh waxing, and the chalkboards are slicked clean, belying the twelve years of my lessons which have been written on them. A new American flag hangs in the center front between two bare bulletin boards. Not a speck of dust rests upon the bookshelves where the Scott Foresmans await distribution to this year's classes. Windows sparkle in the August sunlight, fresh after their annual washing and polishing. In the air lingers the faint odor of Murray's School Disinfecting Cleaner, but not a trace of chalk dust or body odor can be scented.

The room is the product of the janitorial staff's summer labors. There is about it a hushed anticipation of all that this year's students and parents expect to be accomplished here. Within these four freshly painted walls the community expects new ideas to be born and the great, mysterious event known as learning to take place. Books will be read and discussed, issues will be reported and debated, and papers will be written and graded.

Reprinted with permission of the author.

I open the filing cabinet now bulging with years of accumulated study guides, vocabulary lists, tests, and quizzes. I begin sorting through the materials stored here trying to make decisions about where to begin, what to cover, and where we will be when the bell rings on that last day of school nine months from now. Doubts and insecurities begin invading my mind. How can I be sure anything at all will be accomplished? And if there is any measurable product, will it be because of me or in spite of me? Why is it that this profession of teaching raises such questions?

I gaze around the room to confirm that those who work to clean and refurbish the school through the summer have no reason to doubt their labors. The maintenance crew must find fulfillment when they compare the dingy, unkempt appearance of the room in which they began their work last May with the shining, tidy room that this teacher enters at the end of August. The product of their labors can be seen and touched and smelled. Likewise, as I look through my window at the construction site across the street, I observe that where the crew was pouring a foundation in May, a fully completed building now stands. And in the field on the other side of the highway where in May the farmer tilled and planted his ground, a crop of nearly ripe corn rustles in the breeze. Even as I look at my new class lists lying on my desk, I see the fruits of another kind of labor. My own daughter's name is there among the names of the other juniors. The baby I held in my arms sixteen years ago has grown to young womanhood.

But how do I define and measure my product as a teacher? My work cannot be seen or touched or heard or smelled or weighed. It is so elusive that sometimes I wonder if there is any product at all. I try to calm myself. Maybe I am more nervous this year because my own daughter will be among my students, and in the dual roles of teacher and parent I will be anxious over her progress, concerned about her future. However, to dismiss my concerns as the new school year anxieties of a nervous parent offers too simple a solution.

I have struggled with the question before. What am I doing there? Where are my students going? Are they learning? Does anything we do here make any difference? I find the long-saved file of some of my best students' work and pull it from the filing cabinet. Slowly I begin leafing through the papers and remembering the names and faces. Some I wonder about. Where are they? What are they doing? Others have been recognized for their accomplishments. Phil has written a book about archaeology. Paul graduated from West Point with high honors. Sarah has published several of her poems. Some have kept in touch. Four of them are English teachers themselves, and they have come back to say nice things: "Thanks for encouraging me." "You really made a difference." "I remember the book we studied here. I'm going to teach the same book to my students."

Yes, the good students have done well. But what about the troubled kids? Well, I did convince Paul to stay in school. I was able to help Mike find a job. And Laura appreciated the support as she carried the unwanted pregnancy through her senior year. And Mark and John and Chuck—at least they aren't in jail. Can I claim to have had a small part in these and other lives? Yes, I believe that I can.

When Christa McAuliffe was chosen to be a member of the Challenger crew, she improved the image of all teachers when she said, "I touch the future." She was talking about an intangible, some looked-toward, ultimate time when her work would indeed be manifested. She believed she could touch that time with certainty even without being there. She could believe in something that she would never see. If we cannot believe in the unseen, the unheard, and the untouchable, if we cannot be convinced of the presence of an ideal we may never reach but toward which we continue to strive, then what are we doing in this business of teaching at all? I pick up my pen and open my Plan Book. "August 29, 1989. Begin by introducing ourselves."

Once More to the Lake
E. B. White

One summer, along about 1904, my father rented a camp on a lake in Maine and took us all there for the month of August. We all got ringworm from some kittens and had to rub Pond's Extract on our arms and legs night and morning, and my father rolled over in a canoe with all his clothes on; but outside of that the vacation was a success and from then on none of us ever thought

---

"Once More to the Lake" from ESSAYS OF E. B. WHITE by E. B. White. Copyright © 1941 by E. B. White. Reprinted by permission of Harper & Row, Publishers, Inc.

there was any place in the world like that lake in Maine. We returned summer after summer—always on August 1st for one month. I have since become a salt-water man, but sometimes in summer there are days when the restlessness of the tides and the fearful cold of the sea water and the incessant wind which blows across the afternoon and into the evening make me wish for the placidity of a lake in the woods. A few weeks ago this feeling got so strong I bought myself a couple of bass hooks and a spinner and returned to the lake where we used to go, for a week's fishing and to revisit old haunts.

I took along my son, who had never had any fresh water up his nose and who had seen lily pads only from train windows. On the journey over to the lake I began to wonder what it would be like. I wondered how time would have marred this unique, this holy spot—the coves and streams, the hills that the sun set behind, the camps and the paths behind the camps. I was sure that the tarred road would have found it out and I wondered in what other ways it would be desolated. It is strange how much you can remember about places like that once you allow your mind to return into the grooves which lead back. You remember one thing, and that suddenly reminds you of another thing. I guess I remembered clearest of all the early mornings, when the lake was cool and motionless, remembered how the bedroom smelled of the lumber it was made of and of the wet woods whose scent entered through the screen. The partitions in the camp were thin and did not extend clear to the top of the rooms, and as I was always the first up I would dress softly so as not to wake the others, and sneak out into the sweet outdoors and start out in the canoe, keeping close along the shore in the long shadows of the pines. I remembered being very careful never to rub my paddle against the gunwale for fear of disturbing the stillness of the cathedral.

The lake had never been what you would call a wild lake. There were cottages sprinkled around the shores, and it was in farming country although the shores of the lake were quite heavily wooded. Some of the cottages were owned by nearby farmers, and you would live at the shore and eat your meals at the farmhouse. That's what our family did. But although it wasn't wild, it was a fairly large and undisturbed lake and there were places in it which, to a child at least, seemed infinitely remote and primeval.

I was right about the tar: it led to within half a mile of the shore. But when I got back there, with my boy, and we settled into a camp near a farmhouse and into the kind of summertime I had known, I could tell that it was going to be pretty much the same as it had been before—I knew it, lying in bed the first morning, smelling the bedroom, and hearing the boy sneak quietly out and go off along the shore in a boat. I began to sustain the illusion that he was I, and therefore, by simple transposition, that I was my father. The sensation persisted, kept cropping up all the time we were there. It was not an entirely new feeling, but in this setting it grew much stronger. I seemed to be living a dual existence. I would be in the middle of some simple act, I would be picking up a bait box or laying down a table fork, or I would be saying something, and suddenly it would be not I but my father who was saying the words or making the gesture. It gave me a creepy sensation.

We went fishing the first morning. I felt the same damp moss covering the worms in the bait can, and saw the dragonfly alight on the tip of my rod as it hovered a few inches from the surface of the water. It was the arrival of this fly that convinced me beyond any doubt that everything was as it always had been, that the years were a mirage and there had been no years. The small waves were the same, chucking the rowboat under the chin as we fished at anchor, and the boat was the same boat, the same color green and the ribs broken in the same places, and under the floor-boards the same fresh-water leavings and debris—the dead hellgrammite, the wisps of moss, the rusty discarded fishhook, the dried blood from yesterday's catch. We stared silently at the tips of our rods, at the dragonflies that came and went. I lowered the top of mine into the water, tentatively, pensively dislodging the fly, which darted two feet away, poised, darted two feet back, and came to rest again a little farther up the rod. There had been no years between the ducking of this dragonfly and the other one—the one that was part of memory. I looked at the boy, who was silently watching his fly, and it was my hands that held his rod, my eyes watching. I felt dizzy and didn't know which rod I was at the end of.

We caught two bass, hauling them in briskly as though they were mackerel, pulling them over the side of the boat in a business-like manner without any landing net, and stunning them with a blow on the back of the head. When we got back for a swim before lunch, the lake was exactly where we had left it, the same number of inches from the dock, and there was only the merest suggestion of a breeze. This seemed an utterly enchanted sea, this lake you could leave to its own devices for a few hours and come back to, and find that it had not stirred, this constant and trustworthy body of water. In the shallows, the dark, water-soaked sticks and twigs, smooth and old, were undulating in clusters on the bottom against the clean ribbed sand, and the track of the mussel was plain. A school of minnows swam by, each minnow with its small individual shadow, doubling the attendance, so clear and sharp in the sunlight. Some of the other campers were in swimming, along the shore, one of them with a cake of soap, and the water felt thin and clear and unsubstantial. Over the years there had been this person with the cake of soap, this cultist, and here he was. There had been no years.

Up to the farmhouse to dinner through the teeming, dusty field, the road under our sneakers was only a two-track road. The middle track was missing, the one with the marks of the hooves and the splotches of dried, flaky manure. There had always been three tracks to choose from in choosing which track to walk in; now the choice was narrowed down to two. For a moment I missed terribly the middle alternative. But the way led past the tennis court, and something about the way it lay there in the sun reassured me; the tape had loosened along the backline, the alleys were green with plantains and other weeds, and the net (installed in June and removed in September) sagged in the dry noon, and the whole place steamed with midday heat and hunger and emptiness. There was a choice of pie for desert, and one was blueberry and one was apple, and the waitresses were the same country girls, there having been no passage of time, only the illusion of it as in a dropped curtain—the waitresses were still fifteen; their hair had been washed, that was the only difference—they had been to the movies and seen the pretty girls with clean hair.

Summertime, oh summertime, pattern of life indelible, the fade-proof lake, the woods unshatterable, the pasture with the sweetfern and the juniper forever and ever, summer without end; this was the background, and the life along the shore was the design, the cottages with their innocent and tranquil design, their tiny docks with the flagpole and the American flag floating against the white clouds in the blue sky, and the little paths over the roots of the trees leading from camp to camp and the paths leading back to the outhouses and the can of lime for sprinkling, and at the souvenir counters at the store the miniature birchbark canoes and the post cards that showed things looking a little better than they looked. This was the American family at play, escaping the city heat, wondering whether the newcomers in the camp at the head of the cove were "common" or "nice," wondering whether it was true that the people who drove up for Sunday dinner at the farmhouse were turned away because there wasn't enough chicken.

It seemed to me, as I kept remembering all this, that those times and those summers had been infinitely precious and worth saving. There had been jollity and peace and goodness. The arriving (at the beginning of August) had been so big a business in itself, at the railway station the farm wagon drawn up, the first smell of pine-laden air, the first glimpse of the smiling farmer, and the great importance of the trunks and your father's enormous authority in such matters, and the feel of the wagon under you for the long ten-mile haul, and at the top of the last long hill catching the first view of the lake after eleven months of not seeing this cherished body of water. The shouts and cries of the other campers when they saw you, and the trunks to be unpacked, to give up their rich burden. (Arriving was less exciting nowadays, when you sneaked up in your car and parked it under a tree near the camp and took out the bags and in five minutes it was all over, no fuss, no loud wonderful fuss about trunks.)

Peace and goodness and jollity. The only thing that was wrong now, really, was the sound of the place, an unfamiliar nervous sound of the outboard motors. This was the note that jarred, the one thing that would sometimes break the illusion and set the years moving. In those other summertimes all motors were inboard; and when they were at a little distance, the noise they made was a sedative, an ingredient of summer sleep. They were one-cylinder and two-cylinder engines, and some were make-and-break and some were jump-spark but they all made a sleepy sound across the lake. The one-lungers throbbed and fluttered, and the twin-cylinder ones purred and purred, and that was a quiet sound too. But now the campers all had outboards. In the daytime, in the hot mornings, these motors made a petulant, irritable sound; at night, in the still evening when the afterglow lit the water, they whined about one's ears like mosquitoes. My boy loved our rented outboard, and his great desire was to achieve singlehanded mastery over it, and authority, and he soon learned the trick of choking it a little (but not too much), and the adjustment of the needle valve. Watching him I would remember the things you could do with the old one-cylinder engine with the heavy fly-wheel, how you could have it eating out of your hand if you got really close to it spiritually. Motor boats in those days didn't have clutches, and you would make a landing by shutting off the motor at the proper time and coasting in with a dead rudder. But there was a way of reversing them, if you learned the trick, by cutting the switch and putting it on again exactly on the final dying revolution of the flywheel, so that it would kick back against compression and begin reversing. Approaching a dock in a strong following breeze, it was difficult to slow up sufficiently by the ordinary coasting method, and if a boy felt he had complete mastery over his motor, he was tempted to keep it running beyond its time and then reverse it a few feet from the dock. It took a cool nerve, because if you threw the switch a twentieth of a second too soon you would catch the flywheel when it still had speed enough to go up past center, and the boat would leap ahead, charging bull-fashion at the dock.

We had a good weekend at the camp. The bass were biting well and the sun shone endlessly, day after day. We would be tired at night and lie down in the accumulated heat of the little bedrooms after the long hot day and the breeze would stir almost imperceptibly outside and the smell of the swamp drift in through the rusty screens. Sleep would come easily and in the morning the red squirrel would be on the roof, tapping out his gay routine. I kept remembering everything, lying in bed in the mornings—the small steamboat that had a long rounded stern like the lip of a Ubangi, and how quietly she ran on the moonlight sails, when the older boys played their mandolins and the girls sang and we ate doughnuts dipped in sugar, and how sweet the music was on the water in the shining night, and what it had felt like to think about girls then. After breakfast we would go up to the shore and the things were in the same place—the minnows in a bottle, the plugs and spinners disarranged and pawed over by the youngsters from the boys' camp, the fig newtons and the Beeman's gum. Outside, the road was tarred and cars stood in front of the store. Inside, all was just as it had always been, except there was more Coca-Cola and not so much Moxie and root beer and birch beer and sarsaparilla. We would walk out with a bottle of pop apiece and sometimes the pop would backfire up our noses and hurt. We explored the streams, quietly, where the turtles slid off the sunny logs and dug their way into the soft bottom; and we lay on the town wharf and fed worms to the tame bass. Everywhere we went

I had trouble making out which was I, the one at my side, the one walking in my pants.

One afternoon while we were there at that lake a thunderstorm came up. It was like the revival of an old melodrama that I had seen long ago with childish awe. The second-act climax of the drama of the electrical disturbance over a lake in America had not changed in any important respect. This was the big scene, still the big scene. The whole thing was so familiar, the first feeling of oppression and heat and a general air around camp of not wanting to go very far away. In midafternoon (it was all the same) a curious darkening of the sky, and a lull in everything that had made life tick; and then the way the boats suddenly swung the other way at their moorings with the coming of a breeze out of the new quarter, and the premonitory rumble. Then the kettle drum, then the snare, then the bass drum and cymbals, then cracking light against the dark, and the gods grinning and licking their chops in the hills. Afterward the calm, the rain steadily rustling in the calm lake, the return of light and hope and spirits, and the campers running out in joy and relief to go swimming in the rain, their bright cries perpetuating the deathless joke about how they were getting simply drenched, and the children screaming with delight at the new sensation of bathing in the rain, and the joke about getting drenched linking the generations in a strong indestructible chain. And the comedian who waded in carrying an umbrella.

When the others were swimming my son said he was going in too. He pulled his dripping trunks from the line where they had hung all through the shower, and wrung them out. Languidly, and with no thought of going in, I watched him, his hard little body, skinny and bare, saw him wince slightly as he pulled up around his vitals the small, soggy, icy garment. As he buckled up the swollen belt suddenly my groin felt the chill of death.

IV

You may have noticed that E. B. White's essay doesn't exactly fit the three part form of the meditation that I outlined at the beginning of this chapter. "Once More to the Lake," in fact, illustrates that even the use of the form can be ambiguous. White focuses on a place (the lake), and he explores the ideas that the place inspires: ideas about the relationship of past and present; about parents reliving experience through their children; about how things change and remain the same. And he reaches some conclusions, sometimes tentative, sometimes ambiguous, about time and change and mortality. All the parts of the meditation are there, but White mixes them together, usually within a narrative structure. While I recommend that you follow the more straightforward structure, you should appreciate White's variation of it: All "rules" can be broken, if there is a justification for doing so.

While you're appreciating things, note the specific details that White uses to recreate the scene for us. Those aren't just trees in the woods, they're pines. And he doesn't just notice insects flying around. Rather, he "saw the dragonfly alight on the tip of [his] rod as it hovered a few inches from the surface of the water." Larkin and Cording accomplish this same re-creation of setting and events, each providing enough homely, ordinary details to let us see and hear and feel the places they are describing.

Once again, your reading may help you to expand your list of the features of effective writing you started at the beginning of the semester. And once again, working with your group will help you clarify what these features are. Work with the others to come up with another five or six qualities of good writing to record in your journal.

I realize, of course, that this is not your usual way of reading. It's not mine either. No one makes a practice of reading an essay only to keep track of the author's writing techniques and gimmicks, and I'm not suggesting that you ought to always read this way. We're paying attention to these identifiable qualities of effective writing now because, as a rule, when we read we only experience the effect. Paying attention to how the effects are created can let us learn how to better lead *our* readers to experience the effects of *our* writing.

And you have the opportunity now to test those effects. You have real readers in your group who can provide you with some reactions to your meditation before you finish it. Take full advantage of the opportunity. You'll need a readable draft of your paper for the others to look at. Furthermore, to take full advantage of your readers, you'll need to have thought a bit to formulate the questions still in your own mind about the assignment. Honest self-evaluation is called for here.

Next you'll need to let the members of your group know what these questions are: They may be about sections of the paper where you are having trouble, places you're not sure are clear enough, places where you're not sure where to go next. You should also ask the group members to pay particular attention to the details of your description. In addition they can evaluate how well you integrate the three parts of your essay. Finally, your readers may have questions of their own about things they'd like to know that your essay doesn't tell them.

Of course as others are reading your work, you will be reading theirs. Try to be as considerate a reader for your group members as you hope they will be for you. Pay attention to the questions they asked about their work, and try to offer constructive suggestions. While you're at it, be sure to mention the good features of each essay. Not only is this an appropriately generous thing to do, but it will assure that the writers won't change some things that already work well.

Appendix Four contains some additional advice for this group evaluation of essays, along with some additional questions that readers might respond to. And your instructor may provide a particular evaluation form for you to use. The most important advice I can offer, however, is to take this activity seriously. Read other people's essays carefully, and demand that they do the same for you.

V

Now you have one more thing to do before this paper is finished: you need to make use of the readers' reactions as you revise your essay. This process involves sorting through the comments you receive to determine which ones demand attention and which ones you can safely ignore. As a rule, whenever a reader calls for more specific detail, you should respond. And if someone is confused by a portion of your essay, you need to clarify. My rule (which you may remember from the description of my writing process in Chapter Three) is to take seriously any comment a reader makes. I may not agree with the particular revision the reader suggests, but the fact that someone had to make a comment on a particular phrase or sentence means that I may have to do some more work at this point. Some kind of revision or clarification is needed.

Furthermore, I don't depend on a reader to catch everything that needs improvement in my essay. Often I find that just the fact of giving my work to someone else to read makes me aware of the additional work I need to do. Sometimes I even find myself wanting to interrupt the reading to explain, "When you get to page three, what I was really trying to say was . . . ." Pay attention to those flashes of insight you get when someone reads your work. Remember them. Make the necessary changes. For me, those changes often involve adding whole paragraphs to include ideas that I left out, or that I realized too late should have been there. (As a matter of fact, this entire section on revision is one such addition. It wasn't here in the first draft of the chapter.)

Besides paying attention to completeness, I also try to analyze the organization of my essay. I need to be sure that one point leads logically to the next, and that the relationships between the parts are clear. It's not enough to have the connections evident in my mind; they have to be there on paper too. My reader has to be able to follow my thoughts from point to point. To assure that, I may need to cut some digressions and irrelevancies. That can sometimes be hard to do. Since each sentence (let alone whole paragraphs!) represents my hard work, it can be very difficult to push the delete button and send my words off to oblivion. Nonetheless, I sometimes have to do it. Digressions that lead readers away from the main points of the essay can create some unnecessary and unpleasant confusion.

And speaking of confusion, did you ever notice how confusing it can be to read the final exam schedule in the class schedule book?

You have to figure out which category your classes fall into (that is, periods with asterisks and those without) and then find the right number on the chart to find the right exam time. It's a miracle that anyone shows up to exams at the right time. There has to be a simpler system!

See what I mean about digressions? As important as the issue of the final exam schedule may be, it's out of place here. It distracts from the points about revision that I'm trying to present, and creates far more confusion than enlightenment. Away with it!

A concluding observation about the revision process: The introduction of word processing has significantly changed the way writers can approach revision. Before word processors, each revision of a piece of writing could mean retyping whole pages of text. No more. The ability of the computer to store text in memory means that we can revise the necessary parts, adding and deleting whole sections, changing words and sentences, without disturbing the work that is already finished. Far from being a dreaded task, revision can actually become fun. (Well, perhaps finding it "fun" may be a little perverted. At least revision is much easier with the computer.)

And it means that each of us has a better chance than ever to produce what Toss Murray (in Chapter Three) characterized as "self-satisfying" writing. With revision we can get it right. And we have a better chance of satisfying our readers as well.

Rewriting isn't virtuous. It isn't something that ought to be done. It is simply something that most writers find they have to do to discover what they have to say and how to say it.

Donald M. Murray

Chapter **6**

Discovering Diversity

I

So far in your writing you have been examining aspects of your own experience, seeing familiar experience in perhaps unfamiliar ways. Now it is time to turn attention to unfamiliar experiences, the experiences of others.

A college campus is a diverse community, with people from a wide variety of backgrounds. There are students here from different racial and ethnic backgrounds, people of different ages, people with different class backgrounds. Students come from the country, the suburbs, the city; some have military experience; some are married, some divorced; some have a different sexual orientation; some are temporary residents from other countries; some have impaired mobility, or sight, or hearing. Among your classmates are recovering alcoholics, single parents, Peace Corps volunteers, former gang members, dyslexics, and recent immigrants. For your next writing assignment, you will meet someone who is significantly different from you and record his or her experiences.

Interview a person whose background, experience, class, race, nationality, or challenges are different from your own. Learn as much as you can about this person's experience, focusing on specific stories.

In your essay, present the person to your reader, telling his or her story (or stories). As much as possible, use your subject's own words.

Some preparation will be necessary before beginning this project. First some self-examination. Use your journal to remember a time in your life when you felt like an outsider: Perhaps you were the shortest person on a basketball team, or the only person in your class to fail the biology mid-term. Or maybe:

The last person to get picked in gym class
The youngest person at your older sister's birthday party for her friends
The "teacher's pet" in third grade
The only member of a racial or ethnic group at a gathering
The only one of your friends without a date for the Christmas dance
The only person not drinking at a party
The only single person in a group of married friends

You get the idea. Recall an experience like this, describe it in your journal, then try to explain carefully just what the experience felt like.

A second preparatory exercise, again to write about in your journal: What groups do you identify with?—These may be groups such as a sorority, a residence hall floor, a sports team, a religious denomination, a nationality, a neighborhood, an ethnic group, a club, a political party. How did you become a member of the group? What do the members have in common with one another? Do they have a common language? Or behavior patterns? Or rituals? Or beliefs? How do the members differ from one another? How much difference is tolerated? Encouraged?

The third exercise is to read a poem:

---

41 Phone Book Names, Benecia, California

Mary Harlan

> ivalou lantrip
> harry shoup
> sterling wakefield
> adele whittle
> pierre bidou
> mrs ginger cady

From PROBES by William Harlan. Copyright © by Mary Harlan. Reprinted with permission.

6. Discovering Diversity

evelyn peais
harry gee
perry buffum
carl book
coy whitecotton
harold horchem
mrs ethel buzzard
joseph l fincher
earl rexroat
pearl tuvey
leslie bobbitt
karrie ioakimedes
harold boatman
mel jimera
al creekmore
chester frame
ritter vestes
floyd tom boardman
segfrid gibb
owen hotle
brendan o coyne
bert mcguirk
john crum
gerard earp
rudy a o ai
fred fick
gene urquhart
r frapwell
paul wetmore
roger lapant
lester kalk
claude counselman
o blossom
carole schimpa
charles stifle

Is it a poem? Does it have a "meaning"? What do you know about any of these people on this list? How do you know it?

These preparatory exercises are designed to increase your sensitivity toward the person you will write about for this assignment. It's time now to select that person. Begin by reviewing the people you have met on campus (or off) and determining who among them you consider to have experiences, background, culture, or challenges different from your own. The emphasis is on the difference *from you*. Even if you are in a minority group yourself, or consider yourself in some way different from the other students around you, the focus for this paper is not on your experience, but the experience of someone who is noticeably different from you.

You will need to exercise some sensitivity at this point. Not all your acquaintances will be willing to be the subject for your composition assignment. Try to put yourself in their position as you approach them with your request, and be sure to let them know that you will understand if they refuse.

Finally, you will need to prepare carefully for the actual interview. Remember how you interviewed your partner in the Chapter Three exercise. What worked well? What didn't? For this interview, as for that one, you will need to have several prepared questions to prompt your subject to talk (though when it comes to the actual interview, you may find yourself taking a different direction). Some work with your group (either in class or on your own) will help you to form the appropriate questions.

Remember, as you prepare, that your purpose is to get your subject's story, not to judge or evaluate. Ask open-ended questions that will get your subject talking and recalling experience in his or her own words. And you want to encourage specific stories which will reveal the nature of that experience, rather than a lot of vague generalizations. Here's the *start* for the list of questions your group will prepare:

> What groups do you identify with?
> What events do you remember that have helped you identify who you are?
> When did you first realize that you were a member of your (ethnic, gender, minority) group?
> Do you remember events when you felt out of place, or maybe felt like the victim of prejudice?

Once again, you should try as much as possible to lead your partner to tell specific stories which illustrate and explain his or her generalizations. This may mean asking follow-up questions from time to time. Don't talk too much, though. A good interviewer lets the subject do the talking.

A good interviewer also has a plan for recording the subject's responses. One method might be to use a tape recorder. That would mean you wouldn't need to take extensive notes during the interview (it was the method used by Studs Terkel in the three profiles in Part II below). Be sure, however, that your tape recorder is working. Test it to see that it's recording clearly. And be sure to get your subject's permission to be taped. If you don't get it, you will need to take notes.

Note-taking during an interview can be challenging. You will need some kind of shorthand (abbreviating words, leaving out words that you can supply later in context) in order to provide as fair a record as possible. It will be important to transcribe your notes as soon as possible after the interview, while it is still fresh in your memory. If you're not sure that you got it right, you can always show your subject your transcription of the conversation, so he or she can correct any errors you made. Finally, whether you tape your interview or take notes, remember to *listen* carefully. You need to hear what the other person is saying if you are to report on it fairly.

II

Here are some examples of an author reporting objectively on the experiences of another, primarily in the subject's own words. The first is from Henry Mayhew's *London Labour and the London Poor*, a massive sociological study first published in 1861.

I'm Used to It
Henry Mayhew

Several showily-dressed, if not actually well-attired women, who are to be found walking about the Haymarket, live in St. Giles's and about Drury Lane. But the lowest class of women, who prostitute themselves for a shilling or less, are the most curious and remarkable class in this part. We have spoken of them before as growing grey in the exercise of their profession.

From Henry Mayhew, LONDON LABOUR AND THE LONDON POOR, Volume IV, pp. 239–41. Copyright © 1968 by Dover Publications, New York. Reprinted with permission.

One of them, a woman over forty, shabbily dressed, and with a disreputable, unprepossessing appearance, volunteered the following statement for a consideration of a spirituous nature.

"Times is altered, sir, since I come on the town. I can remember when all the swells used to come down here-away, instead of going to the Market; but those times is past, they is, worse luck, but, like myself, nothing lasts for ever, although I've stood my share of wear and tear, I have. Years ago Fleet Street and the Strand, and Catherine Street, and all round there was famous for women and houses. Ah! those were the times. Wish they might come again, but wishing's no use, it ain't. It only makes one miserable a thinking of it. I come up from the country when I was quite a gal, not above sixteen I dessay. I come from Dorsetshire, near Lyme Regis, to see a aunt of mine. Father was a farmer in Dorset, but only in a small way—tenant farmer, as you would say. I was mighty pleased, you may swear, with London, and liked being out at night when I could get the chance. One night I went up the area and stood looking through the railing, when a man passed by, but seeing me he returned and spoke to me something about the weather. I, like a child, answered him unsuspectingly enough, and he went on talking about town and country, asking me, among other things, if I had long been in London, or if I was born there. I not thinking told him all about myself; and he went away apparently very much pleased with me, saying before he went that he was very glad to have made such an agreeable acquaintance, and if I would say nothing about it he would call for me about the same time, or a little earlier, if I liked, the next night, and take me out for a walk. I was, as you may well suppose, delighted, and never said a word. The next evening I met him as he appointed, and two or three times subsequently. One night we walked longer than usual, and I pressed him to return, as I feared my aunt would find me out; but he said he was so fatigued with walking so far, he would like to rest a little before he went back again; but if I was very anxious he would put me in a cab. Frightened about him, for I thought he might be ill, I preferred risking being found out; and when he proposed that we should go into some house and sit down I agreed. He said all at once, as if he had just remembered something, that a very old friend of his lived near there, and we couldn't go to a better place, for she would give us everything we could wish. We found the door half open when we arrived. 'How careless,' said my friend, 'to leave the street-door open, any one might get in.' We entered without knocking, and seeing a door in the passage standing ajar we went in. My friend shook hands with an old lady who was talking to several girls dispersed over different parts of the room, who, she said, were her daughters. At this announcement some of them laughed, when she got very angry and ordered them out of the room. Somehow I didn't like the place, and not feeling all right I asked to be put in a cab and sent home. My friend made no objection and a cab was sent for. He, however, pressed me to have something to drink before I started. I refused to touch any wine, so I asked for some coffee, which I drank. It made me feel very sleepy, so sleepy indeed that I begged to be allowed to sit down on the sofa. They accordingly placed me on the sofa, and advised me to rest a little while, promising, in order to allay my anxiety, to send a messenger to my aunt. Of course I was drugged, and so heavily I did not regain my consciousness till the next morning. I was horrified to discover that I had been ruined, and for some days I was inconsolable, and cried like a child to be killed or sent back to my aunt.

"When I became quiet I received a visit from my seducer, in whom I had placed so much silly confidence. He talked very kindly to me, but I would not listen to him for some time. He came several times to see me, and at last said he would take me away if I liked, and give me a house of my own. Finally, finding how hopeless all was I agreed to his proposal, and he allowed me four pounds a week. This went on for some months, till he was tired of me, when he threw me over for some one else. There is always as good fish in the sea as ever came out of it, and this I soon discovered.

"Then for some years—ten years, till I was six-and-twenty—I went through all the changes of a gay lady's life, and they're not a few, I can tell you. I don't leave off this sort of life because I'm in a manner used to it, and what could I do if I did? I've no character; I've never been used to do anything, and I don't see what employment I stand a chance of getting. Then if I had to sit hours and hours all day long, and part of the night too, sewing or anything like that, I should get tired. It would worrit me so; never having been accustomed, you see, I couldn't stand it. I lodge in Charles Street, Drury Lane, now. I did live in Nottingham Court once, and Earls Street. But, Lord, I've lived in a many places you wouldn't think, and I don't imagine you'd believe one half. I'm

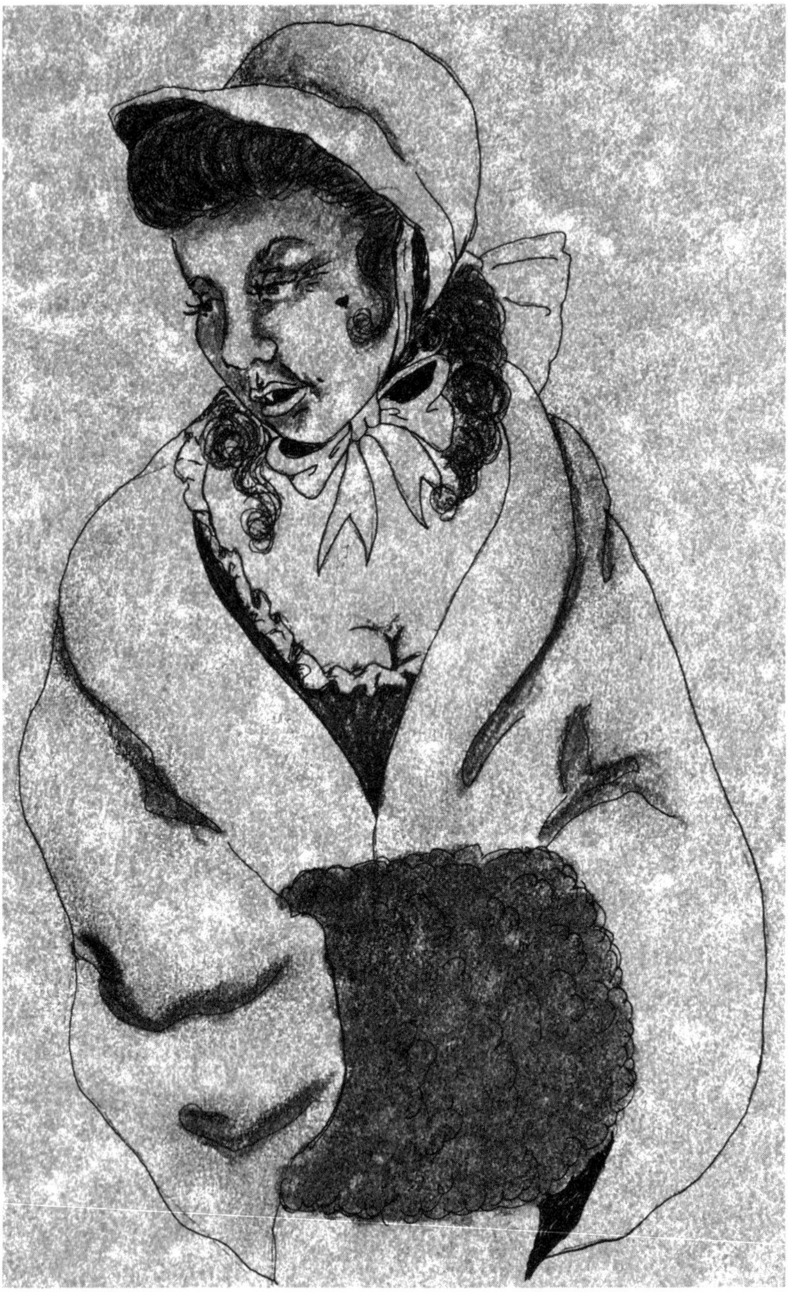

always a-chopping and a-changing like the wind as you may say. I pay half-a-crown a week for my bed-room; it's clean and comfortable, good enough for such as me. I don't think much of my way of life. You folks as has honour, and character, and feelings, and such, can't understand how all that's been beaten out of people like me. I don't feel. I'm used to it. I did once, more especial when mother died. I heard on it through a friend of mine, who told me her last words was of me. I did cry and go on then ever so, but Lor', where's the good of fretting? I arn't happy either. It isn't happiness, but I get enough money to keep me in victuals and drink, and it's the drink mostly that keeps me going. You've no idea how I look forward to my drop of gin. It's everything to me. I don't suppose I'll live much longer, and that's another thing that pleases me. I don't want to live, and yet I don't care enough about dying to make away with myself. I arn't got that amount of feeling that some has, and that's where it is I'm kinder 'fraid of it."

Mayhew's report on the lives of the London poor is based primarily on interviews with people like this unnamed woman. In our time, writer Studs Terkel has made similar studies, leading to his very successful books on World War II *(The Good War)*, the depression *(Hard Times),* and the lives of workers in America *(Working).* The following three selections are from *Working,* and they reveal the very different attitudes, experiences, feelings, and expectations of three different people.

The Mason: Carl Murray Bates
Studs Terkel

We're in a tavern no more than thirty yards from the banks of the Ohio. Toward the far side of the river, Alcoa smokestacks belch forth: an uneasy coupling of a bucolic past and an industrial present. The waters are polluted, yet the jobs out there offer the townspeople their daily bread.

From WORKING: PEOPLE TALK ABOUT WHAT THEY DO ALL DAY AND HOW THEY FEEL ABOUT WHAT THEY DO, by Studs Terkel. Copyright © 1972, 1974 by Studs Terkel. Reprinted by permission of Pantheon Books, a division of Random House, Inc.

He is fifty-seven years old. He's a stonemason who has pursued his craft since he was seventeen. None of his three sons is in his trade.

As far as I know, masonry is older than carpentry, which goes clear back to Bible times. Stone mason goes back way *before* Bible time: the pyramids of Egypt, things of that sort. Anybody that starts to build anything, stone, rock, or brick, start on the northeast corner. Because when they built King Solomon's Temple, they started on the northeast corner. To this day, you look at your courthouses, your big public buildings, you look at the cornerstone, when it was created, what year, it will be on the northeast corner. If I was gonna build a septic tank, I would start on the northeast corner. (Laughs.) Superstition, I suppose.

With stone we build just about anything. Stone is the oldest and best building material that ever was. Stone was being used even by the cavemen that put it together with mud. They built out of stone before they even used logs. He got him a cave, he built stone across the front. And he learned to use dirt, mud, to make the stones lay there without sliding around—which was the beginnings of mortar, which we still call mud. The Romans used mortar that's almost as good as we have today.

Everyone hears these things, they just don't remember 'em. But me being in the profession, when I hear something in that line, I remember it. Stone's my business. I, oh, sometimes talk to architects and engineers that have made a study and I pick up the stuff here and there.

Every piece of stone you pick up is different, the grain's a little different and this and that. It'll split one way and break the other. You pick up your stone and look at it and make an educated guess. It's a pretty good day layin' stone or brick. Not tiring. Anything you like to do isn't tiresome. It's hard work; stone is heavy. At the same time, you get interested in what you're doing and you usually fight the clock the other way. You're not lookin' for quittin'. You're wondering you haven't got enough done and it's almost quittin' time. (Laughs.) I ask the hod carrier what time it is and he says two thirty. I say, "Oh, my Lord, I was gonna get a whole lot more than this."

I pretty well work by myself. On houses, usually just one works. I've got the hod carrier there, but most of the time I talk to myself, "I'll get my hammer and I'll knock the chip off there." (Laughs.) A good hod carrier is half your day. He won't work as hard as a poor one. He knows what to do and make every move count makin' the mortar. It has to be so much water, so much sand. His skill is to see that you don't run out of anything. The hod carrier, he's above the laborer. He has a certain amount of prestige.

I think a laborer feels that he's the low man. Not so much that he works with his hands, it's that he's at the bottom of the scale. He always wants to get up to a skilled trade. Of course he'd make more money. The main thing is the common laborer—even the word common laborer—just sounds so common, he's at the bottom. Many that works with his hands takes pride in his work.

I get a lot of phone calls when I get home: how about showin' me how and I'll do it myself? I always wind up doin' it for 'em. (Laughs.) So I take a lot of pride in it and I do get, oh, I'd say, a lot of praise or whatever you want to call it. I don't suppose anybody, however much he's recognized, wouldn't like to be recognized a little more. I think I'm pretty well recognized.

One of my sons is an accountant and the other two are bankers. They're mathematicians, I suppose you'd call 'em that. Air-conditioned offices and all that. They always look at the house I build. They stop by and see me when I'm aworkin'. Always want me to come down and fix somethin' on their house, too. (Laughs.) They don't buy a house that I don't have to look at it first. Oh sure, I've got to crawl under it and look on the roof, you know . . .

I can't seem to think of any young masons. So many of 'em before, the man lays stone and his son follows his footsteps. Right now the only one of these sons I can think of is about forty, fifty years old.

I started back in the Depression times when there wasn't any apprenticeships. You just go out and if you could hold your job, that's it. I was just a kid then. Now I worked real hard and carried all the blocks I could. Then I'd get my trowel and I'd lay one or two. The second day the boss told me: I think you could lay enough blocks to earn your wages. So I guess I had only one day of apprenticeship. Usually it takes about three years of being a hod carrier to start. And it takes another ten or fifteen years to learn the skill.

I admired the men that we had at that time that were stonemasons. They knew their trade. So naturally I tried to pattern after them. There's been very little change in the work. Stone is still stone, mortar is still the same as it was fifty years ago. The style of stone has changed a little. We use a lot more, we call it golf. A stone as big as a baseball up to as big as a basketball. Just round balls and whatnot. We just fit 'em in the wall that way.

Automation has tried to get in the bricklayer. Set 'em with a crane. I've seen several put up that way. But you've always got in-between the windows and this and that. It just doesn't seem to pan out. We do have a power saw. We do have an electric power mix to mix the mortar, but the rest of it's done by hand as it always was.

In the old days they all seemed to want it cut out and smoothed. It's harder now because you have no way to use your tools. You have no way to use a string, you have no way to use a level or a plumb. You just have to look at it because it's so rough and many irregularities. You have to just back up and look at it.

All construction, there's always a certain amount of injuries. A scaffold will break and so on. But practically no real danger. All I ever did do was work on houses, so we don't get up very high—maybe two stories. Very seldom that any more. Most of 'em are one story. And so many of 'em use stone for a trim. They may go up four, five feet and then paneling or something. There's a lot of skinned fingers or you hit your finger with a hammer. Practically all stone is worked with hammers and chisels. I wouldn't call it dangerous at all.

Stone's my life. I daydream all the time, most times it's on stone. Oh, I'm gonna build me a stone cabin down on the Green River. I'm gonna build stone cabinets in the kitchen. That stone door's gonna be awful heavy and I don't know how to attach the hinges. I've got to figure out how to make a stone roof. That's the kind of thing. All my dreams, it seems like it's got to have a piece of rock mixed in it.

If I got some problem that's bothering me, I'll actually wake up in the night and think of it. I'll sit at the table and get a pencil and paper and go over it, makin' marks on paper or drawin' or however . . . this way or that way. Now I've got to work this and I've only got so much. Or they decided they want it that way when you already got it fixed this way. Anyone hates tearing his work down. It's all the same price but you still don't like to do it.

These fireplaces, you've got to figure how they'll throw out heat, the way you curve the fireboxes inside. You have to draw a line so they reflect heat. But if you throw out too much of a curve, you'll have them smoke. People in these fine houses don't want a puff of smoke coming out of the house.

The architect draws the picture and the plans, and the draftsman and the engineer, they help him. They figure the strength and so on. But when it comes to actually makin' the curves and doin' the work, you've got to do it with your hands. It comes right back to your hands.

When you get into stone, you're gettin' away from the prefabs, you're gettin' into the better homes. Usually at this day and age they'll start into sixty to seventy thousand and run up to about half a million. We've got one goin' now that's mighty close, three or four hundred thousand. That type of house is what we build.

The lumber is not near as good as it used to be. We have better fabricating material, such as plywood and sheet rock and things of that sort but the lumber itself is definitely inferior. Thirty, forty years ago a house was almost entirely made of lumber, wood floors. . . . Now they have vinyl, they have carpet, everything, and so on. The framework wood is getting to be of very poor quality.

But stone is still stone and the bricks are actually more uniform than they used to be. Originally they took a clay bank. . . . I know a church been built that way. Went right on location, dug a hole in the ground and formed bricks with their hands. They made the bricks that built the building on the spot.

Now we've got modern kilns, modern heat, the temperature don't vary. They got better bricks now than they used to have. We've got machines that make brick, so they're made true. Where they used to, they were pretty rough. I'm buildin' a big fireplace now out of old brick. They run wide, long, and it's a headache. I've been two weeks on that one fireplace.

The toughest job I ever done was this house, a hundred years old plus. The lady wanted one room left just that way. And this doorway had to be closed. It had deteriorated and weathered for over a hundred years. The bricks was made out of broken pieces, none of 'em were straight. If you lay 'em crooked, it gets awful hard right there. You spend a lifetime tryin' to learn to lay bricks straight. And it took a half-day to measure with a spoon, to try to get the mortar to match. I'd have so much dirt, so much soot, so much lime, so when I got the recipe right I could make it in bigger quantity. Then I made it with a coffee cup. Half a cup of this, half a cup of that . . . I even used soot out of a chimney and sweepin's off the floor. I was two days layin' up a little doorway, mixin' the mortar and all. The boss told the lady it couldn't be done. I said, "Give me the time, I believe I can do it." I defy you to find where that door is right now. That's the best job I ever done.

There's not a house in this country that I haven't built that I don't look at every time I go by. (Laughs.) I can set here now and actually in my mind see so many that you wouldn't believe. If there's one stone in there crooked, I know where it's at and I'll never forget it. Maybe thirty years, I'll know a place where I should have took that stone out and redone it but I didn't. I still notice it. The people who live there might not notice it, but I notice it. I never pass that house that I don't think of it. I've got one house in mind right now. (Laughs.) That's the work of my hands. 'Cause you see, stone, you don't prepaint it, you don't camouflage it. It's there, just like I left it forty years ago.

I can't imagine a job where you go home and maybe go by a year later and don't know what you've done. My work, I can see what I did the first day I started. All my work is set right out there in the open and I can look at it as I go by. It's something I can see the rest of my life. Forty years ago, the first blocks I ever laid in my life, when I was seventeen years old. I never go through Eureka—a little town down there on the river—that I don't look that away. It's always there.

Immortality as far as we're concerned. Nothin' in this world lasts forever, but did you know that stone—Bedford limestone, they claim—deteriorates one-sixteenth of an inch every hundred years? And it's around four or five inches for a house. So that's gettin' awful close. (Laughs.)

Telephone Operator: Heather Lamb

Studs Terkel

For almost two years she has been working as a long distance telephone operator at Illinois Bell. A naval base is nearby. She works three nights a week, split shift, during the high-school season and a full forty hours in the summertime. She is turning eighteen.

From WORKING: PEOPLE TALK ABOUT WHAT THEY DO ALL DAY AND HOW THEY FEEL ABOUT WHAT THEY DO, by Studs Terkel. Copyright © 1972, 1974 by Studs Terkel. Reprinted by permission of Pantheon Books, a division of Random House, Inc.

It's a strange atmosphere. You're in a room about the size of a gymnasium, talking to people thousands of miles away. You come in contact with at least thirty-five an hour. You can't exchange any ideas with them. They don't know you, they never will. You feel like you might be missing people. You feel like they put a coin in the machine and they've got you. You're there to perform your service and go. You're kind of detached.

A lot of the girls are painfully shy in real life. You get some girls who are outgoing in their work, but when they have to talk to someone and look them in the face, they can't think of what to say. They feel self-conscious when they know someone can see them. At the switchboard, it's a feeling of anonymousness.

There are about seven or eight phrases that you use and that's it: "Good morning, may I help you?" "Operator, may I help you?" "Good afternoon." "Good evening." "What number did you want?" "Would you repeat that again?" "I have a collect call for you from so-and-so, will you accept the charge?" "It'll be a dollar twenty cents." That's all you can say.

A big thing is not to talk with a customer. If he's upset, you can't say more than "I'm sorry you've been having trouble." If you get caught talking with a customer, that's one mark against you. You can't help but want to talk to them if they're in trouble or if they're just feeling bad or something. For me it's a great temptation to say, "Gee, what's the matter?" You don't feel like you're really that much helping people.

Say you've got a guy on the line calling from Vietnam, his line is busy and you can't interrupt. God knows when he'll be able to get on his line again. You know he's lonesome and he wants to talk to somebody, and there you are and you can't talk to him. There's one person who feels badly and you can't do anything. When I first started, I asked the operator and she says, "No, he can always call another time."

One man said, "I'm lonesome, will you talk to me?" I said, "Gee, I'm sorry, I just can't." But you *can't*. (Laughs.) I'm a communications person but I can't communicate.

I've worked here almost two years and how many girls' first names do I know? Just their last name is on their headset. You might see them every day and you won't know their names. At Ma Bell they speak of teamwork, but you don't even know the names of the people who are on your team.

It's kind of awkward if you meet someone from the company and say, "Hi there Jones," or whatever. (Laughs.) It's very embarrassing. You sit in the cafeteria and you talk to people and you don't even know their names. (Laughs.) I've gone to a lot of people I've been talking to for a week and I've said, "Tell me your name." (Laughs.)

You have a number—mine's 407. They put your number on your tickets, so if you made a mistake they'll know who did it. You're just an instrument. You're there to dial a number. It would be just as good for them to punch out the number.

The girls sit very close. She would be not even five or six inches away from me. The big thing is elbows, especially if she's left-handed. That's why we have so many colds in the winter, you're so close. If one person has a cold, the whole office has a cold. It's very catchy.

You try to keep your fingernails short because they break. If you go to plug in, your fingernail goes. You try to wear your hair simple. It's not good to have your hair on top of your head. The women don't really come to work if they've just had their hair done. The headset flattens it.

Your arms don't really get tired, your mouth gets tired. It's strange, but you get tired of talking, 'cause you talk constantly for six hours without a break.

Half the phones have a new system when the quarter is three beeps, a dime is two beeps, and a nickel is one beep. If the guy's in a hurry and he keeps throwing in money, all the beeps get all mixed up together (laughs), and you don't know how much money is in the phone. So it's kinda hard.

When you have a call, you fill it out on this IBM card. Those go with a special machine. You use a special pencil so it'll go through this computer and pick up the numbers. It's real soft lead, it just goes all over the desk and you're all dirty by the time you get off. (Laughs.) And sometimes your back hurts if your chair isn't up at the right height and you have to bend over and write. And keeping track. You don't get just one call at a time.

There is also the clock. You've got a clock next to you that times every second. When the light goes off, you see the party has answered, you have to write down the hour, the minute, and the second. Okay, you put that in a special slot right next to the cord light. You're ready for another one. Still you've got to watch the first one. When the light goes on, they disconnect and you've got to take the card out again and time down the hour, the minute, and the second—plus keeping on taking other calls. It's hectic.

If you work the day shift, conversations are short, so they come down in time amount to trying to take down a man's credit card number and collecting another man's money. One man waiting for his overtime, another man waiting for you to put his call through. Sometimes your tickets get all messed up—and that makes people even madder. And it doesn't help when people are crabby and they don't talk loud enough.

Businessmen get very upset if they have to repeat their credit card number. Sometimes they're taking to you and they're talking to their partner and you're trying to listen for the number. They'll say something to their partner and you think it's for you and they get irritated. You get very sensitive to people's voices. Sometimes you get mad. Why should this man be yelling at me? I do feel put-down a lot.

But other times there's a real sense of power. I can tell you when you have to stop talking. You have to pay me the money. If you don't pay me the money, I can do this and this to you. You feel that more when you're talking to people who have to pay for their calls, like sailors at the base. But with the businessmen, you get a feeling of helplessness. He can ruin you. You've got real power over the poorer people. They don't even have a phone, so they can't complain. This businessman can write a letter to Ma Bell. I'm more tolerant of the people who are calling from a pay phone and haven't got much money. But businessmen, I make him pay for every second of his call. (Laughs.) I'm more powerful than him at the moment. (Laughs.)

I think telephone prices are really too high. Dialing direct is cheap, but the poorer people who don't have private phones and have to use pay phones, the costs are exorbitant. It's preying on poor people.

You can always get a date over the phone if you want. I've gotten asked so many times. (Laughs.) You always make some little comment, especially when you're bored late at night. I talk with a Southern accent or a Puerto Rican accent. Or try to make your voice real sexy, just to see what kind of reaction. . . . No, no, I never accepted dates. (Laughs.) Nobody ever sounded . . . .

A lot of times, they leave the phone and bill it to others. You call the number they gave and they say, "I don't know him."

The operator isn't charged for any of this, but they do keep track. How many calls you take, how well you mark your tickets, how many errors you make. You're constantly being pushed.

If you're depressed 'cause the day hasn't gone right, it shows in how you talk to people. But again, some days are hysterically funny. I don't keep with all the regulations. I always try to make a couple of jokes. Especially if you're working late at night. Sometimes people on the lines are so funny, you'll just sit there and laugh and laugh until tears roll down your face. (Laughs.)

Do I listen in on conversations? (Lowers voice.) Some girls really do. I've never had the temptation to flip the switch. I don't know why. This company is the kind who watches you all the time. The supervisor does listen to you a lot. She can push a button on this special console. Just to see if I'm pleasant enough, if I talk too much to the customers, if I'm charging the right amount, if I make a personal call. Ma Bell is listening.

And you don't know. That's why it's smart to do the right thing most of the time. Keep your nose clean.

They never asked me to listen in. 'Cause they'd be reversing all the things they ever said: secrecy of communications, privacy for the customers. I don't think I would anyway. They can have the job.

Most people who have stayed as telephone operators are older women. Not too many young girls are there forever. Girls are more patient than older women. I was sitting next to one today. This man evidently left the phone and she was trying to get money from him. She yells, "Look at that bastard!" She started ringing real hard, "You come back here, you owe me money!" Really crabbily. If I did that, the supervisor would yell at me. But this lady's been there for twenty years. They're very permissive with their older ladies. A lot of them have ugly voices. But again, you've been working there twenty years and saying the same things for twenty years, my God, can you blame them? After twenty years you get real hard.

It's a hard feeling when everyone's in a hurry to talk to somebody else, but not to talk to you. Sometimes *you* get a feeling of need to talk to somebody. Somebody who wants to listen to you other than "Why didn't you get me the right number?"

It's something to run into somebody who says, "It's a nice day out, operator. How's your day, busy? Has it been a rough day?" You're so thankful for these people. You say, "Oh yes, it's been an awful day. Thank you for asking."

Gravedigger: Elmer Ruiz
Studs Terkel

Not anybody can be a gravedigger. You can dig a hole any way they come. A gravedigger, you have to make a neat job. I had a fella once, he wanted to see a grave. He was a fella that digged sewers. He was impressed when he seen me diggin' this grave—how square and how perfect it was. A human body is goin' into this grave. That's why you need skill when you're gonna dig a grave.

He has dug graves for eight years, as the assistant to the foreman. "I been living on the grounds for almost twelve years." During the first four years "I used to cut grass and other things. I never had a dream to have this kind of job. I used to drive a trailer from Texas to Chicago." He is married and has five children, ranging in age from two to sixteen. It is a bitter cold Sunday morning.

The gravedigger today, they have to be somebody to operate a machine. You just use a shovel to push the dirt loose. Otherwise you don't use 'em. We're tryin' a new machine, a ground hog. This machine is supposed to go through heavy frost. It do very good job so far. When the weather is mild, like fifteen degrees above zero, you can do it very easy.

But when the weather is below zero, believe me, you just really workin' hard. I have to use a mask. Your skin hurts so much when it's cold—like you put a hot flame near your face. I'm talkin' about two, three hours standin' outside. You have to wear a mask, otherwise you can't stand it at all.

Last year we had a frost up to thirty-five inches deep, from the ground down. That was difficult to have a funeral. The frost and cement, it's almost the same thing. I believe cement would break easier than frost. Cement is real solid, but when you hit 'em they just crack. The frost, you just hit 'em and they won't give up that easy. Last year we had to use an air hammer when we had thirty-five inches frost.

From WORKING: PEOPLE TALK ABOUT WHAT THEY DO ALL DAY AND HOW THEY FEEL ABOUT WHAT THEY DO, by Studs Terkel. Copyright © 1972, 1974 by Studs Terkel. Reprinted by permission of Pantheon Books, a division of Random House, Inc.

The most graves I dig is about six, seven a day. This is in the summer. In the winter it's a little difficult. In the winter you have four funerals, that's a pretty busy day.

I been workin' kinda hard with this snow. We use charcoal heaters, it's the same charcoal you use to make barbecue ribs or hot dogs. I go and mark where the grave is gonna be tomorrow and put a layer of charcoal the same size of a box. And this fifteen inches of frost will be completely melt by tomorrow morning. I start early, about seven o'clock in the morning, and I have the park cleaned before the funeral. We have two funerals for tomorrow, eleven and one o'clock. That's my life.

In the old days it was supposed to be four men. Two on each end with a rope, keep lowerin' little by little. I imagine that was kinda hard, because I imagine some fellas must weigh two hundred pounds, and I can feel that weight. We had a burial about five years ago, a fella that weighed four hundred pounds. He didn't fit on the lowerin' device. We had a big machine tractor that we coulda used, but that woulda looked kinda bad, because lowerin' a casket with a tractor is like lowerin' anything. You have to respect. . . . We did it by hand. There were about a half a dozen men.

The grave will be covered in less than two minutes, complete. We just open the hoppers with the right amount of earth. We just press it and then we lay out a layer of black earth. Then we put the sod that belongs there. After a couple of weeks you wouldn't know it's a grave there. It's complete flat. Very rarely you see a grave that is sunk.

To dig a grave would take from an hour and a half to an hour and forty-five minutes. Only two fellas do it. The operator of the ground hog or back hoe and the other fella, with the trailer, where we put the earth.

When the boss is gone I have to take care of everything myself. That includes givin' orders to the fellas and layin' graves and so on. They make it hard for me when the fellas won't show. Like this new fella we have. He's just great but he's not very dependable. He miss a lot. This fella, he's about twenty-four years old. I'm the only one that really knows how to operate that machine.

I usually tell 'em I'm a caretaker. I don't think the name sound as bad. I have to look at the park, so after the day's over that everything's closed, that nobody do damage to the park.

Some occasions some people just come and steal and loot and do bad things in the park, destroy some things. I believe it would be some young fellas. A man with responsibility, he wouldn't do things like that. Finally we had to put up some gates and close 'em at sundown. Before, we didn't, no. We have a fence of roses. Always in cars you can come after sundown.

When you tell people you work in a cemetery, do they change the subject?

Some, they want to know. Especially Spanish people who come from Mexico. They ask me if it is true that when we bury somebody we dig 'em out in four, five years and replace 'em with another one. I tell 'em no. When these people is buried, he's buried here for life.

It's like a trade. It's the same as a mechanic or a doctor. You have to present your job correct, it's like an operation. If you don't know where to make the cut, you're not gonna have a success. The same thing here. You have to have a little skill. I'm not talkin' about college or anything like that. Myself, I didn't have no grade school, but you have to know what you're doin'. You have some fellas been up for many years and still don't know whether they're comin' or goin'. I feel proud when everything became smooth and when Mr. Bach congratulate us. Four years ago, when the foreman had a heart attack, I took over. That was a real rough year for myself. I had to dig the graves and I had to show the fellas what to do.

A gravedigger is a very important person. You must have heard about the strike we had in New York about two years ago. There were twenty thousand bodies layin' and nobody could bury 'em. The cost of funerals they raised and they didn't want to raise the price of the workers. The way they're livin', everything wanna go up, and I don't know what's gonna happen.

Can you imagine if I wouldn't show up tomorrow morning and this other fella—he usually comes late—and sometimes he don't show. We have a funeral for eleven o'clock. Imagine what happens? The funeral arrive and where you gonna bury it?

We put water, the aspirins, in case somebody pass out. They have those capsules that you break and put up by their nose—smelling salts. And we put heaters for inside the tents so the place be a little warm.

There are some funerals, they really affect you. Some young kid. We buried lots of young. You have emotions, you turn in, believe me, you turn. I had a burial about two years ago of teen-agers, a young boy and a young girl. This was a real sad funeral because there was nobody but young teen-agers. I'm so used to going to funerals every day—of course, it bothers me—but I don't feel as bad as when I bury a young child. You really turn.

I usually will wear myself some black sunglasses. I never go to a funeral without sunglasses. It's a good idea because your eyes is the first thing that shows when you have a big emotion. Always these black sunglasses.

This grief that I see every day, I'm really used to somebody's crying every day. But there is some that are real bad, when you just have to take it. Some people just don't want to give up. You have to understand that when somebody pass away, there's nothing you can do and you have to take it. If you don't want to take it, you're gonna make your life worse, become sick. People seems to take it more easier these days. They miss the person, but not as much.

There's some funerals that people, they show they're not sad. This is different kinds of people. I believe they are happy to see this person—not in a way of singing—because this person is out of his sufferin' in this world. This person is gone and at rest for the rest of his life. I have this question lots of times: "How can I take it?" They ask if I'm calm when I bury people. If you stop and think, a funeral is one of the natural things in the world.

I enjoy it very much, especially in summer. I don't think any job inside a factory or an office is so nice. You have the air all day and it's just beautiful. The smell of the grass when it's cut, it's just fantastic. Winter goes so fast sometimes you just don't feel it.

When I finish my work here, I just don't remember my work. I like music so much that I have lots more time listenin' to music or playin'. That's where I spend my time. I don't drink, I don't smoke. I play Spanish bass and guitar. I play accordion. I would like to be a musician. I was born and raised in Texas and I never had a good school. I learned music myself from here and there. After I close the gate I play. I don't think it would be nice to play music when the funeral's goin' by. But after everything . . . .

I believe we are not a rich people, but I think we're livin' fair. We're not sufferin'. Like I know lotsa people are havin' a rough time to live on this world because of crises of the world. My wife, sometimes she's tired of stayin' in here. I try to take her out as much as possible. Not to parties or clubs, but to go to stores and sometimes to go to drive-ins and so on.

She's used to funerals, too. I go to eat at noon and she asks me, "How many funerals you got today? How many you buried today?" "Oh, we buried two." "How many more you got?" "Another." Some other people, you go to your office, they say, "How many letters you write today?" Mine says, "How many funerals you had today?" (Laughs.)

My children are used to everything. They start playin' ball right against the house. They're not authorized to go across the road because it's the burial in there. Whenever a funeral gonna be across from the house, the kids are not permitted to play. One thing a kid love, like every kid, is dogs. In a way, a dog in here would be the best thing to take care of the place, especially a German Shepherd. But they don't want dogs in here. It's not nice to see a dog around a funeral. Or cats or things like that. So they don't have no pet, no.

I believe I'm gonna have to stay here probably until I die. It's not gonna be too bad for me because I been livin' twelve years already in the cemetery. I'm still gonna be livin' in the cemetery. (Laughs.) So that's gonna be all right with me whenever I go. I think I may be buried here, it look like.

Thus far I haven't followed the various essays I've asked you to read with the "discussion questions" that many textbooks include. This time, however, I would like to direct your attention with some questions. If you don't have an opportunity to talk about these points with the members of your group, be sure to explore them in your journal:

What did you learn about each of these four people?
How would you summarize each of their experiences? How could you briefly characterize each person?
What techniques do the authors use to convey a full sense of who these people are?

I want now to make one observation in response to my last question. Notice that all these people, whose experiences and backgrounds are very different from those of authors Mayhew and Terkel, are allowed to speak in their own words. Or, if not in their exact words, at least in an honest approximation of those words. And they are treated with fairness and consideration. The authors didn't have to editorialize or generalize. The reported words and stories are themselves enough to reveal both the person and the experience.

III

Mayhew and Terkel's technique of letting their subjects speak for themselves, with only minimal authorial commentary, is an especially effective way to report on the experience of someone else, particularly if the person can speak fluently about that experience. Of course both Mayhew and Terkel did considerable editing, choosing which of their subjects' words they would use. And in Mayhew's case, there was also considerable re-writing of the woman's speech, since he had to work without benefit of tape-recorder.

In some instances, however, it is necessary for the author to be more of a participant in the action, to explain more and to describe more. In other words, the resulting essay is, in part, a description of the author's own experience, although the other person still emerges as the center of the essay. And while there are fewer of the subject's own words, the author still makes use of dialog to let the subject come to life. (A journal entry: try transcribing a conversation that you overhear, just to get practice in recording the way people really speak.)

The following essay exemplifies this narrative method of profiling another person whose experience differs from the author's. It was written by a Western student for the *Courier*.

It Doesn't Only Happen in America

Siraj Habib

1.

With the issue of abortion and teen-age pregnancy in the news media almost every day, have we thought about what it would be like to be an unmarried pregnant woman in another country (not in the Western world)?

Years ago, back in my hometown in Malaysia, several blocks away from my home, there was a grocery store where my friend Ani worked. Ani was almost seventeen, and she worked there as a cashier. She was short, yet very pretty. Her long hair fell to her hips and fluttered as she moved around cashing in change during busy hours.

When she smiled, her shiny set of teeth gleamed, and her dimples showed. Men flocked around the grocery store like bees to honey, just to chat with her and tease her. Ani's warm and friendly manners won the hearts of not only men but women as well. She always appeared happy and often had a kind word or two for everyone who walked into the store. She was like a mentor to the youngsters in that neighborhood.

One evening, as I walked into the store to get my daily share of candies, there was a change of mood on Ani's face. She wasn't herself; she appeared sullen. Her eyes were red as though she had just dried the tears that had been flowing the whole morning.

I did not have the nerve to ask her what was wrong, for I was younger than she, and as I adored her so very much, I felt that it was impolite to ask. But as I was leaving the store, Ani grabbed my hands and begged to talk to me.

We left the store, walking as we talked. Ani told me she was in love with the store owner's son, Mat. Mat had talked her into marrying him, and this led to her becoming pregnant. Now that

---

Reprinted from Siraj Habib, "It doesn't only happen in America," and "Leaving town was the best solution." Western COURIER, November 1, 1989, © Western COURIER.

Ani was pregnant, he had betrayed her by calling the marriage off. Ani was devastated.

Premarital sex was a serious crime in that Muslim community, and she knew any plea for help would fall on deaf ears. She would be outcast by her family and relatives. Poor Ani had no one to turn to.

"What should I do?" asked Ani.

I stood there, stunned and unable to even think of such a situation happening to me. I had no words of advice for her. I just looked at her with despair. I thought of all the things that could happen to her once they found out. My hands turned numb, and I shook.

"Ani, what are you going to do?" I asked.

"In a village nearby there lives Machik Pah, who can abort the baby. Will you accompany me there?" she asked. Machik Pah was the village medicine woman. Now I shook even more, and at this point I could not stop my tears. I was scared and wished that Ani had never asked me these questions.

2.

On the other hand, what would Ani do? There was no community mental health services or any other place she could go for help. Instead there were people who would torment her, blame her, and probably punish her severely for sinning. Adultery and promiscuity between unmarried individuals are not tolerated among the Muslims.

We did not talk for very long. We parted, and as I walked home, I was thinking of Ani's fate. She was in very deep trouble. Should I accompany her to Machik Pah's house? I was very confused.

The next day I met Ani, and she told me she had decided what to do. She was not going to abort the child. Instead she was going to have the child and live through her sin.

A week later, I accompanied Ani to the train station where she boarded the train to Kuala Lumpur, the capital city of Malaysia. The twenty ringgit bill that I managed to get from my piggy bank was damp in my hands. I was distressed to see my friend leave with such a heavy heart. At the sound of the whistle, I thrust the twenty ringgits into Ani's hands and wished her luck. She waved as the train moved and shouted back, "I'll write to you."

A year passed after Ani left, and there was no news from her. Then one evening, as I came home from school, a letter from Ani awaited me. I ran to my room, locked the door, and sat on my bed to read it. In that letter she recapitulated the account of her departure and told about subsequent events.

Tears of joy and nostalgia choked me as I read her letter and studied the picture of her with her son in her arms. She had faced many hurdles to bear her son. Now, even though I have lost contact with Ani, I know that my memories of her will be with me forever.

Notice how Siraj uses narrative structure to talk about Ani. The essay tells a story. And like most stories, this one begins at the beginning, with a few paragraphs of background leading to Ani's confession of her pregnancy. Then the story moves chronologically through the events of the next day.

Notice, too, that the story has an ambiguous ending. Ani and her son were well, but we know that their lives will not be easy. And the writer, in this country now, has lost touch with them. Siraj doesn't try to force the story to have a happier ending than it actually does. The ambiguity is honest. Further, Siraj resists the temptation to end the story with a moralizing conclusion. The first paragraph suggests that we compare our life in America with life in the Malaysian village, with the focus on the issue of Ani's pregnancy. The conclusion could make that comparison for us. That it doesn't increases the effect. The story is left to make its point for each of us by itself.

Have you found Appendix Six yet? It has a selection of essays by a wide variety of writers, including some that deal with a variety of life experiences. You might want to read now about the experiences described in the essays by Nancy Mairs and Ebrima Jow. (Okay, I know "You might want to . . . ." is a teacher-type thing to say. What I mean, of course, is that I'd like you to read them. They are both effective essays about different kinds of experience.)

All of these essays about other people are powerfully written, and they may seem to set a high standard for your paper. Don't worry about that. You're not really expected to achieve professional levels just yet, though you are expected to aim in that direction. Think of all the driveway or schoolyard basketball players, shouting in their preadolescent voices "I'm Michael Jordan" as they jump toward the basket. Sure they miss the basket a bit more frequently than Jordan does, but that doesn't affect their vision of themselves as professional ball players.

It's that vision that helps them to learn and to improve. By aiming high, by setting high standards, and of course by practicing, they develop their skills. They also have a lot of fun. And it can be the same with writing. With each paper, each revision, each challenge, you'll learn. It's important to keep that challenge before you, though, in order to continue developing as a writer and in order to get the greatest pleasure from your accomplishments.

It's important, too, to keep track of what you're learning. As you finish your essay on the person you interviewed, take some time to reflect on the experience in your journal. What have you learned as a result of this exercise: About writing? About other people? About yourself?

IV
On Revision Again

In Chapter Five I spent some time discussing the process of revising your essays. I wish I could say that I had covered the ground there, and that if you'd follow the suggestions in that chapter your work would always be as good as it could be, and you'd be done. But that's not so.

In fact, revision is a process that goes on and on, for just as long as you let it. Your writing has the opportunity to mature and develop each time you return to it. Indeed, sometimes only the need to hand in a paper, submit a report, or mail a manuscript to meet a deadline brings the revision process to an end. And sometimes not even then. Sometimes authors continue to revise their work even after it has appeared in print.

The poet W. H. Auden is one example. He wrote a poem in honor of fellow-poet William Butler Yeats (called, appropriately, "In Memory of W. B. Yeats") in 1940. The poem was widely reprinted and anthologized, and became quite well-known. Nonetheless, when Auden put together a volume of his collected poems in 1966, he changed it, leaving out two stanzas he didn't like any more and changing a line that he decided sounded too mechanistic. The fact that the poem was well known did not deter him from revising it further.

It's that way with my writing too, though on a much less public scale. This textbook is certainly working that way. Even though I'm working now on Chapter Six, I have, earlier today, gone back to Chapters Three and Five to make some revisions that were suggested by the people who read the drafts. And yesterday I messed around a bit with Chapter One. And I will probably continue to do the same thing until the day the book is finally published. And even then I will keep on revising, noting all of the changes I will want to make for the second edition.

What does this mean for writers in a college class? First, it is a suggestion that you take full opportunity of the time you have available for revision. Even when your writing is largely reporting on what someone else has written or said, you can always find room to improve transitions, cut out a digression, clarify a point, or describe an attitude. Your writing is always in process, and you should not consider it finished after the first draft, or even after the first revision. Or the second. There is always more work to be done. On the other hand, you can take comfort in knowing that other writers (a great many writers) have to bow eventually to the tyranny of deadlines and submit work that they know they could work on further. Keep at it, but don't despair.

And what to look for while keeping at it? Well, besides all the points that your readers from your group have suggested, you might look at the lists of writing features that you have been keeping in your journal. Check your own work against the points on these lists. Further, you will probably have learned something about what works and what doesn't by reading and hearing other people's essays. With each revision you should try to make all the changes that your analysis of your work indicates will be necessary, including all of the other changes that these first changes will necessitate.

When that revision is done, re-read your work the way you imagine your reader is going to read it. Picture that person, sitting alone in an easy chair, your paper in hand. Try to imagine his or her reactions, questions, feelings, interests, and annoyances. Another way to review your work is to try to read it as if it had been written by someone else and you were encountering it for the first time. Admittedly, this last exercise isn't too easy to do and requires some practice. It helps if you can get away from the paper for a while first; then it will be easier to read it with a fresh eye.

Approached this way, you will surely be able to see details that should be added, paragraphs that could be rearranged, corrections that need to be made, confusions that need to be eliminated. And again, with each change you make, however small, you will need to check for other changes which are now made necessary. And so it goes, until you have to stop. As I do now. For now.

Half my life is an act of revision.

John Irving

Chapter 7

Discovering Information

I

As I've already noted (and you already knew), there's a good chance that you will not be asked to examine your personal experience or write a meditation in most of your college classes. Not that such writing might not be valuable in other disciplines, but in fact, most academic writing involves working with information: facts, theories, test results, reports, hypotheses, and ideas. This chapter is designed to give you some practice in writing about information.

In your college classes you'll sometimes be asked to record information about an activity, such as a lab experiment or field work, that you've participated in. You will describe what you did, and what happened as a result. Other examples of this writing about your activities include responding to a book or article you've read, reviewing a play, reporting on an internship experience, or summarizing events you've witnessed. Note that you, the writer, are involved in these events, at least as an observer, so this type of writing is not, in fact, totally removed from personal experience writing.

A second type of academic writing asks you to discover new information and report on it. This is most typically done by searching for that information in the library, although interviews, questionnaires, and personal observation are also available to you as ways of learning about a subject. The questioning, reading, interviewing, and discovering which must precede the writing all become part of the prewriting process.

A third type of information-based writing asks you to record information that you've already learned, as a way of proving that you

111

have learned it. This third type is probably already familiar enough to you: it's encountered regularly in essay exams. The techniques for writing successful college essay exams are the subject of Chapter Eight. For now, however, I'm going to give you the opportunity to use writing as a way to discover information.

> Identify something that you already know a little bit about, or have some experience of. It should, of course, be something that you have enough interest in to sustain you through the writing process. Consider what you already know and what more you need to know. Then, through reading, interviewing, or other means, get any additional information that's necessary to develop your expertise in the subject.
>
> Write a report on this information for readers who would like to increase their understanding and appreciation of this subject by reading what you, as an authority, have to say about it.

You'll notice that this assignment is somewhat broader than the previous invitations to write. This time you're merely asked to write about "something." That vagueness is deliberate. Part of the challenge of this assignment is to choose an appropriate topic, one that you're interested in, that you already know something about, and that you're willing to become an "expert" about.

You may, in fact, already have a pretty clear idea what you'd like to write about. Some people are just lucky that way. Otherwise, the list below may help to trigger a possibility. Alternatively, your instructor may ask the whole class to work on the same topic. Or perhaps the members of your group will all work on the same project together, sharing ideas, resources, expertise, and research.

Topic suggestions:

An ethnic custom, such as dancing the hora, wearing a veil, deer hunting, taking siestas, decorating a house with Christmas lights.
The water problem in Macomb.

A current danger to the environment: acid rain, non-biodegradable garbage, the loss of the rain forest, an endangered species.

Career opportunities available to people graduating in your major.

A common event or occurrence, like sneezing, jet lag, potholes, frostbite, tornadoes, plane crashes.

Alcoholism among college students (or in their families).

A common object, like baseballs, potatoes, cocker spaniels, house flies, chimneys, ball point pens.

The story behind the "Flags of Love" in Chandler Park.

The story behind Chandler Park.

The story of a landmark, such as Lincoln's Tomb, Leavenworth Penitentiary, Dickson Mounds, Mt. Rushmore, Sherman Hall.

The story of a public building, such as a theatre, court house, or school.

Student newspapers at WIU.

Plagiarism: causes, practices, punishment.

Remember listing as a prewriting activity? This might be a good time to come up with your own list of possible topics. At least ten items would make an appropriate list. That number will assure that you have enough choices to move confidently to the next step: selecting which item on your list you want to spend some time exploring and writing about.

II

While you're making that important decision, here are two newspaper articles to read. Newspapers are generally devoted to reporting information (after all, the writers are called "reporters"), so these articles, along with most of the articles in today's paper, can serve to demonstrate some "real life" uses of this kind of writing.

The first article is from *Nexus,* the newsletter of Western's Office of Minority and Special Student Services. It is a report based on an interview with Nazareth Hattwick, the Director of Casa Latina. The second article, from the *Macomb Journal,* reports on shoplifting, a subject which Kay Norton already knew enough about to know who to interview and what questions to ask.

Promoting Hispanic Culture

Rose Lopez
Nexus, 11/29/89

In the spring of 1973, Casa Latina Cultural Awareness Center was established thanks to the efforts of the Hispanic students on campus. Since then, Casa Latina (Latin Home) has become more than a meeting place for its members. The students go to the center to voice their concerns, discuss their educational goals and socialize with members who speak their language. In short, it is a home away from home.

Nazareth Hattwick has been the director of the center for the past ten years. Many changes have taken place since then. Recently, the students voiced their concerns to President Wagoner on how Casa needed major renovations and secretarial help. Casa Latina now has a kitchen for the use of its members, a full-time secretary has been hired, a face-lift has been given to Casa and a budget for a graduate assistant is available. Nazareth stated, "It was a long time coming but progress is being made."

Casa Latina strives to promote an informed understanding of the Hispanic culture to WIU's student population and to Macomb's community. At the community's request, Casa Latina's dance troupe often performs traditional dances, not only in Macomb, but in different cities in Illinois and Iowa. Recently they were invited to perform at the Wesley Village Retirement Center. The annual Recruitment Dance is scheduled to be held in Galesburg.

Swirling to traditional dances from Veracruz and Nuevo Leon, Mexico, performers with the Tradicion Hispana Dance Troupe share new steps and learn them through hard work. Casa Latina Cultural Awareness Center sponsors shows whenever possible. The dances are both educational and entertaining. The director for Tradicion Hispana is Rose Newman.

It is important to the Hispanic population on campus to have a place where they feel at home. Knowing that there is a center that will make them feel welcome and not alienated is helpful to

From Rose Lopez, "Promoting the Hispanic Culture," NEXUS, © 1989 by NEXUS. Reprinted with permission.

the students. Having a structured support system is important to help them successfully complete their undergraduate degrees.

Casa sponsors Monday Night conversations in Spanish open to all students who wish to improve their Spanish vocabulary. And as the holidays approach, Casa has celebrated with their annual Thanksgiving dinner and a Christmas party.

The philosophy of Casa Latina is to create and to maintain a Bilingual and Bicultural environment to be shared with everyone who visits, regardless of their background or language. Casa hopes to be a supportive structure for all Hispanic students, their families and friends.

Holiday Shoplifting Carries Big Price Tag

Kay Norton
Macomb Journal
12/17/89

This may be the season to be jolly, but Macomb police and local merchants say those who succumb to the temptation to shoplift will find their holidays anything but merry.

"Our retail thefts definitely go up (during the Christmas season)," said Police Chief Richard Clark. In Illinois, 45 percent of all retail theft, or shoplifting, takes place in November and December. "We'd be right along with the state average."

Since April of 1988 there have been 65 shoplifting charges filed by the Macomb Police Department. And according to Detective Joe Wazny, the price tag for a conviction is high. "Shoplifting is a crime," said Wazny. "You create yourself a police record that stays with you all your life."

Wazny said some shoplifters steal for "a dare, a thrill, an adventure, boredom, or frustration." Some may be pressured by peers to try it. But, he added, the consequences can be severe. According to the Illinois Retail Theft Act, if the items stolen are less than $300 in value, the charge is a Class A misdemeanor, punishable by one year in jail and a $1,000 fine. A charge of theft

From Kay Norton, "Holiday Shoplifting Carries Big Price Tag," © 1989 by The Macomb JOURNAL. Reprinted with permission.

over $300, a Class 4 felony, or a second misdemeanor conviction, could result in a $10,000 fine and one to three years in jail.

Most stores in Macomb, Clark said, follow similar rules in regard to procedure, and most decide to prosecute. The procedure for booking a shoplifter can be a humiliating experience. If a person is suspected of shoplifting, he or she will be approached by a store employee and taken to the manager's office. The police are called, and a report is made. "The person is placed under arrest," said Wazny, "then handcuffed, escorted from the store (usually out the front door in front of other shoppers), placed in a police car and taken to the station."

Once at the station, officers take a personal history of the suspect, as well as fingerprints and pictures. Suspects are not jailed unless they are unable to post bond in a "reasonable" period of time, Clark said.

"One of the strangest things," Clark noted, "is that most people reach in their pockets and get the $100 bond money." Most others are able to raise the bond money in a very short period of time, he said. "It could all be for a $1.25 bottle of nail polish."

The individual is usually advised by the store where the incident occurred never to return. "If they do," said Clark, "they can be arrested for criminal trespass."

Wazny and Clark agreed there is no such thing as a "typical" shoplifter, although the majority are juveniles. "People who shoplift can be kleptomaniacs and be extremely rich or can be extremely poor and stealing for something to eat," said Wazny.

Juveniles (under age 17) are handled in the same way as adults at the scene, and then they are taken to the station where they are turned over to juvenile authorities and handed over to their parents with an appointment to see a juvenile officer later.

State statistics show more women than men shoplift. Macomb figures indicate that of the 65 charges filed since computer records have been kept, 33 were made against females and 32 against males.

Common shoplifting methods include "palming," or simply taking items out of the store in the hand, working in crowds, handling several items at once and only returning a few, using accomplices, and employing concealment techniques, such as suitcases, packages or bulky clothing.

The most frequently taken items include jewelry, perfumes, cosmetics, small appliances, records, tapes and compact discs. Other items that seem to be easy prey are clothing and tools. Meat and cigarettes are the most frequent targets at supermarkets, not immune from shoplifting incidents. Gas stations and convenience stores also seem to be easy targets, and "drive-aways" from filling stations (pumping gas into a car and driving away without paying for it) also occur.

Clark said that at this time of the year most of the stores use "employee awareness" and beef up their security operations. The Macomb patrol has a special "Santa Patrol" which goes in and out of stores around the square, spending 15–20 minutes in a store. And police escorts of merchants carrying unusually heavy deposits to the banks increase. But there are no extra patrols assigned. "The responsibility is primarily that of the management to prevent shoplifting," said Clark.

Sharon Curry, in-store loss prevention associate with Wal-Mart, said the primary focus of security there is "preventive aggression from the store clerks." Curry, who also is the district employee trainer for Wal-Mart, added, "Most shoplifters are amateurs and they shoplift on impulse—we don't know why." The store, whose policy it is to prosecute shoplifters, makes sure employees "know what to expect" and know how to spot a possible shoplifter. All employees, including seasonal workers, are shown films on shoplifting as part of their training.

"We constantly test our in-store employees with shopper checks," said Curry, who has been with Wal-Mart for about a year and a half. The store uses security teams, which travel to various Wal-Marts in the district, to perform security "blitzes." "Nobody knows where we'll be, or when," said Curry. "It's very effective."

Macomb K-Mart manager Mark Schuetz said his store, too, beefs up security efforts during the holiday season. "We double our coverage on the floor during the Christmas season," said Schuetz, who has been with the chain a little more than a year. K-Mart also uses a loss prevention team concept in conjunction with its Canton store, and Schuetz said it has helped cut their losses.

Not surprisingly, the store's highest foot traffic occurs from Thanksgiving to Christmas, but Schuetz said the Macomb K-Mart's losses are "significantly high" year-round.

Both Curry and Schuetz said high periods of shoplifting coincide with times when WIU is in session. "I'm sorry to say, the 'slow time' is in the summer when WIU is out of session," said Schuetz.

The K-Mart manager said employees monitor dressing rooms carefully, since the clothing department is one place where the store faces "significant losses." Schuetz said some people will pile on clothes under bulky winter garments, "and all you have left is an empty hanger."

K-Mart also has a policy to prosecute shoplifters, and Schuetz said he feels more have been caught in the act this year than last year. He attributes the increased rate of prosecution to the team concept of security. "I would say we had the losses last year," he said. "We just didn't catch them."

An exercise: Neither of these articles is a "hot news" story, a story, that is, whose purpose is to inform the reader about important recent events. Both have, instead, some rather different purposes. First of all, define for yourself what you think the purpose (or purposes) of each article is. Then read a recent *Courier*. How many different purposes lie behind the different articles in the paper? How do the purposes help to determine what information the authors chose to include in the articles? How do they help determine what is left out?

III

Do you know yet what your essay will be about? If you haven't decided, you might recall that you will be working with this subject for a while, so you would do well to choose a topic that you're especially interested in. That's not just for your sake; it's for your reader's sake too. Think about it. If you, as writer, aren't particularly interested in a subject, how can you possibly get your reader interested in it? And if your reader loses interest, your essay will not be very effective.

Of course there will be many times (I'm sure you've experienced them already) when you will be asked to write about a subject you don't find wonderfully compelling. The trick then is to find some aspect of your subject, some angle, some perspective which you *can* develop an interest in. Though the French Reign of Terror may not be a stimulating topic for you, you might apply your interest in the capital punishment controversy to that period, and explore the attitudes toward life and death which allowed the large number of public executions. Or a health class paper on drug abuse can take on significance for you if you recall the experience and behavior of a friend in light of the new information you have learned.

In any event, you must find a way to become involved and to care deeply; you must also be able to speak with authority. You need to know a great deal about your subject, and that includes identifying everything that you still need to know. In fact, you are going to need to know more than you tell in your paper. If you are to give information to your reader, you must do so as an insider, as an authority, as someone to be trusted.

Please make up your mind about your topic before you read any further. The rest of this chapter contains additional essays to read and discuss in class, along with some advice about how to proceed with your work. But you can't put off getting started any longer.

And now that you've got a topic (you do, don't you?), you can move immediately to the next step. You now need to discover what you already know about your subject and what you still need to find out. Use whatever prewriting techniques seem appropriate: write in your journal; make notes in a computer file; try cubing or clustering; and start preparing to collect new information. One of your notes to yourself might be a list of the sources you can go to to discover the information you need: the people you need to talk to, the articles you need to read, the places you need to visit. Your experience as an interviewer should come in handy as you keep track of the questions you need to find answers to.

As you work through this part of the process, you may find some ideas or inspiration from these two essays, both written by WIU students for a composition class. Both students wrote about subjects that interested them, and the result is two essays that we readers can get interested in too. Both also built on the things they knew already by doing some research to discover answers to their questions. The first essay is in response to the invitation to write about a public building. Even though Darby Crouse keeps her personal experience in the background, she clearly had some knowledge and some interest in the Timber Lake Playhouse before she began her research.

In the second essay Judy Eberle was able to draw on her knowledge and feelings about disciplining children, but before she wrote she supplemented her knowledge by reading what two parenting authorities had to say on the subject. Notice, as you read, the ways both essays make it clear when they are reporting information learned from others.

Theater at Its Best
Darby Crouse

Thirty miles from the nearest major metropolitan area, Timber Lake Playhouse sits proudly within a dense timber, proving every season its commitment to high quality theater. As the second longest-running summer stock theater in Illinois, it is unique not only in its location but also in its history and its operation.

Timber Lake Playhouse had an interesting beginning. It was first conceived in 1961 by Mr. Andy Bro, a chaplain at Shimer

Reprinted with permission of the author.

College in Mt. Carroll, IL. He was put in charge of plays at the college campus, and from that experience he thought of starting a summer theater. Mr. Bro came into contact with Mr. Don McKay, the owner of the Timber Lake Resort, later that year and it was at that time that the idea began to really materialize. In August of 1961, a committee was formed in which several possibilities were discussed, including theater names such as Shimer College's Theater Lake Playhouse. The idea sprouted as more meetings were held and information began to circulate. Although there was no place to stage the performances, the summer of 1962 was set as a target date for opening the playhouse. Don McKay donated the land across from the Timber Lake Resort and so only a building was needed. Through loans and donations the building was completed and Timber Lake Playhouse was no longer just a dream.

According to an article published in the *Carroll County Review* ("Playhouse's Founding Father Departs. 1979), Bro said that things were "nip and tuck" for a while. June 28, 1962 arrived, and TLP's first production, *Teahouse of the August Moon*, was a smooth success. At first attendance was good and then it seemed to slowly decline until something magic happened.

"Don McKay and I were sitting on a bench in front of the theater talking about the small crowds," recalled Bro in the *Carroll County Review*. "As we were talking, the people kept coming in for that night's performance. They went over capacity and had to take in the bench we were sitting on for extra seating." Further, Mr. Bro refers to 1973 as a "golden summer" for TLP "when everything seemed to fall into place."

Timber Lake has always been committed to providing a center of cultural opportunity for developing artists. The playhouse has presented more than 180 plays since 1962 with over 1,300 performances.

It was in 1974, during an electrical storm, that this dream was reduced to ashes. Lightning struck the theater engulfing it in flames. Determined to have their dream of a summer stock theater, these people clung to the theme "The show must go on!" and so it did. Through public support, including a radiothon over WCCI-FM in Savannah, IL, the sooty remains of the original theater were replaced with a brand new building. The theater that stands today can comfortably accommodate 400 people. The 40-by-60-foot stage is equipped with a rotating center which aids in quick scene changes.

The history of TLP is not the only part that is intriguing as the present operation still fulfills the expectations of those who established it. Victoria Freeman has been linked with the theater for several years and explained what goes on during the productive summer months. Freeman is the only year-round employee of the establishment.

"I just completed my fourth season and currently hold the position of Executive Assistant," the quiet but business-like voice informed me. Her duties include managing the box office during the summer as well as running the winter office. While playing her role as box office manager in the summer, which includes reservations and ticket sales, Freeman also keeps the accounting books, assists the Artistic Director and completes any tasks given her by the board.

"The season usually begins the first week in June and ends the end of August or first week in September," the Timber Lake veteran recalled. "Musicals are the most popular, along with comedies," she added.

The theater is well kept and seems to be able to accomplish big tasks in a short time. "All of the company members except the guest actors participate in the upkeep of the theater," Freeman stated. In this particular operation certain duties such as sweeping the theater, cleaning the public restrooms and cleaning the front of the theater are assigned to the company members. Here free time is rare, since those who have it are willing and expected to pitch in to make a show happen or to get the needed tasks accomplished. The Executive Assistant chuckled as she recalled some of her odd jobs, "like painting the company restrooms, returning a tent that had been used as a prop or cleaning the concession stand and finding workers."

In addition to the extra duties assigned, the company members have their own rigorous schedule. They begin rehearsal around 9:00 and break at 11:30. From 11:30 to 1:30 they are expected to eat lunch and complete their extra company duties around the theater. Beginning again at 1:30 the actors and actresses rehearse until around 5:00. They eat at 5:00 and then have a break until they must prepare for that evening's performance. Usually lasting around two hours, the performances let out around 10:00. This cycle is constant until the last performance of a play.

Seemingly without a break, the actors and actresses, as well as the rest of the company, begin "strike" as soon as the patrons have left the theater. "Striking" the set refers to dissecting and removing the set that's on the stage. This can begin around 10:00 or 11:00 and run into the wee hours of the morning. The end of this sleepless period is far from over as the TLP company enters the next tech week (fondly referred to as hell week). Tech week is the week before a new show opens when all technical details must be covered. During this time the new set must be built, lighting cues learned, lights adjusted, and many other complicated details attended to.

With the constant hard work involved, one may wonder, "Who works at TLP?" Freeman answered this frequently asked question with ease, "The actors and actresses come mostly from the midwest, but we do have people who come from all over the country as well as from overseas." With 15–20 actors, as well as a number of apprentices (young people who work at TLP just for the experience, with no monetary payment), the company varies in size. "The actors and actresses can range from about 21 years old to 50 or 60," Freeman estimated. The apprentices' ages range from 15–20. Freeman explained that, "Most have had experience in community or regional theater as well as in college theater."

The semi-professional, non-equity theater holds usual auditions and produces quality plays. Non-equity theater refers to the fact that the actors and actresses do not belong to the union. "Auditions," Freeman stated, "are usually held in the spring around March and April." The audition sites include Chicago, Madison, St. Louis, Peoria, Champaign, Des Moines as well as TLP's hometown, Mt. Carroll. In Timber Lake's past they have done such plays as *On Borrowed Time, Oklahoma, The Nerd, The Music Man, Biloxi Blues, Grease,* and *Annie.* As theater goers we can look forward to seeing such plays as *Pump Boys and Dinettes, Big River, Run For Your Wife, Broadway Bound,* and several others in Timber Lake's next season.

As Timber Lake Playhouse sits quietly for the next several months, it prepares itself for another exciting year of cultural opportunity for the artists as well as quality theater for those who attend. The thrill of live theater is something one must experience in order to feel the true excitement. Information on auditions or performances is available at the Timber Lake box office, (815) 244-2035.

To Spank or Not to Spank: A Question for Everyone Who Likes Kids

Judy Eberle

If you're not a parent already, chances are you eventually will be. Even if you're sure you don't want children of your own, you will probably find yourself in a disciplinary situation with a child sooner or later. Since kids are people in the process of learning right from wrong, we can safely assume that they will break the rules, sometimes in a major way. I think we owe ourselves and the kids we discipline some thoughtful consideration of the issues involved with corporal punishment so that we can make informed decisions as to its use. Blind acceptance is not necessary. We should all examine its wisdom and effectiveness.

Corporal punishment is defined in *Webster's Handy College Dictionary* (New American Library, 1981) as "punishment inflicted on the body, as flogging" (125). Flogging sounds awfully brutal when compared with spanking, which is "to strike on the buttocks with the open hand; punish." When used as a noun, spank means "a slap" (502). No matter which terms are used, I believe most of us have experienced corporal punishment in one form or another.

Physical punishment of children appears to be a widespread tradition, which is generally accepted in most societies. Sweden is the only exception, to my knowledge. Citizens there are prohibited by law from inflicting bodily harm upon a child as a means of punishment. In American society, spanking is often considered not only a parental right but a parental duty. Parents frequently see spanking as a measure consistent with the concept of their moral responsibility to provide society with law abiding, decent citizens.

The decision to use physical force in child rearing remains an individual one. Government keeps a "hands off" attitude concerning the issue—until and unless punishment suggesting child abuse comes to the attention of authorities. However, it seems that we will tolerate or even sometimes accept in our families, friends

Reprinted with permission of the author.

and neighbors, anything short of child abuse because we feel so strongly that parents have the "right" to "discipline" their children as they see fit. In some cases, kids are treated as possessions, not unlike the family dog, which can be whacked with a newspaper for each and every offense.

Those who favor the use of spanking often refer to the hazards of over-permissiveness. They cite extreme examples of parents who let their kids walk all over them. I cannot deny that a child who is given little or no behavioral limits is a fearsome and pitiful creature. I think the parents of such a child are sort of scary, too. Kids need and deserve discipline. It can also be argued that mild corporal punishment can be effective in some situations. For example, a sharp hand slap can be used as emphasis for teaching a child to avoid a dangerous or life threatening situation. Children are often unable to control their natural curiosity and self-preservation can lose its significance when they're caught up in exuberant or fantasy type play.

It may be helpful, at this point, to consider what is meant by the word "discipline." Frequently its common meaning is confused and even equated with punishment of the physical variety. The dictionary tells us that discipline means "mental and moral training, obedience to rules, a set of rules; regimen, correction" (157). Please note that spanking is not included in the description. I prefer to think of discipline as a way of guidance. We can guide our children toward proper behavior. We don't have to punish them into it.

Misinterpretation of the meaning of discipline has led to extremes when it comes to corporal punishment. These actions are always justified in some way. Usually, the degree of "badness" (as perceived by the parent) must be met or exceeded by the intensity of parental action. Children are viewed as a kind of moral extension of the parents and as such, their behavior creates the parents' image. We wish to be seen as "good parents" and will often go to great lengths to achieve and maintain that status.

Swiss psychoanalyst Alice Miller, in her book *For Your Own Good: Hidden Cruelty in Child-Rearing and the Roots of Violence* (Farrar, Straus, Giroux, 1983), states:

> The conviction that parents are always right and [that] every act of cruelty, whether conscious or unconscious, is an expression of their love is deeply rooted in human beings be-

cause it is based on the process of internalization that takes place during the first months of life. (7)

It is precisely this kind of perception that can have very negative effects for child and disciplinarian alike. People who have committed terrible cruelties in the name of discipline commonly say that their actions were right and necessary because *the child was so bad.* They contend that their punishment fit the child's crime of disobedience. They wrongly allowed the child's behavior to regulate their own negative impulses to hit or hurt in response.

Some other forms of justification may be more familiar, such as, "Spare the rod, spoil the child." This common cliche, which is derived from the Bible, suggests that kids are more or less inherently wicked and must be hurt in order for both the parent and the child to be really good. When the justifying punisher says, "This will teach you a lesson," they come close to the real truth about spanking, yet the statement is loaded with misperception for both people involved. One of the real lessons being taught is dominance over others. Another is how to lie in order to avoid future spankings. Spanking becomes the thing to be avoided, not the wrong behavior which preceded it. Dr. Haim Ginott, a popular author on parenting, asserts that spanking teaches kids ineffective ways of dealing with anger and frustration. Alternative (nonviolent) means of coping with this kind of stress are not shown or role-modeled as an outlet for what he calls "savage" feelings *(Between Parent and Child,* Macmillan, 1969, 125).

When parents who espouse love for their children inflict pain on them (often in the heat of reactionary anger when their physical power is intensified), they send a very clear and profoundly conflicting message: "I am your caring, protective parent. I am purposely causing you great pain." The connotative message is love, but the denotive message is quite the opposite. Both parts of the message are accentuated by the pain. The parent probably knows this and has employed some kind of justification for the behavior. The child definitely knows this, although unable to resolve the psychological dilemma that results. Child psychologist Selma Fraiberg says that this psychological conflict can interfere with a child's development of conscience. They develop a "bookkeeping" approach and permit themselves to misbehave, to go into debt on one side of the "ledger"; they pay this off in weekly or monthly spanking "installments." The child is freed from misbehavior by enduring corporal punishment (quoted in Ginott 125). I wonder how many children make this kind of maladjustment.

It is especially detrimental when children are not allowed to express feelings after spankings. Dr. Miller offers helpful insight regarding childhood emotions:

> If the child is prevented from reacting to his inner emotions because the parent can't tolerate the reactions (crying, sadness, rage), the child will learn to be silent, i.e., to repress. This silence is a danger signal pointing to future pathology. *Neurosis is the result of the act of repression, not of events themselves.* (56, emphasis added)

In other words, if children can't show their legitimate feelings toward the pain and humiliation they have just experienced, they bury them very deeply in their minds. These feelings inevitably come out later in life in very unhealthy, usually violent and/or self-destructive behaviors.

The long range effects of corporal punishment often become known as a result of the more extreme cases, such as serial killings and multiple personalities. I'm sure we have all heard the alarming statistics about the large number of incarcerated violent offenders who were abused as children. The long lasting effects of less severe experiences are much more difficult to pinpoint. However, common sense should tell us that violence usually begets violence. People learn basic values and morals within the family unit, first and foremost. We begin to learn this at a very early age. Children watch our actions very closely and emulate many of our behaviors.

Parents are responsible for providing their kids with role models that enable them to grow into happy, healthy, law-abiding adults. We can do this by examining our own values and behaviors first and then by educating ourselves in the art of parenting. I don't think we should expect behaviors in our kids that we don't expect in ourselves.

There are many alternatives to the use of spanking. Sources of information on child development and non-violent discipline are available to those who seek them out. An informed decision is one we can be sure of and can be happy about. We owe it to ourselves, the children and our common future to take the time to do this.

IV

By now you're probably busy searching for the information you need to add to what you already know in order to write your paper. This process will probably involve talking to people, giving you a chance to use what you already know about interviewing techniques. It may also involve reading articles or books that you already have handy. Or it may involve looking for the books and articles you need in the library. There's a chance, though, that you don't yet have much experience using Western's library, and you might even be a little intimidated at the prospect of locating the things you need among the six floors of books, documents, and periodicals.

Always ready to help, I have next for you an essay about the WIU library. It provides some initial orientation and also includes instructions for using the computerized card catalog system. Just as I suggested that you read the introduction to WordPerfect while sitting at a computer, I now propose that you take this essay to the library and read it there. The descriptions and instructions will make more sense if you are on the premises.

The Western Illinois University Library

Rick Clemons

Because college-level education often requires research, most students will find it necessary to use the Library's resources at various times during their university studies, no matter what their major or minor. With more than 400,000 volumes and 3800 periodical titles, the Library can present a considerable challenge to the newcomer. In addition to its large size, the Library presents another challenge to many new students—a computerized card catalog. In May, 1988, the library staff stopped adding new acquisitions to the printed card catalog, so clients must use the LCS (Library Computer System)/Illinet computers to find books acquired after that date. Armed with advance information and prepared to do some exploring, everyone can, however, easily

Reprinted with permission of the author.

learn to use the Library in order to enrich and enhance their academic experience.

The first step in gaining a comfortable working relationship with the Library is to discover the organization of books throughout the building. Western's Library uses the Library of Congress system to catalog and shelve books. This system organizes books by general subject matter using letters to denote the subject. For instance, the letter D indicates History: General and Old World. A second letter following the first indicates a subcategory: DA identifies history books about Great Britain. Finally the call number will include some numbers that further narrow the subject and another letter to indicate the author or editor, or a special category.

Books in the stacks—the shelves—are arranged alphabetically and numerically, by call number, and are easily found once you understand the system. The stacks begin at A on the fourth floor and end at Z on the sixth floor of the Library. Signs over the entrances to the stacks will help you find the right general location. Inside, the shelves themselves are labeled. If, however, you are searching for science (Q) or music (M) materials, you will need to go to Currens Hall or Sallee Hall respectively, where these books are housed in special libraries.

The reference section on the main—second—floor of the Library is the place to start any research project. Here you will find the card catalog (divided into author, title, and subject catalogs), periodical abstracts and indexes, general reference works, and reference librarians to assist you. Surrounding the card catalog are computer terminals that give you access to the LCS and Illinet catalog systems (more on using the computers to search for materials later). Also located on the main floor are the circulation desk and the reserve desk.

Up one flight of stairs on the third floor are periodical holdings. These include newspapers, popular magazines, and scholarly journals. After finding references to pertinent periodical articles through an index or another source, you must go to the third floor to retrieve the specific item. The entire floor is devoted to magazines, journals and newspapers, and finding the article you need can be somewhat tricky unless you know how the floor is arranged. The section called "current periodicals" contains recent issues of newspapers and the current year of magazines and journals which come out weekly or monthly. If a journal is issued less frequently (as most academic journals are), the current issues will be shelved in the stacks with older periodicals. All periodicals are arranged alphabetically by title, and, as in the book collection, all the shelves are labeled. Some older material, particularly newspapers, are on microfilm or microfiche, both of which are stored on the third floor in a clearly identified area.

Up one more flight of stairs, the fourth floor is where the stacks of books begin. In addition, there is another important source of information located on the fourth floor—government documents. The umbrella title of government documents includes U.S. and Illinois state government publications, the law library, and ERIC (Education Resources Information Center). Much of this material is *not* catalogued in the main library computer or the card catalog. Instead, you must search for this material through special indexes or special computer programs. The three primary indexes for publications by the federal government, the largest publisher in the world, are the "Monthly Catalog," the "Index to U.S. Government Periodicals," and the "CIS Index," all of which are located near the government documents desk. You may do your search much more quickly, if not as completely, on the computer. It normally takes about fifteen minutes or more to learn the program. ERIC has its own printed index, which is also computerized; ERIC terminals are located near the government documents desk and near the reference desk. If you learn the basic commands for ERIC, you learn them for government publications too.

Besides government publications, the Library has three other specialized areas: audio-visual holdings, located on the first (basement) floor; archives, located on the sixth floor; and the map library, which is in Tillman Hall. There are librarians in each of the three areas to help patrons locate materials.

Although the librarians are extremely knowledgeable and helpful, students should try to become self-sufficient, especially when it comes to learning how the LCS/Illinet computer system works. Even if you are a computer novice, it takes only a few minutes to learn the LCS commands, and not much longer to master Illinet. I know this is true because I did it. Information about the two systems is found near all the terminals, and may be called up on the screen by typing "help" or "info."

An important difference between the LCS and Illinet systems should be noted. The LCS program searches WIU holdings, and can be asked to search 29 other academic libraries in Illinois by inserting a school code after the normal command. The Illinet system searches the WIU Library, and can be asked to search more than 800 other Illinois libraries. Instructions on how to search these other libraries can be found on Library handouts.

The basic commands to search for books are provided by the Library near every terminal. Of the commands, available, the LCS author-title search is the fastest and most accurate way to find the call number of a book. To use the command, type "ats/" and the first four letters of the author's last name and the first five letters of the first significant word in the title. For example, if you were trying to locate Allan Bloom's *The Closing of the American Mind,* your command would look like this:

ats/blooclosi

("The" is not considered a significant word.) After you type in your search command, press the enter key and the computer will search for every book title that has a first word beginning "closi" and match those books with an author whose last name begins with "bloo." Generally, this command will find the exact book you are searching for, but occasionally there will be more than one match. If this occurs, use the line search to check the matches until you find the right book. A line search is conducted by typing "dsl/" and the line number of the match you want to check.

There will, however, be times when you know only the author's name or only the title. If you know the author's name, you can search for all of that author's books in the Library by using the command "aut/" and the first six letters of the last name and the first three letters of the first name. Books by Allan Bloom could be found by using this command:

aut/bloom all

(Leave a space when the name or word does not have enough letters to fill the designated number for any command.)

Now assume that only the title of the book is known. You then must use the "tls/" command with the first four letters of the first *significant* word in the title and with the first five letters of the second significant word. When Judy Eberle wanted to consult *Between Parent and Child,* her title search would have looked like this:

tls/betwparen

The shortcoming of the LCS program, as may be apparent, is the inability to search by subject matter, a capability the printed card catalog has. Rather than spending a time-consuming search in the printed card catalog, students can do a much faster subject search on the computer by using the Illinet system. In order to do a subject search, you must find the *exact* subject heading from the *Library of Congress Subject Headings* books; these books are found near the card catalog. An alternate way to discover what subject heading to search is to examine the entry for one book you already know on the subject. That entry will indicate what subject headings it is listed under. You can then search those subjects.

To use the subject search, type "f s" and the heading. The command "f s Vietnamese Conflict, 1961–1975" will produce a number of matches concerning the Vietnam War. Any time the computer finds more than one match it will either list briefly the matches if there are ten or less, or it will simply show the number of matches if there are more than ten. To see the complete record for the book—the same information that would be on a card—you must type "s" and the line number. If the computer found more than ten matches, you can look at brief records of the books by selecting a few at a time: "s 1–9." Finally, once you find a book that appears to be useful you must link to the LCS system by typing "l" (a small letter "L") and the number of the record displayed. The computer will then show the call number of the book and whether it is available or checked out.

In addition to the subject search, the Illinet system can be used to search authors' names (f a) or book titles (f t). Library handouts explain clearly how to conduct these various searches.

Taking the time to learn the operations of the LCS and Illinet systems, as well as other programs such as ERIC and PsychLIT, can make researching a topic a much more pleasant experience. Having general knowledge about where materials are located in the Library can cut the time spent looking for books, periodicals, and other sources. Of course the information presented here is a very basic guide, and it is now up to you to explore the Library and learn the various computer systems. Good hunting.

V

Once you've begun discovering the information you need to know, you can start thinking about the most effective way to present it to a reader. The next few paragraphs may help with that part of the process. As usual, I'm not really going to give a lot of rules here so much as discuss a series of ideas, hints, and suggestions that you can think about and apply as appropriate.

I've already suggested that choosing a topic you are interested in will help you to keep your reader interested. It will also help if you try to develop a sense of who that reader is. You can assume, generally, that your audience is someone who doesn't have as much information as you do, and who would like to learn something about your subject, provided it is presented in an interesting way. It sometimes may be useful, however, to personalize your reader even more.

Imagine the one person who will sit down with your essay. It may be your teacher, who will, of course, read your paper. It may be a member of your group, who might read the paper or have it read to them. Or it may be someone you don't know at all, if your paper should be circulated, or reproduced, or even printed (perhaps in the second edition of this book). It's that unknown reader that I'm going to ask you to imagine now.

So how should you do that? How can you imagine this unknown reader? For an answer, you might look again at the two students' essays you just read in section II of this chapter. What do you know about the reader Darby Crouse had in mind for "Theater at its Best"? (Pause for your answer.) Since she invites her reader to attend the Timber Lake Playhouse, that reader must live in or near Mt. Carroll, Illinois. Further, she seems to assume that her reader is interested in summer theater; at least he or she is open to the possibilities of this form of entertainment. Finally, Darby's reader hasn't worked in a theater (she has to explain what "striking the set" means), though there is apparently some curiosity about what goes on behind the scenes.

Do you fit that description of her reader? Neither do I. Yet something happens when I read Darby's essay. For a while I find myself drawn into her audience. I may be fairly sure that I'll never attend a performance at the Timber Lake Playhouse; certainly I'll never work there. Yet while I'm reading, I'm willing to imagine myself enjoying the pleasures of the place. In other words, I'm willing to *become* the reader that she wrote for.

Look now at the beginning of Judy Eberle's essay. She is very explicit about telling us, as readers, who she expects us to be and what she expects our concerns to be. And again, I am willing to go along with her. Even if disciplining children (something I have had remarkably little experience with) is not on my mind as I begin reading, I find that I get involved; I get interested; I trust her and I want to hear what she has to say. I become the audience she imagined.

Rhetorical theorist Walter Ong has suggested that this is the normal relationship between a writer and a reader. As a writer, you can *create* your own reader by clearly imagining who you want to have as your audience, what that ideal audience knows and is interested in, and what your relationship to that audience should be. Then you write to that specific, imagined audience. Ong suggests that your readers will, when they read your essay, each become the person you have imagined (just as I did when I read Darby and Judy's essays).

Still not convinced? Consider this example: Imagine that you're sitting for an hour and a half waiting to see a doctor. Of course none of the magazines in the waiting room are anything you're interested in. In desperation you pick up a travel magazine and start reading an article about the joys of a two week luxury cruise up the Nile. The author seems to assume that you, the reader, are an experienced traveler, that you have always longed to visit Egypt, and that you can easily afford the several-thousand-dollar fee. You're told how to bargain for gold jewelry, how to recognize a licensed dealer in antiquities, and where to buy an inlaid leather camel saddle. Still, the photograph of the temple of Abu Simbel attracts your attention, and before long you're reading intently, easily imagining yourself as the rich traveler through Egypt. In other words, you have become the audience the article is addressed to.

All of this is not to claim that you as writer will have your reader *entirely* in your control. You can't, for instance, imagine a reader who is infinitely patient and forgiving, willing to follow you into digressions, able to provide any missing details, eager to figure out what you really meant to say. You can't imagine that your reader will be able to read your mind.

Look at it this way: the purpose in creating your imagined ideal reader (the one you want your real reader to become) is to give you some clues about how you can best present your material to that reader. It will help you to know what details you need to provide, what stories to tell, what facts to cite, what proof to offer. Thinking of the person you want to have read your work will also let you see how important it is to organize your ideas in a way that your ideal reader (let's call this person Kim) can follow.

The information in your essay is, after all, all new to Kim. If it weren't, there would be no need for you to write it. And since it's new, you will need to provide Kim with as much help as you can. You will need to present your information clearly, logically, completely, and coherently. You'll need to make it as easy as possible to understand. The next few paragraphs focus on one way to do that: developing a clear organization.

Of course the way you're going to organize and present your material to your reader will not be your initial concern in the writing process. You shouldn't worry about it during the invention part of the process. First you have to gather all the information you need and begin to figure out for yourself what it all means.

Once you understand the subject, however, you need to examine what you have and organize it suitably for Kim. No, I'm not going to suggest a formal outline with Roman numerals and capital letters. If that kind of planning works for you, by all means continue to use it. But for many people it doesn't work. And for them (you?), there are alternatives. Even without a formal outline, all writers can pay attention to the organization of their papers, rather than just presenting ideas in a paper as they occur. During your prewriting you have generated a great many ideas. Working through those notes before you start to write, numbering points in the order you'll use them, will provide you with at least an initial organizational plan.

One conventional way of organizing information, a way that is particularly popular in academic writing, is to compose a sentence that clearly states the main point of the essay. Though you probably won't be able to compose this sentence till most (or all) of the paper is drafted, it is usually placed somewhere in the introduction. That way your reader can learn right at the start what to expect.

And this sentence (called the "thesis statement") not only helps the reader. It also helps you to keep your focus clear. You can check (several times) to make sure that everything in the essay does, in fact, build on the promise that the thesis makes. If you find yourself going in a direction that differs from the thesis, you can either alter that direction, or else change your thesis.

To be sure, this kind of organization around a thesis statement isn't always appropriate. It is often useful for a paper that presents information, but when you are telling a story, or exploring a topic from several angles, or reporting an interview, you will not be using a single sentence summary of your essay at the beginning. It would be silly to try. Other times, when you are leading your reader (or yourself) toward a solution of a problem or a conclusion about an issue, you'll want to hold off your main point until the end.

You will still, with or without a thesis statement, always have some organization, some logical reason for moving from point to point, from paragraph to paragraph. Remember that Kim (your ideal reader, remember?) will have to stay with you and follow your thought processes all the way through the paper. In order for that to happen, all of the connections and relationships must be clear. It's not enough for the points to fit together in your mind. They must do so in the paper too. How to make sure you've accomplished that? For now, I suggest using the readers in your group to help you clarify your organization. Let each of them play the role of Kim, telling you whenever they can't follow the logic of your movement from one point to the next. After that, there are some additional suggestions in Appendix Two.

A final point on organizing an essay: The computer can really help. When writing by hand, most writers reorganize material by numbering paragraphs, or drawing arrows, or writing in the margins, or cutting up a draft and taping the pieces together in a new order. That same reorganization can be accomplished with a few key-strokes on the computer. The blocking and moving functions of WordPerfect, which allow this easy movement, are explained in Appendix Five.

This ability of a word-processing program to move bits of text around lets us easily experiment with different arrangements until we find the one that works the best. Printing out a hard copy of the new arrangement (and perhaps doing more work with notes and arrows) will help complete the process. To use myself as an example one more time, I have moved large sections of this chapter around several times since I first drafted it. In an early version the two newspaper articles and the two student essays were collected together in one section without commentary. The readers of the draft, playing Kim, suggested that they be separated. That change led to others as I moved blocks of text back and forth. The result is a final draft which looks radically different from the version I started with.

VI

Now as you continue organizing, drafting, and revising your paper, here is another selection to read. This essay, from Stephen Jay Gould's book *Ever Since Darwin,* presents information that the author has learned about Darwin's biography and journals. Gould examines this information in order to reach his own answer to the question why Darwin waited twenty years to publish his findings on evolution.

Darwin's Delay

Stephen Jay Gould

Few events inspire more speculation than long and unexplained pauses in the activities of famous people. Rossini crowned a brilliant operatic career with *William Tell* and then wrote almost nothing for the next thirty-five years. Dorothy Sayers abandoned Lord Peter Wimsey at the height of his popularity and turned instead to God. Charles Darwin developed a radical theory of evolution in 1838 and published it twenty-one years later only because A. R. Wallace was about to scoop him.

Five years with nature aboard the *Beagle* destroyed Darwin's faith in the fixity of species. In July, 1837, shortly after the voyage, he started his first notebook on "transmutation." Already convinced that evolution had occurred, Darwin sought a theory to explain its mechanism. After much preliminary speculation and a few unsuccessful hypotheses, he achieved his central insight while reading an apparently unrelated work for recreation. Darwin later wrote in his autobiography:

> In October 1838 . . . I happened to read for amusement Malthus on *Population,* and being well prepared to appreciate the struggle for existence which everywhere goes on from long continued observation of the habits of animals and plants, it at once struck me that under these circumstances favorable variations would tend to be preserved and unfavorable ones to be destroyed. The result of this would be the formation of new species.

Darwin had long appreciated the importance of artificial selection practiced by animal breeders. But until Mathus's vision of struggle and crowding catalyzed his thoughts, he had not been able to identify an agent for natural selection. If all creatures produced far more offspring than could possibly survive, then natural selection would direct evolution under the simple assump-

---

"Darwin's Delay" is reprinted from EVER SINCE DARWIN, Reflections in Natural History, by Stephen Jay Gould, by permission of W. W. Norton & Company, Inc. Copyright © 1977 by Stephen Jay Gould. Copyright © 1973, 1974, 1975, 1976, 1977 by The American Museum of Natural History.

tion that survivors, on the average, are better adapted to prevailing conditions of life.

Darwin knew what he had achieved. We cannot attribute his delay to any lack of appreciation for the magnitude of his accomplishment. In 1842 and again in 1844 he wrote out preliminary sketches of his theory and its implications. He also left strict instructions with his wife to publish these alone of his manuscripts if he should die before writing his major work.

Why then did he wait for more than twenty years to publish his theory? True, the pace of our lives today has accelerated so rapidly—leaving among its victims the art of conversation and the game of baseball—that we may mistake a normal period of the past for a large slice of eternity. But the span of a man's life is a constant measuring stick; twenty years is still half a normal career—a large chunk of life even by the most deliberate Victorian standards.

Conventional scientific biography is a remarkably misleading source of information about great thinkers. It tends to depict them as simple, rational machines pursuing their insights with steadfast devotion, under the drive of an internal mechanism subject to no influence but the constraints of objective data. Thus, Darwin waited twenty years—so the usual argument runs—simply because he had not completed his work. He was satisfied with his theory, but theory is cheap. He was determined not to publish until he had amassed an overwhelming dossier of data in its support, and this took time.

But Darwin's activities during the twenty years in question display the inadequacy of this traditional view. In particular, he devoted eight full years to writing four large volumes on the taxonomy and natural history of barnacles. Before this single fact, the traditionalists can only offer pap—something like: Darwin felt that he had to understand species thoroughly before proclaiming how they change; this he could do only by working out for himself the classification of a difficult group of organisms—but not for eight years, and not while he sat on the most revolutionary notion in the history of biology. Darwin's own assessment of the four volumes stands in his autobiography.

> Besides discovering several new and remarkable forms, I made out the homologies of the various parts . . . and I proved the existence in certain genera of minute males complemental to

and parasitic on the hermaphrodites. . . . Nevertheless, I doubt whether the work was worth the consumption of so much time.

So complex an issue as the motivation for Darwin's delay has no simple resolution, but I feel sure of one thing: the negative effect of fear must have played at least as great a role as the positive need for additional documentation. Of what, then, was Darwin afraid?

When Darwin achieved his Malthusian insight, he was twenty-nine years old. He held no professional position, but he had acquired the admiration of his colleagues for his astute work aboard the *Beagle*. He was not about to compromise a promising career by promulgating a heresy that he could not prove.

What then was his heresy? A belief in evolution itself is the obvious answer. Yet this cannot be a major part of the solution; for, contrary to popular belief, evolution was a very common heresy during the first half of the nineteenth century. It was widely and openly discussed, opposed, to be sure, by a large majority, but admitted or at least considered by most of the great naturalists.

An extraordinary pair of Darwin's early notebooks may contain the answer (see H. E. Gruber and P. H. Barrett, *Darwin on Man*, for text and extensive commentary). These so-called M and N notebooks were written in 1838 and 1839, while Darwin was compiling the transmutation notebooks that formed the basis for his sketches of 1842 and 1844. They contain his thoughts on philosophy, esthetics, psychology, and anthropology. On rereading them in 1856, Darwin described them as "full of metaphysics and morals." They include many statements showing that he espoused but feared to expose something he perceived as far more heretical than evolution itself: philosophical materialism—the postulate that matter is the stuff of all existence and that all mental and spiritual phenomena are its by-products. No notion could be more upsetting to the deepest traditions of Western thought than the statement that mind—however complex and powerful—is simply a product of brain. Consider, for example, John Milton's vision of mind as separate from and superior to the body that it inhabits for a time (*Il Penseroso*, 1633).

> Or let my lamp, at midnight hour
> Be seen in some high lonely tower,

> Where I may oft outwatch the Bear,
> With thrice-great Hermes,[1] or unsphere
> The spirit of Plato, to unfold
> What worlds or what vast regions hold
> The immortal mind that hath forsook
> Her mansion in this fleshly nook.

The notebooks prove that Darwin was interested in philosophy and aware of its implications. He knew that the primary feature distinguishing his theory from all other evolutionary doctrines was its uncompromising philosophical materialism. Other evolutionists spoke of vital forces, organic striving, and the essential irreducibility of mind—a panoply of concepts that traditional Christianity could accept in compromise, for they permitted a Christian God to work by evolution instead of creation. Darwin spoke only of random variation and natural selection.

In the notebooks Darwin resolutely applied his materialistic theory of evolution to all phenomena of life, including what he termed "the citadel itself"—the human mind. And if mind has no real existence beyond the brain, can God be anything more than an illusion invented by an illusion? In one of his transmutation notebooks, he wrote:

> Love of the deity effect of organization, oh you materialist! . . .
> Why is thought being a secretion of brain, more wonderful than gravity a property of matter? It is our arrogance, our admiration of ourselves.

This belief was so heretical that Darwin even sidestepped it in *The Origin of Species* (1859), where he ventured only the cryptic comment that "light will be thrown on the origin of man and his history." He gave vent to his beliefs, only when he could hide them no longer, in the *Descent of Man* (1871) and *The Expression of the Emotions in Man and Animals* (1872). A. R. Wallace, the codiscoverer of natural selection, could never bring himself to apply it to the history of life. Yet Darwin cut through 2,000 years of philosophy and religion in the most remarkable epigram of the M notebook;

> Plato says in *Phaedo* that our "imaginary ideas" arise from the preexistence of the soul, are not derivable from experience—read monkeys for preexistence.

In his commentary on the M and N notebooks, Gruber labels materialism as "at that time more outrageous than evolution." He documents the persecution of materialistic beliefs during the late eighteenth and early nineteenth century and concludes:

> In virtually every branch of knowledge, repressive methods were used: lectures were proscribed, publication was hampered, professorships were denied, fierce invective and ridicule appeared in the press. Scholars and scientists learned the lesson and responded to the pressures on them. The ones with unpopular ideas sometimes recanted, published anonymously, presented their ideas in weakened forms, or delayed publication for many years.

Darwin had experienced a direct example as an undergraduate at the University of Edinburgh in 1827. His friend W. A. Browne read a paper with a materialistic perspective on life and mind before the Plinian Society. After much debate, all references to Browne's paper, including the record (from the previous meeting) of his intentions to deliver it, were expunged from the minutes. Darwin learned his lesson, for he wrote in the M notebook:

> To avoid stating how far, I believe, in Materialism, say only that emotions, instincts, degrees of talent, which are hereditary are so because brain of child resembles parent stock.

The most ardent materialists of the nineteenth century, Marx and Engels, were quick to recognize what Darwin had accomplished and to exploit its radical content. In 1869, Marx wrote to Engels about Darwin's *Origin:*

> Although it is developed in the crude English style, this is the book which contains the basis in natural history for our view.

Marx later offered to dedicate volume 2 of *Das Kapital* to Darwin, but Darwin gently declined, stating that he did not want to imply approval of a work he had not read. (I have seen Darwin's copy of volume 1 in his library at Down House. It is inscribed by Marx who calls himself a "sincere admirer" of Darwin. Its pages are uncut. Darwin was no devotee of the German language.)

Darwin was, indeed, a gentle revolutionary. Not only did he delay his work for so long, but he also assiduously avoided any public statement about the philosophical implications of his theory. In 1880, he wrote to Karl Marx:

> It seems to me (rightly or wrongly) that direct arguments against Christianity and Theism hardly have any effect on the public; and that freedom of thought will best be promoted by that gradual enlightening of human understanding which follows the progress of science. I have therefore always avoided writing about religion and have confined myself to science.

Yet the content of his work was so disruptive to traditional Western thought that we have yet to encompass it all. Arthur Koestler's campaign against Darwin, for example, rests upon a reluctance to accept Darwin's materialism and an ardent desire once again to invest living matter with some special property (see *The Ghost in the Machine* or *The Case of the Midwife Toad*). This, I confess, I do not understand. Wonder and knowledge are both to be cherished. Shall we appreciate any less the beauty of nature because its harmony is unplanned? And shall the potential of mind cease to inspire our awe and fear because several billion neuron reside in our skulls?

I can't resist pointing out Gould's many references to Darwin's diaries and notebooks. Apparently Darwin was another life-long journal-keeper, going so far as to keep different journals for the exploration of different subjects and ideas. An admirable example to us all.

Don't let that example slip by. This would be a particularly appropriate time to use your journal to respond to your reading. For starters, you might try applying some of the points I've discussed in this chapter to Gould's essay. Who is the audience that Gould creates for the essay? How does he help us to become part of that audience? What is his main point (or points) about Darwin? How does the essay trace Gould's discovery of that main point? How does he organize his essay to support that point?

---

1. "The Bear" refers to the constellation of Ursa major (the Great Bear), better known to us by its tail and hindquarters—the big dipper. "Thrice great Hermes" is Hermes Trismegistus (a Greek name for Toth, Egyptian god of wisdom). The "hermetic books," supposedly authored by Toth, are a collection of metaphysical and magical works that exerted great influence in seventeenth century England. They were equated by some with the Old Testament as a parallel source of pre-Christian wisdom. They waned in importance when exposed as a product of Alexandrian Greece, but survive in various doctrines of the Rosicrucians, and in our phrase "hermetic seal."

Now so long as you have your journal open (or your journal disk in the computer), how about some reflection about your experience writing your essay for this chapter? What have you learned so far? How has the experience of working on this paper differed from your experience with the other papers this semester?

And now a final reading. So far, this chapter has discussed the discovery and presentation of information in newspaper articles and in academic writing. Here, just to show that information can be provided in a wide variety of formats, I've included a poem by Illinois poet Dave Etter, titled "Flora Rutherford: Postcard to Florida." In this poem the fictional speaker writes to her mother in Florida to give her information about the coming of spring in Illinois.

Flora Rutherford: Postcard to Florida
Dave Etter

What brightens up this prairie town in spring?
Not tulip, not dandelion, not willow leaf,
but New Holland, Massey-Ferguson, and John Deere.
Right, the brand-new farm equipment
glistening now in the rooster-strutting sun.
And oh what colors they have given us:
strawberry red, sweet-corn yellow, pie-apple green.
A fragrant breeze drifts in from the plowed earth.
The excitement of crops seeds my furrowed brain.
Mother, we have come through another wintertime,
and I had to write to tell you this.

VII
So What About Grammar, Anyway?

You will have noticed, no doubt, that up till now this text has said nothing about prepositional phrases, dangling modifiers, coor-

From Dave Etter, ALLIANCE, ILLINOIS, copyright © by Spoon River Poetry Press. Reprinted with permission.

dinating conjunctions, or comma splices. Perhaps your instructor has commented on these or other features of your writing, and may even have discussed them with you in conferences or in class. But the text has been strangely silent.

It's time to correct that. After all, it is the work of English textbooks to teach grammar, or at least that's what we've been led to believe. So here we go: Think for a moment (in writing, perhaps) about your experience with grammar instruction. What exactly has that experience been? Which classes included it? What did you learn? In what ways has it helped you to be a better writer? What use do you make of your knowledge of English grammar when you write?

Are you about to keep reading? Without answering the questions? Once again these are real questions that I'd really like you to think about. And if the questions so far haven't inspired you, here's another, which would be an especially good topic for a journal entry: Why should we study grammar in a writing class? Or why not? (The space below is to give you time to write.)

* * * *

Chances are that you don't know the names of a lot of grammatical constructions, even if they were covered in one of your high school classes. Nor do you usually take time to analyze the grammatical structure of your sentences as you are writing. In fact, most writers don't. That's not to say that grammar study is useless. On the contrary, grammar study gives us a way to examine our language, allowing us to better understand how we say things and why we say them that way. Further, it lets us analyze the various ways we use words and structures in order to communicate, indeed, in order to think.

But the study of grammar (part of the discipline of linguistics) is different from the study of writing, and this is a writing course. Most research into the relationship between grammar study and writing has demonstrated very little connection. (If you are one of the many Western students who learned English as a second language, that statement, which *is* true of your native language, will not apply to your use of English. Until you achieve near-native fluency, you will need to recall the grammatical rules you've learned whenever you write.)

Research has shown that native speakers of English don't usually need to be able to define the grammatical structure of the language in order to write. So what *do* you need to know? With just a few exceptions, you know it already: it's the structure of the language that you learned years ago when you first learned to talk.

Here's proof. Do you know the grammatical rule in English for the placement of adjectives of age, number, and nationality before a noun? Trust me, you do. Consider: There are four boys sitting at a table. All four are Swiss. They are all young. Now fill in the blanks: _____ _____ _____ boys are sitting at the table.

The words will fall into the same order every time, no matter what the number, or the age, or the nationality. It's a rule of English grammar. And you knew it, just like you know most of the other rules and conventions of your language. They're there in your head. You couldn't talk without them.

So why do you (and I) make mistakes when we write? Well, there are probably a number of reasons. Sometimes we really don't know how to put a particular sentence together, usually when we've let the sentence get too complex and confusing. Other times we make a mistake because, for some reason, we missed out learning a rule or convention when we were young, or because we don't know what kind of construction an unfamiliar word requires. Yet other times we get into trouble because we've learned where mistakes are likely to occur (what are the rules for a semi-colon, anyway?) and instead of learning how to do it right, we just freeze up and make it worse. These are all problems that can be corrected with a little work, most effectively on a one-to-one basis with a teacher or Writing Center tutor.

The great majority of errors, however, are simply the result of carelessness. When the writing's going well, and the ideas are coming quickly, it's easy to leave the ending off a verb or to misplace a comma. And during revision, it's not unusual to change one part of a sentence and forget to make the necessary changes in the rest. Then, once an essay has been drafted and revised and re-revised, it can be very hard to go back to it one more time to proofread carefully. Even a quick read-through can sometimes be nearly impossible. Result: a paper full of silly mistakes.

Not, of course, that all the mistakes are really that serious. The reader will probably be able to figure out what you were trying to say, even if there are a few commas where you meant to put periods. But remember what I said a few pages back about your relationship with your reader? That can be one of the most important considerations when you write. Anything that gets in the way of that relationship can destroy the effectiveness of your writing. Anything—whether talking over the reader's head, or assuming she knows something she doesn't, or omitting necessary details, *or* distracting her with careless errors. And imagining a reader who doesn't care about your errors, in the hope that your real reader will go along, just doesn't seem to work.

That's the reason for paying attention to the mechanical details of your writing. They distract. They interfere with communication. They annoy. They may even make your reader lose respect for you. So when you've got a pretty good essay, it's senseless to let your failure to proofread create such disastrous effects.

Of course you have to have something pretty good to start with. Accuracy alone won't make a dull, dishonest, or purposeless paper any better. But if you've done your work well so far, you should be sure to finish the job. Read the paper through from beginning to end. Then look at it again starting at the end and working backwards. This backwards reading will let you see what's really on the page, rather than what you think is there. And if you have a question, ask your teacher or a tutor in the Writing Center. Make use of what you know already, *and* draw on the resources that are available to you. It's worth the effort.

The art of writing is the art of applying the seat of the pants to the seat of the chair.

Mary Heaton Vorse

Chapter 8
Interlude: Writing Essay Exams

I

Here, after the very long Chapter Seven, is a very short Chapter Eight. And not only is it short, it doesn't have an essay assignment! All you have to do is read it, learn it, and I hope, make use of it the next time you have to take an essay test.

Actually, this chapter is very short because it was supposed to be a part of the last chapter. From the time I made my third revision of the Table of Contents I intended to include a section with advice on writing essay exams in Chapter Seven. It made sense to include it there. It should have fit. After all, what else are essay exams but occasions to present information?

But it didn't fit. I tried to insert it in several places in the chapter, but no matter where I put it it read like a digression. Even introducing it by calling it a digression didn't seem to work. So I recalled some of my own advice, gave the chapter to other people to read, and talked it over with them. It was a productive conversation, leading me directly to another piece of advice that I offered back in Chapter Five: Digressions, however interesting, usually confuse, distract, and annoy. They need to be cut.

Accordingly, I cut my essay on essay exams out of Chapter Seven. But thanks to the computer's ability to move large sections of text around, I was able to move it here, into a new Chapter Eight. Should you ever need to move text around this way, you can find the instructions in Appendix Five. (I'd put them here, but that would be another digression.)

II
Writing Essay Exams

At the beginning of Chapter Seven I suggested that there were three typical situations when you will present information in a college class. The first two involve using writing to discover information as well as to share it with a reader. The third kind of writing, I said, requires you to write to prove that you have already learned a subject. Most often this writing will occur in essay exams.

Essay exams are, of course, much dreaded. Somehow a computer-graded multiple-choice tester seems easier. There is, however, an important difference in the philosophy between these two types of tests, a difference in what is being tested. Understanding that difference may help you see what needs to be done on an essay exam.

Objective tests, the kinds with pencils and computer-graded answer sheets or else a series of blanks for short answers, are usually designed to discover what you *don't* know. They are graded by looking for mistakes, and may in fact include invitations to error (the so-called "trick questions"). On the other hand, an essay question gives you the opportunity to demonstrate what you *do* know.

That means that in writing the answer to an essay question, just as in writing other essays that present information, you need to sound like an authority on the subject. Of course you will have read the assigned material, attended class meetings, and reviewed carefully. Now you need to include as much appropriate information as you can in your essay answer. Don't leave anything out. Don't assume that the reader already knows it. This time you have a clearly defined relationship with your reader. Your teacher is not merely an interested reader seeking to learn from you. Rather, she will be evaluating how much information you have.

Here's another fact about your reader that you need to keep well in mind as you write. Your teacher will likely have to read a great many essays on the same subject, and will probably need to evaluate them fairly quickly. Some teachers may, in fact, have over a hundred responses to read. To the same question. Oh, I know, she's the one who decided to give you the test in the first place, so it's hard to feel sorry for her. Nonetheless, if you can think of the things that will make her job any easier or pleasanter, you can be sure it will be appreciated.

Here are the things that you can do to make your reader's job easier:

1. Answer the question that is asked. The question will probably ask you to compare two things, or contrast them; or it will ask you to define a term or concept; or else to analyze causes, or effects; or explain the parts; or place the thing in a larger context; or give examples. Whatever the question asks you to do should be the thing that you actually do do.

2. Put a carefully worded one-sentence answer to the question right at the start. (See my discussion of the thesis statement in Chapter Seven or else in Appendix Two.) The sentence can be something like "The three major differences between A and B are: one, two, and three." Or else "The four causes of A were O, P, Q, and R." Or else, "The personality of character H determines his fate by leading him first to do M and then to do N." This statement will let the reader immediately anticipate what the rest of the essay will be about and how it will be organized. (A hint: The form your thesis statement should take is often determined by the form of the question. Sometimes just rewriting the question as a declarative sentence will give you the first part of your thesis.)

3. Be sure that your whole essay is, indeed, about the subject announced in that first sentence. If, as you write, you discover that you have something quite different to say, go back and change the first sentence.

4. Make the relationships among the parts of your essay clear. Indicate "first," "second," "third," "in addition," "on the other hand," or "in conclusion." While it is always important to lead your reader carefully from point to point, on an essay exam it is absolutely essential.

5. Include as many specific facts as you can. Instead of merely generalizing, list *specific* examples, events, ideas, dates, names, theories, characteristics, and quotations which lead to your conclusion. Show what you know.

6. Don't pad your answer with a lot of unnecessary words. Say what you need to directly and clearly. (Write: "Darwin had three main reasons for delaying publication of his theory of natural selection." Don't write: "In my humble opinion, there were countless reasons for the great and famous scientist Charles Darwin to have been tempted to delay announcing his revolutionary theories about

evolutionary ideas, but after careful and thoughtful consideration of all of the issues involved, I have come to the final conclusion that three main reasons are of chief and primary significance and should be listed here.") Extra words that don't contribute to your answer are an annoyance, and it's unwise to annoy.

In addition to including the right things in your essay, your exam-taking behavior can also influence your success. First, show up on time. That's obvious, except to the two or three people in every class who show up, confused or panicked, twenty minutes after the exam began. Second, relax: Breathe deeply, stretch, get comfortable. Don't go to sleep, of course, but don't let anxiety keep you from doing your best. And third, look at the whole test before you start to answer the first question. Knowing what's ahead will help you to effectively manage the time allowed.

Fourth, use all of the available time. After you've figured out how much time you should spend on each question, try to stick to that schedule. The exam is not a race, and there is no honor in being the first one finished. In fact, finishing first may be a clue that you have not answered the questions as completely as you were expected to. In my experience, the first person to finish a test rarely has the best grade.

Fifth, apply what you know about the writing process, or rather, about *your* writing process. This attention to process can begin before the exam time, as you prepare for it. Use writing to get ready for writing. Try to anticipate some probable test questions and practice writing out answers to them. Even if you don't come up with the same questions your teacher does, the practice will be valuable.

Then, when the exam time arrives, take some time at the beginning to think, take notes, and, if necessary, use one of the simpler invention techniques (the reporter's formula, listing). Many people have found that a few minutes of free writing is a good way to get started. Next, as you draft your answer, write on every other line (unless instructed otherwise). Not only will your answer be easier to read, but also you'll have room to add or replace as you revise, which of course you will do. If you've paid attention to the time, you should have a few minutes left at the end to look over your answers and make appropriate changes.

Sixth, be sure to answer all the questions. Don't skip any. Even if you don't think you know the answer, write something. Do the best you can. Show what you know. (On the other hand, be sure to read the instructions and determine how many questions you are supposed to answer. Essay tests often allow you some choice. If the instructions ask you to answer four questions, don't try to answer seven!)

Seventh and last, approach the whole experience with confidence. If you begin an essay exam (or any exam for that matter) with a feeling of doom and despair, you may well fulfill your own prophecy. On the other hand, if you have studied as well as you could, rested sufficiently, and reviewed the advice I've offered, you should have no reason to panic. You might even look forward (just a little bit) to the opportunity to demonstrate what you know.

I write as straight as I can, just as I walk as straight as I can, because that is the best way to get there.

H. G. Wells

Chapter **9**

Discovering Values

I

In this chapter you will be asked to write about an ethical issue. You'll once again examine your experience, this time to analyze the values and beliefs that help you to make choices and determine action.

That may sound like a demanding assignment. Okay, it probably is. The challenge will be worth it, however, since this writing project has the potential to lead you to a better understanding of yourself, even as it gives you some practice in the analysis of ideas. Don't let the words "values" or "ethics" throw you off. We're not going to be talking about religion, or rules, or impossible standards.

On the contrary, we'll consider ethical issues that are part of daily experience, influencing everything from your most recent conflict with your parents, to your relationship with your roommate, to your understanding of racial conflict, to your goals for your career, to your decision to read these pages your instructor assigned. Indeed, some of the essays you've already written for this class will have revealed some aspects of your ethical system. In this chapter we'll focus more specifically on these issues.

To provide a context for this focus, it will help to have some further background in the nature of ethical choices. That means that unlike the other chapters, this one will delay making a writing assignment for a while. I've chosen an essay by Peter Singer, "About Ethics," to provide the initial background information. It comes from a philosophy text exploring the variety of ways we can study and understand the subject of ethics. The essay is also a good example of the kind of writing we looked at in Chapter Seven; that is, it's an essay which presents information to a reader who is interested but not yet fully informed.

I'll warn you from the beginning: Singer's essay is challenging. The difficulty is not that it's badly written (quite the opposite), but that the material is complex and probably unfamiliar. You'll need to read it more slowly than usual. You might also need to practice some strategies for reading complex material. These include previewing, active reading, and reviewing. If you've ever struggled through a difficult text, only to emerge with no idea what it was about, you'll see the advantage of taking time to practice these strategies.

PREVIEWING

First of all, it's very helpful to provide your own context for the experience of reading the essay. Do you know anything already about the author? Does the place the essay appears (a textbook, a scientific journal, a popular magazine, a newspaper) suggest to you anything that you should expect? What does the title tell you? What does it lead you to expect? What do you already know about the subject of the essay? Taking just a few seconds to answer these questions can get you ready to read. Notice that they are primarily based on your knowledge and expectations as a reader.

In Chapter Seven I suggested that in an essay presenting information, it is important for you to understand and meet your reader's expectations. As a writer you need to make it possible for your reader to move through the essay understanding the relationships among your various points.

As a reader, you can assume that the writer will give you the same kind of help; your job now is to watch for the clues about structure and relationships that the writer has provided. Many of these can be detected before you get too deeply into the essay. The second part of previewing is to look at the divisions of the essay, if any, or the suggestions about organization contained in the opening paragraphs.

For example, glance through the essay on ethics. You'll see that there are two subheadings: "What Ethics Is Not" and "What Ethics Is: One View." These subheadings make it quite clear how the author is going to proceed. Next look at the first paragraph. What predictions does it contain that will let you follow the rest of the essay?

ACTIVE READING

As you read you can continue to notice the predictions about what to expect next. There will be plenty of clues that can establish your expectations. These include *lists* (a sentence beginning "first" usually predicts that there will be a "second," and maybe a "third"), *contrasts* ("on the one hand" suggests that a contrasting view will follow), *examples* ("for example" is a sure give-away), or *indications of relationships* ("at the same time," "also," "as a result," "therefore," "in conclusion," "furthermore," or "of course"). In addition, the first sentence of each paragraph will usually give some indication of what that paragraph will be about. You should find that being able to predict the direction of a sentence or paragraph (or indeed, the whole essay) will let you read it more fluently. This "predictability," according to people who study reading habits, is an essential ingredient in successful reading. As you begin to recognize and appreciate the ways that certain verbal clues help you to anticipate what is to come, you may want to add them to your own list of writing strategies.

Active reading involves more than just consciously predicting what will come next. It also involves thinking about the subject, comparing what you read with what you already know, providing additional examples from your experience, asking questions, and noting what you don't yet understand. For experienced readers, all this means reading with a pencil in hand, underlining passages and making notes in the margins of the text. These marks and notes will help you to review the essay once you are finished, as well as to determine at the end what questions still remain.

REVIEWING

Once you have finished reading an essay, the temptation will be to sigh with relief, take a break, and get on with something else. (In other words, it's much like the temptation to quit working on a paper assignment as soon as the last paragraph is reached.) The danger of moving on too quickly is that most of what you read will soon be forgotten. A few minutes of review, looking again at those underlined passages and notes, will help you remember the important points and features. If you're especially ambitious, or if the material is particularly important, or if it is assigned, you might use your journal to record your reaction to the essay, including the main points, the things you learned, the questions you still have, and your feeling about it all.

After that long introduction, here, finally, is the background discussion of ethics that I promised:

About Ethics
Peter Singer

This essay is about practical ethics, that is about the application of ethics or morality—I shall use the words interchangeably—to practical issues like the treatment of racial minorities, equality for women, the use of animals for food and research, abortion, euthanasia and the obligation of the wealthy to help the poor. No doubt the reader will want to get on to these issues without delay; but there are some preliminaries which must be dealt with at the start. In order to have a useful discussion within ethics, it is necessary to say a little about ethics so that we have a clear understanding of what we are doing when we discuss ethical

From Peter Singer, PRACTICAL ETHICS. Copyright © 1979 by Peter Singer. Reprinted by permission of Cambridge University Press.

questions. In order to prevent this essay from growing into an entire volume, it is brief and at times dogmatic. I cannot take the space properly to consider all the different conceptions of ethics that might be opposed to the one I shall defend.

What Ethics is Not

Some people think that morality is now out of date. They regard morality as a system of nasty puritanical prohibitions, mainly designed to stop people having fun. Traditional moralists who claim to be the defenders of morality, when they are only defending one particular moral code, rather than morality as such, have been allowed to pre-empt the field to such an extent that when a newspaper headline reads BISHOP ATTACKS DECLINING MORAL STANDARDS we expect to read yet again about promiscuity, homosexuality, pornography, and so on, and not about corporations bribing government officials, or the puny amounts we give as overseas aid to poorer nations.

So the first thing ethics is not, is a set of prohibitions particularly concerned with sex. Sex raises no special moral issues at all. Decisions about sex may involve considerations of honesty, concern for others, prudence, and so on, but there is nothing special about sex in this respect, for the same could be said of decisions about driving a car. (In fact the moral issues raised by driving a car, both from an environmental and from a safety point of view, are much more serious than those raised by having sex.) Accordingly this essay contains no discussion of sexual morality. There are more important ethical issues to be considered.

The second thing that ethics is not, is an ideal system which is all very noble in theory but no good in practice. The reverse of this is closer to the truth: an ethical judgment that is no good in practice must suffer from a theoretical defect as well, for the whole point of ethical judgments is to guide practice.

People sometimes believe that ethics is inapplicable to the real world because they believe that ethics is a system of short and simple rules like "Do not lie," "Do not steal," and "Do not kill." It is not surprising that those who hold this model of ethics should also believe that ethics is not suited to life's complexities. In unusual situations, simple rules conflict; and even when they do not, following a rule can lead to disaster. It may normally be wrong to lie, but if you were living in Nazi Germany and the

Gestapo came to your door looking for Jews, it would surely be right to deny the existence of the Jewish family hiding in your attic.

Like the failure of a restrictive sexual morality, the failure of an ethic of simple rules must not be taken as a failure of ethics as a whole. It is only a failure of one view of ethics, and not even an irremediable failure of that view. Those who think that ethics is a system of rules—the deontologists—can rescue their position by finding more complicated and more specific rules which do not conflict with each other, or by ranking the rules in some hierarchial structure to resolve conflicts between them. Moreover there is a long-standing approach to ethics which is quite untouched by the complexities which make simple rules difficult to apply. This is the teleological or consequentialist view. Consequentialists start not with moral rules but with goals. The best-known, though not the only, consequentialist theory is utilitarianism. The classical utilitarian regards an action as right if it produces as much or more of an increase in the happiness of all affected by it than any alternative action, and wrong if it does not.

The consequences of an action vary according to the circumstances in which it is performed. Hence a utilitarian can never properly be accused of a lack of realism, or of a rigid adherence to ideals in defiance of practical experience. The utilitarian will judge lying bad in some circumstances and good in others, depending on its consequences.

The third thing ethics is not, is something intelligible only in the context of religion. I shall treat ethics as entirely independent of religion.

Some theists say that ethics cannot do without religion because the very meaning of "good" is nothing other than "what God approves." Plato refuted a similar claim more than two thousand years ago by arguing that if the gods approve of some actions it must be because those actions are good, in which case it cannot be the gods' approval that makes them good. The alternative view makes divine approval entirely arbitrary: if the gods had happened to approve of torture and disapprove of helping our neighbors, torture would have been good and helping our neighbors bad. Some modern theists have attempted to extricate themselves from this type of dilemma by maintaining that God is good and so could not possibly approve of torture; but these theists are caught in a trap of their own making, for what can they possibly mean by the assertion that God is good? That God is approved of by God?

Traditionally the more important link between religion and ethics was that religion was thought to provide a reason for doing what is right, the reason being that those who are virtuous will be rewarded by an eternity of bliss while the rest roast in hell. Not all religious thinkers have accepted this: Immanuel Kant, a most pious Christian, scorned anything that smacked of a self-interested motive for obeying the moral law. We must obey it, he said, for its own sake. Nor do we have to be Kantians to dispense with the motivation offered by traditional religion. There is a long line of thought which finds the source of ethics in the attitudes of benevolence and sympathy for others that most people have. This is, however, a complex topic and I shall not pursue it here. It is enough to say that our everyday observation of our fellows clearly shows that ethical behavior does not require belief in heaven and hell.

The fourth, and last, claim about ethics that I shall deny is that ethics is relative or subjective. At least, I shall deny these claims in some of the senses in which they are often made. This point requires a more extended discussion than the other three.

Let us take first the often-asserted idea that ethics is relative to the society one happens to live in. This is true in one sense and false in another. It is true that, as we have already seen in discussing consequentialism, actions that are right in one situation because of their good consequences may be wrong in another situation because of their bad consequences. Thus casual sexual intercourse may be wrong when it leads to the existence of children who cannot be adequately cared for, and not wrong when, because of the existence of effective contraception, it does not lead to reproduction at all. But this is only a superficial form of relativism. While it suggests that a specific principle like "Casual sex is wrong" may be relative to time and place, it says nothing against such a principle being objectively valid in certain specified circumstances, or against the universal applicability of a more general principle like "Do what increases happiness and reduces suffering."

The more fundamental form of relativism became popular in the nineteenth century when data on the moral beliefs and practices of far-flung societies began pouring in. To the strict reign of Victorian prudery the knowledge that there were places where sexual relations between unmarried people were regarded as perfectly wholesome brought the seeds of a revolution in sexual attitudes. It is not surprising that to some the new knowledge suggested not merely that the moral code of nineteenth-century Europe was not objectively valid, but that no moral judgment can do more than reflect the customs of the society in which it is made.

Marxists adapted this form of relativism to their own theories. The ruling ideas of each period, they said, are the ideas of its ruling class, and so the morality of a society is relative to its dominant economic class, and thus indirectly relative to its economic basis. So they triumphantly refuted the claims of feudal and bourgeois morality to objective, universal validity. But this raises a problem: if all morality is relative, what is so special about communism? Why side with the proletariat rather than the bourgeoisie?

Engels dealt with the problem in the only way possible, by abandoning relativism in favor of the more limited claim that the morality of a society divided into classes will always be relative to the ruling class, although the morality of a society without class antagonisms could be a "really human" morality. This is no longer relativism at all, but Marxism still, in a confused sort of way, provides the impetus for a lot of woolly relativist ideas.

The problem that led Engels to abandon relativism defeats ordinary ethical relativism as well. Anyone who has thought about an ethical decision knows that being told what our society thinks we ought to do does not settle our decision. We have to reach our own decision. The beliefs and customs we were brought up with may exercise great influence on us, but once we start to reflect upon them we can decide whether to act in accordance with them, or go against them.

The opposite view—that ethics is always relative to a particular society—has most implausible consequences. If our society disapproves of slavery, while another society approves of it, we have no basis to choose between these conflicting views. Indeed, on a relativist analysis there is really no conflict—when I say slavery is wrong I am really only saying that my society disapproves of slavery, and when the slaveowners from the other society say that slavery is right, they are only saying that their society approves of it. Why argue? Obviously we could both be speaking the truth.

Worse still, the relativist cannot satisfactorily account for the nonconformist. If "slavery is wrong" means "my society disapproves of slavery" then someone who lives in a society which does not disapprove of slavery is, in claiming that slavery is wrong, making a simple factual error. An opinion poll could demonstrate the error of an ethical judgment. Would-be reformers are therefore in a parlous situation: when they set out to change the ethical views of their fellow-citizens they are *necessarily* mistaken; it is only when they succeed in winning most of the society over to their own views that those views become right.

These difficulties are enough to sink ethical relativism; ethical subjectivism at least avoids making nonsense of the valiant efforts of would-be moral reformers, for it makes ethical judgments depend on the approval or disapproval of the person making the judgment, rather than that person's society. There are other difficulties, though, that at least some forms of ethical subjectivism cannot overcome.

If those who say that ethics is subjective mean by this that when I say that cruelty to animals is wrong I am really only saying that I disapprove of cruelty to animals, they are faced with an aggravated form of one of the difficulties of relativism: the inability to account for ethical disagreement. What was true for the relativist of disagreement between people from different societies is for the subjectivist true of disagreement between any two people. I say cruelty to animals is wrong: someone else says it is not wrong. If this means that I disapprove of cruelty to animals and someone else does not, both statements may be true and so there is nothing to argue about.

Other theories often described as "subjectivist" are not open to this objection. Suppose someone maintains that ethical judgments are neither true nor false because they do not describe anything—neither objective moral facts, nor one's own subjective states of mind. This theory might hold that, as C. L. Stevenson suggested, ethical judgments express attitudes, rather than describe them, and we disagree about ethics because we try, by expressing our own attitude, to bring our listeners to a similar attitude. Or it might be, as R. M. Hare has urged, that ethical judgments are prescriptions and therefore more closely related to commands than to statements of fact. On this view we disagree because we care about what people do. Those features of ethical argument that imply the existence of objective moral standards can be explained away by maintaining that this is some kind of error—perhaps the legacy of the belief that ethics is a God-given system of law, or perhaps just another example of our tendency to objectify our personal wants and preferences. J. L. Mackie has defended this view.

Provided they are carefully distinguished from the crude form of subjectivism which sees ethical judgments as descriptions of the speaker's attitudes, these are plausible accounts of ethics. In their denial of a realm of ethical facts which is part of the real world, existing quite independently of us, they are no doubt correct. But does it follow from this that ethical judgments are immune from criticism, that there is no role for reason or argument in ethics and that, from the standpoint of reason, any ethical judgment is as good as any other? I do not think it does, and none of the three philosophers referred to in the previous paragraph denies reason and argument a role in ethics, though they disagree as to the significance of this role.

This issue of the role that reason can play in ethics is the crucial point raised by the claim that ethics is subjective. The nonexistence of a mysterious realm of objective ethical facts need not concern us, as long as it does not imply the nonexistence of ethical reasoning. It may even help, since if we could arrive at ethical judgments only by intuiting these strange ethical facts, ethical argument would be more difficult still. So what has to be shown to put practical ethics on a sound basis is that ethical reasoning is possible. Here the temptation is to say simply that the proof of the pudding lies in the eating, but this is not entirely satisfactory. From a theoretical point of view it is unsatisfactory because we might find ourselves reasoning about ethics without really understanding how this can happen; and from a practical point of view it is unsatisfactory because our reasoning is more likely to go astray if we lack a grasp of its foundations. I shall therefore attempt to say something about how we can reason in ethics.

What Ethics Is: One View

What follows is a sketch of a view of ethics which allows reason an important role in ethical decisions. It is not the only possible view of ethics, but it is a plausible view. Once again, however, I shall have to pass over qualifications and objections worth an essay to themselves. To those who think these undiscussed objections defeat the position I am advancing I can only say, again, that this essay is designed to assist in giving a clear view of what I take ethics to be.

What is it to make a moral judgment, or to argue about an ethical issue, or to live according to ethical standards? How do moral judgments differ from other practical judgments? Why do we regard a woman's decision to have an abortion as raising an ethical issue, but not her decision to change her job? What is the difference between a person who lives by ethical standards and one who doesn't?

All these questions are related, so we only need to consider one of them; but to do this we need to say something about the nature of ethics. Suppose that we have studied the lives of a number of different people, and we know a lot about what they do, what they believe, and so on. Can we then decide which of them are living by ethical standards and which are not?

We might think that the way to proceed here is to find out who believes it wrong to lie, cheat, steal and so on, and does not do any of these things, and who has no such beliefs, and shows no such restraint in their actions. Then those in the first group would be living according to ethical standards and those in the second group would not be. But this procedure mistakenly assimilates two distinctions: the first is the distinction between living according to (what we judge to be) the right ethical standards and living according to (what we judge to be) mistaken ethical standards; the second is the distinction between living according to some ethical standards, and living according to no ethical standards at all. Those who lie and cheat, but do not believe what they are doing to be wrong, may be living according to ethical standards. They may believe, for any of a number of possible reasons, that it is right to lie, cheat, steal and so on. They are not living according to conventional ethical standards, but they may be living according to some other ethical standards.

This first attempt to distinguish the ethical form the nonethical was mistaken, but we can learn from our mistakes. We found that we must concede that those who hold unconventional ethical beliefs are still living according to ethical standards, *if they believe, for any reason, that it is right to do as they are doing.* The italicized condition gives us a clue to the answer we are seeking. The notion of living according to ethical standards is tied up with the notion of defending the way one is living, of giving a reason for it, of justifying it. Thus people may do all kinds of things we regard as wrong, yet still be living according to ethical standards, if they are prepared to defend and justify what they do. We may find the justification inadequate, and may hold that the actions are wrong, but the attempt at justification, whether successful or not, is sufficient to bring the person's conduct within the domain of the ethical as opposed to the non-ethical. When, on the other hand, people cannot put forward any justification for what they do, we may reject their claim to be living according to ethical standards, even if what they do is in accordance with conventional moral principles.

We can go further. If we are to accept that a person is living according to ethical standards, the justification must be of a certain kind. For instance, a justification in terms of self-interest alone will not do. When Macbeth, contemplating the murder of Duncan, admits that only "vaulting ambition" drives him to do it, he is admitting that the act cannot be justified ethically. "So that I can be king in his place" is not a weak attempt at an ethical justification for assassination; it is not the sort of reason that counts as an ethical justification at all. Self-interested acts must be shown to be compatible with more broadly based ethical principles if they are to be ethically defensible, for the notion of ethics carries with it the idea of something bigger than the individual. If I am to defend my conduct on ethical grounds, I cannot point only to the benefits it brings me. I must address myself to a larger audience.

From ancient times, philosophers and moralists have expressed the idea that ethical conduct is acceptable from a point of view that is somehow universal. The Golden Rule attributed to Moses tells us to go beyond our own personal interests and "do unto others as we would have them do unto us." The same idea of putting oneself in the position of another is involved in the Christian commandment that we love our neighbor as ourself. The Stoics held that ethics derives from a universal natural law. Kant developed this idea into his famous formula: "Act only on that maxim through which you can at the same time will that it should become a universal law." Kant's theory has itself been modified and developed by R. M. Hare, who sees "universalizability" as a logical feature of moral judgments. The eighteenth-century British philosophers Hutcheson, Hume and Adam Smith appealed to an imaginary "impartial spectator" as the test of a moral judgment, and this theory has its modern version in the Ideal Observer

Theory. Utilitarians, from Jeremy Bentham to J. C. C. Smart, take it as axiomatic that in deciding moral issues "each counts for one and none for more than one"; while John Rawls, a leading contemporary critic of utilitarianism, incorporates essentially the same axiom into his own theory by deriving basic ethical principles from an imaginary choice in which those choosing do not know whether they will be the ones who gain or lose by the principles they select. Even Continental philosophers like the existentialist Jean-Paul Sartre and the Marxist Jurgen Habermas, who differ in many ways from their English-speaking colleagues—and from each other—agree that ethics is in some sense universal.

One could argue endlessly about the merits of each of these characterizations of the ethical; but what they have in common is more important than their differences. They agree that the justification of an ethical principle cannot be in terms of any partial or sectional group. Ethics takes a universal point of view. This does not mean that a particular ethical judgment must be universally applicable. Circumstances alter causes, as we have seen. What it does mean is that in making ethical judgments we go beyond our own likes and dislikes. From an ethical point of view the fact that it is I who benefit from, say, a more equal distribution of income and you, say, who lose by it, is irrelevant. Ethics requires us to go beyond "I" and "you" to the universal law, the universalizable judgment, the standpoint of the impartial spectator or ideal observer, or whatever we choose to call it.

Can we use this universal aspect of ethics to derive an ethical theory which will give us guidance about right and wrong? Philosophers from the Stoics to Hare and Rawls have attempted this. No attempt has met with general acceptance. The problem is that if we describe the universal aspect of ethics in bare, formal terms, a wide range of ethical theories, including quite irreconcilable ones, are compatible with this notion of universality; if, on the other hand, we build up our description of the universal aspect of ethics so that it leads us ineluctably to one particular ethical theory, we shall be accused of smuggling our own ethical beliefs into our definition of the ethical—and this definition was supposed to be broad enough, and neutral enough, to encompass all serious candidates for the status of "ethical theory." Since so many others have failed to overcome this obstacle to deducing an ethical theory from the universal aspect of ethics, it would be fool-hardy to attempt to do so in a brief introduction with a quite different aim. Nevertheless I shall propose something only a little less ambitious. The universal aspect of ethics, I suggest, does provide a persuasive, although not conclusive, reason for taking a broadly utilitarian position.

My reason for suggesting this is as follows. In accepting that ethical judgments must be made from a universal point of view, I am accepting that my own interests cannot, simply because they are *my* interests, count more than the interests of anyone else. Thus my very natural concern that my own interests be looked after must, when I think ethically, be extended to the interests of others. Now, imagine that I am trying to decide between two possible courses of action—any example would do. Imagine, too, that I am deciding in a complete ethical vacuum, that I know nothing of any ethical considerations—I am, we might say, in a pre-ethical stage of thinking. How would I make up my mind? One thing that would be still relevant would be how the possible courses of action will affect my interests. Indeed, if we define "interest" broadly enough, so that we count anything people desire as in their interests (unless it is incompatible with another desire or desires) then it would seem that at this pre-ethical stage, *only* one's own interests can be relevant to the decision.

Suppose I then begin to think ethically, to the extent of recognizing that my own interests cannot account for more, simply because they are my own, than the interests of others. In place of my own interests, I now have to take account of the interests of all those affected by my decision. This requires me to weigh up all these interests and adopt the course of action most likely to maximize the interests of those affected. Thus I must choose the course of action which has the best consequences, on balance, for all affected. This is a form of utilitarianism. It differs from classical utilitarianism in that "best consequences" is understood as meaning what, on balance, furthers the interests of those affected, rather than merely what increases pleasure and reduces pain. (It has, however, been suggested that classical utilitarians like Bentham and John Stuart Mill used "pleasure" and "pain" in a broad sense which allowed them to include achieving what one desired as a "pleasure" and the reverse as a "pain." If this interpretation is correct, the difference between classical utilitarianism and utilitarianism based on interests disappears.)

What does this show? It does not show that utilitarianism can be deduced from the universal aspect of ethics. There are other ethical ideals—like individual rights, the sanctity of life, justice, purity and so on—which are universal in the required sense, and are, at least in some versions, incompatible with utilitarianism. It does show that we very swiftly arrive at an *initially* utilitarian position once we apply the universal aspect of ethics to simple, pre-ethical decision-making. This, I believe, places the onus of proof on those who seek to go beyond utilitarianism. The utilitarian position is a minimal one, a first base which we reach by universalizing self-interested decision-making. We cannot, if we are to think ethically, refuse to take this step. If we are to be persuaded that we should go beyond utilitarianism and accept non-utilitarian moral rules or ideals, we need to be provided with good reasons for taking this further step. Until such reasons are produced, we have some grounds for remaining utilitarians.

II

Here is a series of exercises which will let you examine some ethical concerns:

Exercise 1. Below is a list of criminals, sinners, wrongdoers, and mischief-makers. How would you rank their misdeeds? Which are the worst offenses? Which are the least serious? This exercise might be profitably discussed in groups; alternatively, it would make a good journal entry.

1. A father gambles away his money and then his property, leaving his family homeless.
2. A judge accepts interest-free loans from a bank where he has invested money from a trust fund he administers.
3. A politician uses his influence to help a local company get a government contract; he then accepts the company's "support" (they paid his expenses) of his fact-finding tour through Europe.
4. An FBI agent sells documents to the Cuban government because he needs money to pay for his daughter's organ transplant operation.
5. A terrorist kills an innocent hostage to protest political injustice.

6. A doctor sells his patients an ordinary facial cream as an anti-aging formula.
7. A writer publishes a novel which is really an adaptation of an obscure book by a now-dead author.
8. A child takes money from his mother's purse, then lets his brother take the blame.
9. A singer popularizes a song that urges young people to use drugs; some fans become addicts.
10. In order to get a promotion, an employee has an affair with a vice-president of the company.
11. A woman who dislikes her neighbor's ethnic group sends threatening messages to make her neighbor move out.
12. A mother keeps her child quiet in the grocery store by letting him open packages of food, sample the contents, and then put them back.
13. A woman lets her boyfriend beat her crying child.
14. A student borrows a paper her roommate wrote and submits it to her teacher in a different section of the course.
15. A landlord neglects to make plumbing and electrical repairs in a student rental apartment.
16. A critic praises a bad film because the theatre where it is being shown buys a lot of expensive advertising in his newspaper.
17. A young man seriously wounds another in a fight when both were drunk.
18. A man forces a woman to have sex with him after an expensive date.

(Adapted from Anne B. Gardiner, "The Teaching of Ethics through Literature and Dante's *Inferno*," *ADE Bulletin*, Fall 1989, 24.)

Exercise 2. "Heinz's dilemma" is a classic problem which has been used by psychologists to measure ethical development. Quite apart from its value in psychological research, it remains an interesting problem to consider:

A man named Heinz has fallen on hard times. He has lost his job and used all of his savings. Now his wife is ill with a disease that causes her great pain and threatens her life. There is one drug available that can lessen her pain and maybe even save her life. Since he has not been able to pay insurance premiums, Heinz now has no way to pay for the drug. He goes to Jones, the druggist, and when Jones learns that Heinz cannot pay for the drug, he will not give it to him. Heinz is considering whether or not to steal the drug which he cannot afford to buy in order to save the life of his wife. Should Heinz steal the drug?

Exercise 3. This exercise presents a problem which needs to be solved by working together with the other members of your group. It's called "Survivors."

An accidental attack on an American battleship has triggered a nuclear war. Chicago has just received heavy bombing, and the radiation fallout has already reached Macomb. You and the other members of your group were able to make it to shelter in a secure building. You are safe from the radiation and you have enough food and water to last you for eight or nine months. You have at least a fair chance of survival, and you suspect that others in town were not so lucky.

Suddenly there is a pounding on the door. There is another survivor out there looking for shelter. You don't know if it is safe to open the door, or if the other person is already dangerously contaminated. Do you take the risk and let the person join you? You must reach unanimous agreement before you can do anything.

Exercise 4. Here is a paragraph from the essay "Fishes and Pike" by Upton Sinclair. The essay appears in Sinclair's book *Money Talks* (Scholarly Press, 1970).

> The Italian educator, Pestalozzi, tells how the little fishes complained of the voracity of the pike, and the pike held a conference, and adjudged the complaint to be justified, and ordained that every year thereafter two little fishes should be permitted to become pike. That most charming fable tells me all I need to know about the moral code of my country. For a million little fishes to be preyed upon by a hundred great pike is all right, because every little fish has an equal chance to become a pike—all he needs is to grow sharp enough teeth, and eat enough of the other little fishes. Any little fish that disputes the fairness of such an arrangement is a "sorehead," and his "grouch" is simply the expression of his conscious dental inferiority. (15)

The story is a parable, and like the parables of the Bible it is used to explore a moral issue. What is the issue? What is the ethical concern? Is it also a political concern? What does ethics have to do with politics?

If your mind works that way, you might have some fun trying to write a parable of your own.

III

This next section of the chapter contains three readings that raise and explore some ethical issues. They not only deal with very different issues, but they also take three different forms. The first is an essay, the second a poem, and the third a short story.

The essay is by John Hallwas, and was published in the *Macomb Journal* on September 9, 1984. It combines an examination of the role of heroes in our lives with a discussion of the major political issue of the day: Ronald Reagan's campaign for re-election to the presidency. Walter Mondale was his Democratic challenger.

The Return of the Hero
John Hallwas

"Ours is an age without heroes," historian Arthur Schlesinger, Jr. remarked in a 1958 article called "The Decline of Heroes." He noted the passing of great leaders like Roosevelt, Churchill, and Gandhi, who had left their imprint on history in the first half of the twentieth century, and he lamented that "Today no one bestrides our narrow world like a colossus; we have no giants who play roles which one can image no one else playing. . . ."

Of course that essay appeared before Martin Luther King, Jr. achieved national and world attention. He will remain the greatest American hero of the 1960's—if not of the later 20th century—but his heroic stature, like Lincoln's, was not fully realized until after his assassination.

During the past fifteen or twenty years there has been a notable lack of heroes on the American scene. Even some of our recent presidents (Nixon, Ford, Carter) have been more like vic-

From John Hallwas, "The Return of the Hero," © 1984 by The Macomb JOURNAL. Reprinted with permission.

tims, of circumstances and their own shortcomings, than heroic figures.

But what about Reagan? As with most considerations surrounding our current president, there is a difference of opinion.

To Republicans, who recently nominated him for another term, Reagan is indeed a hero, the man who led (and still leads) the conservative revolution, who greatly strengthened the Republican party, who engineered a strong economic recovery, and who has reasserted traditional values. To many Democrats, he is an imitation hero, with "a talent for selling illusions to the Indiana Jones generation," as Bruce Bawer put it in a recent *Newsweek* article.

What is Reagan's real relationship to the public? The presidential election will provide considerable insight. But in the meantime, the most helpful framework for considering the matter is a study called "From Hero to Celebrity: The Human Pseudo-Event" by noted historian Daniel J. Boorstin. It appeared in his 1961 book *The Image*.

Like Schlesinger, Boorstin feels that ours is not an age of heroes. But he traces the problem to ourselves, noting that "We see greatness as an illusion. . . ." The rise of critical biography and the scrutinizing of leaders in the media are two reasons for our disillusionment. We suspect that apparent models of human greatness are "not what they seem."

But ironically, we still want to relate to greatness, so we have produced a new kind of eminence, the celebrity. As Boorstin says,

> The celebrity is a person who is known for his well-knownness . . . . He is neither good nor bad, great nor petty. He is the human pseudo-event. He has been fabricated on purpose to satisfy our exaggerated expectations of human greatness. He is morally neutral.

Singers and actors are the most common kinds of celebrities, but politicians, writers, athletes, and others frequently attain that status as well. They differ from true heroes, as Boorstin points out:

> The hero was distinguished by his achievement; the celebrity by his image or trademark. The hero created himself; the celebrity is created by the media. The hero is a big man; the celebrity is a big name.

People magazine is the most well known of many publications devoted to the manufacture and continuance of celebrities. Individuals appear in it because they are known, not because they deserve our admiration.

Unlike celebrities, heroes are not morally neutral: "We revere them . . . because they embody popular virtues. We admire them because they reveal and elevate ourselves." For that reason, heroes create or reshape the society that relates to them.

The spiritual emptiness of our contemporary experience is manifested in our response to celebrities. According to Boorstin,

> We forget that celebrities are known primarily for their well-knownness. And we imitate them as if they were cast in the mold of greatness. Yet the celebrity is usually nothing greater (morally) than a more well-publicized version of us.

What light does Boorstin's analysis shed on President Reagan? Is he a hero or a celebrity?

In spite of the fact that he is a product of Hollywood, that he was first of all a celebrity, Reagan is a hero. His election to the presidency in 1980 did not accomplish the transformation. That simply made him a different kind of celebrity. (Election campaigns are, in fact, the chief means by which we create political celebrities.)

But during his term of office, Reagan has achieved a certain legitimacy as an American hero, a man with a consistent set of values—whether or not they are entirely laudatory—who has been able to accomplish at least his primary goal of turning the economy around.

Moreover, perhaps because of his Hollywood background, he has been more aware of the symbolic potential of his role than any other recent president. He embodied positive aspects of America at a time when the country was tormented by self-doubt, and now that doubt has dissipated. As Tom Morganthau said in the *Newsweek* cover article of August 27,

> Over the past 3 1/2 years, through words and deeds and careful stage management by the White House staff, Reagan has undeniably brought about a revival of patriotism, confidence, and national purpose.

That alone is a great accomplishment, and it demonstrates that President Reagan has been anything but morally neutral in his impact on the American people. Besides, he has made the presidency look manageable—a remarkable, if not heroic achievement in our increasingly complex era.

Reagan may even be striving to make the admiration of heroes a more characteristic feature of our culture, by consistently affirming the uncommon achievements of various Americans: the Marines who invaded Grenada, the Medal of Freedom recipients, the athletes who dominated the Olympics, and others who have been courageous or outstanding.

Reagan's own stature as a hero will have an influence on the election. It will inhibit public recognition of his shortcomings—as was true of Eisenhower, the war-hero candidate, during the 1950's. It will promote the notion that he embodies what America is all about—regardless of how inaccurate that view may be with respect to, for example, the separation of church and state or public commitment to the disadvantaged. It will also inspire his campaign workers, who will feel—as the Dallas convention suggested—that they are morally elevated through their intense identification with him.

How can Walter Mondale successfully contend with that? After all, he is only a celebrity.

Hallwas's essay will help form the basis for one of this chapter's essay assignments (yes, the assignments are coming). So will the poem by Robert Frost which follows. The assignment based on the poem asks you to make a series of journal entries before you start the paper. It might be a good idea to write one of these immediately after your first reading of the poem. Just respond to it, writing down everything that it makes you think about or feel.

The Road Not Taken
Robert Frost

Two roads diverged in a yellow wood,
And sorry I could not travel both
And be one traveler, long I stood
And looked down one as far as I could
To where it bent in the undergrowth;

Then took the other, as just as fair,
And having perhaps the better claim,
Because it was grassy and wanted wear;
Though as for that the passing there
Had worn them really about the same,

And both that morning equally lay
In leaves no step had trodden black.
Oh, I kept the first for another day!
Yet knowing how way leads on to way,
I doubted if I should ever come back.

I shall be telling this with a sigh
Somewhere ages and ages hence:
Two roads diverged in a wood, and I—
I took the one less traveled by,
And that has made all the difference.

Before you go on to the next selection, go back and re-read the poem. As is often the case with poetry, your understanding and appreciation will increase with a second reading. And you might record that increased understanding in your journal.

The next selection is a piece of fiction, a short story by Toni Cade Bambara. The story is narrated by one of the characters in it, a little girl named Sylvia (though we don't learn that that is her name until we're well into the story). Throughout we get Sylvia's view of

From THE POETRY OF ROBERT FROST edited by Edward Connery Lathem. Copyright 1916, 1969 by Holt, Rinehart and Winston. Copyright 1944 by Robert Frost. Reprinted by permission of Henry Holt and Company, Inc.

"Two roads diverged..."
Robert Frost

people and events, as well as her childish interpretation of them. By the end of the story, however, she's on the verge of a more mature understanding. She's learned something, in spite of herself. Note that in addition to presenting Sylvia's point of view, Bambara has taken great care to capture the sound of the girl's voice throughout the story.

The Lesson
Toni Cade Bambara

Back in the days when everyone was old and stupid or young and foolish and me and Sugar were the only ones just right, this lady moved on our block with nappy hair and proper speech and no makeup. And quite naturally we laughed at her, laughed the way we did at the junk man who went about his business like he was some big-time president and his sorry-ass horse his secretary. And we kinda hated her too, hated the way we did the winos who cluttered up our parks and pissed on our handball walls and stank up our hallways and stairs so you couldn't halfway play hide-and-seek without a goddamn gas mask. Miss Moore was her name. The only woman on the block with no first name. And she was black as hell, cept for her feet, which were fish-white and spooky. And she was always planning these boring-ass things for us to do, us being my cousin, mostly, who lived on the block cause we all moved North the same time and to the same apartment then spread out gradual to breathe. And our parents would yank our heads into some kinda shape and crisp up our clothes so we'd be presentable for travel with Miss Moore, who always looked like she was going to church, though she never did. Which is just one of the things the grown-ups talked about when they talked behind her back like a dog. But when she came calling with some sachet she'd sewed up or some gingerbread she'd made or some book, why then they'd all be too embarrassed to turn her down and we'd get handed over all spruced up. She'd been to college and said it was only right that she should take responsibility for the young ones' education, and she not even related by marriage or blood. So they'd go for it. Specially Aunt Gretchen. She was the main gofer in the family. You got some old dumb shit foolishness you want somebody to go for, you send for Aunt Gretchen. She been screwed into the go-along for so long, it's a blood-deep natural thing with her. Which is how she got saddled with me and Sugar and Junior in the first place while our mothers were in a la-de-da apartment up the block having good ole time.

From GORILLA, MY LOVE by Toni Cade Bambara. Copyright © 1972 by Toni Cade Bambara. Reprinted by permission of Random House, Inc.

9. Discovering Values 179

So this one day Miss Moore rounds us all up at the mailbox and it's puredee hot and she's knockin herself out about arithmetic. And school suppose to let up in summer I heard, but she don't never let up. And the starch in my pinafore scratching the shit outta me and I'm really hating this nappy-head bitch and her goddamn college degree. I'd much rather go to the pool or to the show where it's cool. So me and Sugar leaning on the mailbox being surly, which is a Miss Moore word. And Flyboy checking out what everybody brought for lunch. And Fat Butt already wasting his peanut-butter-and-jelly sandwich like the pig he is. And Junebug punchin on Q. T.'s arm for potato chips. And Rosie Giraffe shifting from one hip to the other waiting for somebody to step on her foot or ask her if she from Georgia so she can kick ass, preferably Mercedes'. And Miss Moore asking us do we know what money is, like we a bunch of retards. I mean real money, she say, like it's only poker chips or monopoly papers we lay on the grocer. So right away I'm tired of this and say so. And would much rather snatch Sugar and go to the Sunset and terrorize the West Indian kids and take their hair ribbons and their money too. And Miss Moore files that remark away for next week's lesson on brotherhood, I can tell. And finally I say we oughta get to the subway cause it's cooler and besides we might meet some cute boys. Sugar done swiped her mama's lipstick, so we ready.

So we heading down the street and she's boring us silly about what things cost and what our parents make and how much goes for rent and how money ain't divided up right in this country. And then she gets to the part about we all poor and live in the slums, which I don't feature. And I'm ready to speak on that, but she steps out in the street and hails two cabs just like that. Then she hustles half the crew in with her and hands me a five-dollar bill and tells me to calculate 10 percent tip for the driver. And we're off. Me and Sugar and Junebug and Flyboy hangin out the window and hollering to everybody, putting lipstick on each other cause Flyboy a faggot anyway, and making farts with our sweaty armpits. But I'm mostly trying to figure how to spend this money. But they all fascinated with the meter ticking and Junebug starts laying bets as to how much it'll read when Flyboy can't hold his breath no more. Then Sugar lays bets as to how much it'll be when we get there. So I'm stuck. Don't nobody want to go for my plan, which is to jump out at the next light and run off to the first bar-b-que we can find. Then the driver tells us to get the hell out cause we there already. And the meter reads eighty-five cents. And I'm stalling to figure out the tip and Sugar say give him a dime. And I decide he don't need it bad as I do, so later for him. But then he tries to take off with Junebug foot still in the door so we talk about his mama something ferocious. Then we check out that we on Fifth Avenue and everybody dressed up in stockings. One lady in a fur coat, hot as it is. White folks crazy.

"This is the place," Miss Moore say, presenting it to us in the voice she uses at the museum. "Let's look in the windows before we go in."

"Can we steal?" Sugar asks very serious like she's getting the ground rules squared away before she plays. "I beg your pardon," say Miss Moore, and we fall out. So she leads us around the windows of the toy store and me and Sugar screamin, "This is mine, that's mine, I gotta have that, that was made for me, I was born for that," till Big Butt drowns us out.

"Hey, I'm going to buy that there."

"That there? You don't even know what it is, stupid."

"I do so," he say punchin on Rosie Giraffe. "It's a microscope."

"Whatcha gonna do with a microscope, fool?"

"Look at things."

"Like what, Ronald?" ask Miss Moore. And Big Butt ain't got the first notion. So here go Miss Moore gabbing about the thousands of bacteria in a drop of water and the somethinorother in a speck of blood and the million and one living things in the air around us is invisible to the naked eye. And what she say that for? Junebug go to town on that "naked" and we rolling. Then Miss Moore ask what it cost. So we all jam into the window smudgin it up and the price tag say $300. So then she ask how long'd take for Big Butt and Junebug to save up their allowances. "Too long," I say. "Yeh," adds Sugar, "outgrown it by that time." And Miss Moore say no, you never outgrow learning instruments. "Why, even medical students and interns and," blah, blah, blah. And we ready to choke Big Butt for bringing it up in the first damn place.

"This here costs four hundred eight dollars," say Rosie Giraffe. So we pile up all over her to see what she pointin out. My eyes tell me it's a chunk of glass cracked with something heavy, and different-color inks dripped into the splits, then the whole thing put into a oven or something. But for $480 it don't make sense.

"That a paperweight made of semi-precious stones fused together under tremendous pressure," she explains slowly, with her hands doing the mining and all the factory work.

"So what a paperweight?" asks Rosie Giraffe.

"To weigh paper with, dumbbell," say Flyboy, the wise man from the East.

"Not exactly," say Miss Moore, which is what she say when you warm or way off too. "It's to weigh paper down so it won't scatter and make your desk untidy." So right away me and Sugar curtsy to each other and then to Mercedes who is more the tidy type.

"We don't keep paper on top of the desk in my class," say Junebug, figuring Miss Moore crazy or lyin one.

"At home, then," she say. "Don't you have a calendar and a pencil case and a blotter and a letter-opener on your desk at home where you do your homework?" And she know damn well what our homes look like cause she nosys around in them every chance she gets.

"I don't even have a desk," say Junebug. "Do we?"

"No. And I don't get no homework neither," say Big Butt.

"And I don't even have a home," say Flyboy like he do at school to keep the white folks off his back and sorry for him. Send this poor kid to camp posters, is his specialty.

"I do," says Mercedes. "I have a box of stationery on my desk and a picture of my cat. My godmother brought the stationery and the desk. There's a big rose on each sheet and the envelopes smell like roses."

"Who wants to know about your smelly-ass stationery," say Rosie Giraffe fore I can get my two cents in.

"It's important to have a work area all you own so that..."

"Will you look at this sailboat, please," say Flyboy, cuttin her off and pointin to the thing like it was his. So once again we tumble all over each other to gaze at this magnificent thing in the toy store which is just big enough to maybe sail two kittens across the pond if you strap them to the post tight. We all start reciting the price tag like we in assembly. "Handcrafted sailboat of fiberglass at one thousand one hundred ninety-five dollars."

"Unbelievable," I hear myself say and am really stunned. I read it again for myself just in case the group recitation put me in a trance. Same thing. For some reason this pisses me off. We look at Miss Moore and she lookin at us, waiting for I dunno what.

"Who'd pay all that when you can buy a sailboat set for a quarter at Pop's, a tube of glue for a dime, and a ball of string for eight cents? It must have a motor and a whole lot else besides," I say. "My sailboat cost me about fifty cents."

"But will it take water?" say Mercedes with her smart ass.

"Took mine to Alley Pond Park once," say Flyboy. "String broke. Lost it. Pity."

"Sailed mine in Central Park and it keeled over and sank. Had to ask my father for another dollar."

"And you got the strap," laugh Big Butt. "The jerk didn't even have a string on it. My old man wailed on his behind."

Little Q. T. was staring hard at the sailboat and you could see he wanted it bad. But he too little and somebody'd just take it from him. So what the hell. "This boat for kids, Miss Moore?"

"Parents silly to buy something like that just to get all broke up," say Rosie Giraffe.

"That much money it should last forever," I figure.

"My father'd buy it for me if I wanted it."

"Your father, my ass," say Rosie Giraffe getting a chance to finally push Mercedes.

"Must be rich people shop here," say Q. T.

"You are a very bright boy," say Flyboy. "What was your first clue?" And he rap him on the head with the back of his knuckles, since Q. T. the only one he could get away with. Though Q. T. liable to come up behind you years later and get his licks in when you half expect it.

"What I want to know is," I says to Miss Moore though I never talk to her, I wouldn't give the bitch that satisfaction, "is how much a real boat costs? I figure a thousand'd get you a yacht any day."

"Why don't you check that out," she says, "and report back to the group?" Which really pains my ass. If you gonna mess up a perfectly good swim day least you could do is have some answers. "Let's go in," she say like she got something up her sleeve. Only she don't lead the way. So me and Sugar turn the corner to where the entrance is, but when we get there I kinda hang back. Not that I'm scared, what's there to be afraid of, just a toy store. But I feel funny, shame. But what I got to be shamed about? Got as much right to go in as anybody. But somehow I can't seem to get hold of the door, so I step away for Sugar to lead. But she hangs back too. And I look at her and she looks at me and this is ridiculous. I mean, damn, I have never ever been shy about doing nothing or going nowhere. But then Mercedes steps up and then Rosie Giraffe and Big Butt crowd in behind and shove, and next thing we all stuffed into the doorway with only Mercedes squeezing past us, smoothing out her jumper and walking right down the aisle. Then the rest of us tumble in like a glued-together jigsaw done all wrong. And people lookin at us. And it's like the time me and Sugar crashed into the Catholic church on a dare. But once we got in there and everything so hushed and holy and the candles and the bow-in and the handkerchiefs on all the drooping heads, I just couldn't go through with the plan. Which was for me to run up to the altar and do a tap dance while Sugar played the nose flute and messed around in the holy water. And Sugar kept givin me the elbow. Then later teased me so bad I tied her up in the shower and turned it on and locked her in. And she'd be there till this day if Aunt Gretchen hadn't finally figured I was lying about the boarder takin a shower.

Same thing in the store. We all walkin on tiptoe and hardly touchin the games and puzzles and things. And I watched Miss Moore who is steady watchin us like she waiting for a sign. Like Mama Drewery watches the sky and sniffs the air and takes note of just how much slant is in the bird formation. Then me and Sugar bump smack into each other, so busy gazing at the toys, 'specially the sailboat. But we don't laugh and go into our fat-lady bump-stomach routine. We just stare at that price tag. Then Sugar run a finger over the whole boat. And I'm jealous and want to hit her. Maybe not her, but I sure want to punch somebody in the mouth.

"Watcha bring us here for, Miss Moore?"

"You sound angry, Sylvia. Are you mad about something?" Givin me one of them grins like she tellin a grown-up joke that never turns out to be funny. And she's lookin very closely at me like maybe she plannin to do my portrait from memory. I'm mad, but I won't give her that satisfaction. So I slouch around the store bein very bored and say, "Let's go."

Me and Sugar at the back of the train watchin the tracks whizzing by large then small then gettin gobbled up in the dark. I'm thinking about this tricky toy I saw in the store. A clown that somersaults on a bar then does chin-ups just cause you yank lightly at his leg. Cost $35. I could see me askin my mother for a $35 birthday clown. "You wanna who that costs what?" she'd say, cocking her head to the side to get a better view of the hole in my head. Thirty-five dollars could buy new bunk beds for Junior and Gretchen's boy. Thirty-five dollars and the whole househole could go visit Granddaddy Nelson in the country. Thirty-five dollars would pay for the rent and the piano bill too. Who are these people that spend that much for performing clowns and $1,000 for toy sailboats? What kinda work they do and how they live and how come we ain't in on it? Where we are is who we are, Miss Moore always pointin out. But it don't necessarily have to be that way, she always adds then waits for somebody to say that poor people have to wake up and demand their share of the pie and don't none of us know what kind of pie she talkin about in the first damn place. But she ain't so smart cause I still got her four dollars from the taxi and she sure ain't gettin it. Messin up my day with this shit. Sugar nudges me in my pocket and winks.

Miss Moore lines us up in front of the mailbox where we started from, seem like years ago, and I got a headache for thinkin so hard. And we lean all over each other so we can hold up under the draggy-ass lecture she always finishes us off with at the end before we thank her for borin us to tears. But she just looks at us like she readin tea leaves. Finally she say, "Well, what did you think of F. A. O. Schwartz?"

Rosie Giraffe mumbles, "White folks crazy."

"I'd like to go there again when I get my birthday money," says Mercedes, and we shove her out the pack so she has to lean on the mailbox by herself.

"I'd like a shower. Tiring day," say Flyboy.

Then Sugar surprises me by sayin, "You know, Miss Moore, I don't think all of us here put together eat in a year what that sailboat costs." And Miss Moore lights up like somebody goosed her. "And?" she say, urging Sugar on. Only I'm standin on her foot so she don't continue.

"Imagine for a minute what kind of society it is in which some people can spend on a toy what it would cost to feed a family of six or seven. What do you think?"

"I think," say Sugar pushing me off her feet like she never done before, cause I whip her ass in a minute, "that this is not much of a democracy if you ask me. Equal chance to pursue happiness means an equal crack at the dough, don't it?'' Miss Moore is besides herself and I am disgusted with Sugar's treachery. So I stand on her foot one more time to see if she'll shove me. She shuts up, and Miss Moore looks at me, sorrowfully I'm thinkin. And something weird is going on, I can feel it in my chest.

"Anybody else learn anything today?" lookin dead at me. I walk away and Sugar has to run to catch up and don't even seem to notice when I shrug her arm off my shoulder.

"Well, we got four dollars anyway," she says.

"Uh huuh."

"We could go to Hascombs and get a half a chocolate layer and then go to the Sunset and still have plenty money for potato chips and ice-cream sodas."

"Un hunh."

"Race you to Hascombs," she say.

We start down the block and she gets ahead which is O.K. by me cause I'm goin to the West End and then over to the Drive to think this day through. She can run if she want to and even run faster. But ain't nobody gonna beat me at nuthin.

IV

Here, at last, are the writing assignments for this chapter. The issues raised by a consideration of ethics are complex enough and wide-ranging enough to suggest many different kinds of writing topics, so, unlike the choices in other chapters, these are very different from one another. Your instructor will probably direct you to a particular question. And who knows? You may have opportunity to write about more than one of them.

1. First, reread John Hallwas's essay on heroes. The essay was motivated by the 1984 presidential campaign, in which Ronald Reagan ran for a second term against Democrat Walter Mondale. The personalities in the election gave Hallwas opportunity to consider the ethical dimensions of heroism. How does he define heroism? What are the criteria? How do his examples illustrate his definition? How do the people he quotes reinforce his argument? Why does the essay regularly use male pronouns to refer to heroes? How important is the

political situation of 1984 to the essay? Does Hallwas reveal his own political preferences?

> In Bertolt Brecht's play *Life of Galileo,* a young man reproaches Galileo after he recanted and renounced his scientific teaching. The young man says "Unhappy the land that has no heroes!" To which Galileo replies, "No. Unhappy the land that needs a hero."
>
> Why do we need heroes? What purpose do they play in our personal lives? In our national life? How do they contribute to our ethical development? Be specific, drawing on your experience and using plenty of examples.

Or

> What do you consider to be the essential qualities of a hero? In other words, define your understanding of the term. Draw on your reading (perhaps of some essays in this text) and on your experience in order to profusely illustrate your ideas with specific examples.

2. Reread Robert Frost's "The Road Not Taken" several times, making at least four entries in your journal, noting your reactions to the poem.

Consider:

In what sense is Frost's poem about making an ethical choice?
What factors influenced the speaker's choice in the poem?
Have you ever experienced a "fork in the road" like this?
How did you feel?
What factors helped you make your decision?
What difference has your choice made?
Do you have a choice like this ahead of you?
How will you make that choice?

> Describe an important (and difficult) choice that you have had to make, a choice that has made a difference in your life. Be sure to let your reader see the ethical considerations that informed your decision-making process.

3. This next question invites you to do the kind of investigation to discover information that you practiced in Chapter Seven:

One morning last month you left a print-out of your meditation essay from Chapter Five lying on your desk. That evening you couldn't find it, but you didn't worry about it much because you had it saved on disk. Yesterday you learned from your roommate what happened to it: Someone down the hall from you was having trouble with that same assignment and "borrowed" yours. And that person actually got a better grade on your paper than you did!

> What is plagiarism? How is it defined by the university? By the English department? Why is it wrong? What are the ethical considerations? Is it ever justified? Are there places, or situations, where it is actually appropriate? Should it be punished? How? How can it be prevented?

Or

> As an alternative, apply some of these same questions to the issue of software theft.

4. Ethics on the job

> Write about your experience with an ethical issue on the job. It may be a personal choice that you had to make, or a decision you observed someone else make.

> (For example, a salesman knows that some merchandise is defective, but he sells it anyway. Or, an office worker takes home company software to copy for her own use. Or, a bartender pours himself shots all evening and gets fairly drunk.)

Or

> Analyze one of the major ethical issues which control or influence decision-making in the career you are planning to enter. Explain the issue, and show how it influences (or fails to influence) behavior. (For example, what are the ethical issues in fashion merchandising? In planning a recreational facility? In theatrical performance?)

V
Recursiveness in Writing

From time to time throughout this text I have tried to direct attention to parts of the writing process, the ways that prewriting activities, drafting, and revision can help you to use writing to learn. I've also suggested that what you do at each of these stages is based on your individual preferences. You will do what works best for you. As a final point on the writing process, I want to admit that for me (as for many writers), the three stages often become intertwined.

In other words, I don't always work through all my invention, then move on to drafting, ending with revision and editing. In fact, if you think about it, it can't work that way, since if I make any additions to my text during revision, I have to move back to drafting to get the new material, and quite likely I need to do more invention too. And no matter how complete my prewriting activity has been, I always find that new ideas keep occurring to me as I write my draft, and even as I revise.

In practice, I tend to move easily back and forth among the different activities. Each time I sit down to write I find myself revising completed work, drafting paragraphs or sections of text, and making lists for myself for future reference. I may even work on editing a completed section while still in the midst of drafting another part. (Though this can backfire if I later decide to revise further. That time I spent editing something that I later decide to delete is time wasted. I do better when I hold off editing as long as I can.)

At one time, when I did most of my writing in pencil on yellow legal pads, this recursive method led to a great deal of erasing, crossing out, pointing with arrows, numbering paragraphs, and shuffling pages. Messy, though still necessary. With the computer the process has become far easier. Movement from list to completed text to new paragraph to another list is just a matter of a few key strokes. I can add, delete, and rearrange easily. I can even move material from one file to another, which, though not exactly easy, does come in handy with a long document written in different parts.

Of course I still do have recourse to some of the pencil and paper techniques. Many of my prewriting notes are done by hand, and I always do my final revision from a print-out. I need to be able to see what the text looks like on the page in order to get a sense of the whole. In fact, I do quite a bit of moving back and forth between the page and the screen, just as I move back and forth among the steps in the writing process.

Thus, though I have written about invention, drafting, and revising as separate activities, and praised the advantages of word processing, in my own practice I can't separate any of the elements in my own writing process. The divisions and dichotomies I have set up are not real; they are only necessary as a means for explaining them. I admit all of this now as a way of prompting your thinking about the ways *you* actually work, which will serve now as a transition to Chapter Ten.

I love being a writer. What I can't stand is the paperwork.
Peter deVries

Chapter **10**

Discovering Writing Again

As the last chapter of the book, this chapter *should* summarize everything you've learned this semester, but I hope by now you realize that that's unlikely. I can't very well tell you what you've learned, or even what you are supposed to have learned. That's for you to do, and the purpose of this chapter is to direct your efforts in doing so.

For starters, here is a series of questions to consider. You might talk about them in your group, write about some of them in your journal, or free-write your responses (ten minutes, non-stop).

- Which of the writing assignments did you enjoy the most?
- Which of the assignments let you learn the most about yourself?
- Which of the assignments led you to learn the most about writing?
- Which of the essays you read best exemplified "good writing"? What were the writing qualities you admired?
- Which of the essays you have read from members of the class do you most admire? Why?
- Review your journal entries. What have you learned in the process of keeping a journal?
- How has writing with a computer changed the way you write, or the way you think about writing?
- Would you answer the question in Chapter One (about form and content) any differently today?
- Has the writing process you described in Chapter Three changed in any significant ways?

How would you describe your experience of this course to a student who has not yet taken it?

Now here's the final writing assignment for the course. To complete it successfully you should try to make use of the various ideas about writing and techniques that you have developed during this semester.

What I Have Learned

Write Chapter Ten of this text, summarizing what you have learned about writing as a result of your experience in English 180. Draw on your reading, your writing, your group work, your journal, your answers to the questions above.

I respect faith, but doubt is what gives you an education

Wilson Mizner

Appendix One

Thirty-seven Things to Write About in a Journal

1. Write about your reactions to your college classes. Compare them to classes in high school.
2. Record experiences you want to remember. Be sure to use enough detail to assure that you *will* be able to remember exactly what happened.
3. Keep track of your insights into the writing process. Write about the different methods of writing that you try out. Note which ones work and which ones fail. Done regularly, these entries will give you a record, at the end of the semester, of everything you've learned about writing.
4. Copy a quotation you've read or heard and react to it. Here are a few starters:

   A foolish consistency is the hobgoblin of little minds.
   (Emerson)
   A rose by any other name would smell as sweet.
   (Shakespeare)
   How do I know what I think until I see what I say?
   (E. M. Forster)
   Few things are harder to put up with than the annoyance of a good example.
   (Mark Twain)
   A rose is a rose is a rose.
   (Gertrude Stein)

5. Close your eyes, listen carefully, and describe the sounds you hear.
6. Describe what happened when you first met your roommate.
7. Define something by telling what it is.

"A rose by any other name would smell as sweet."

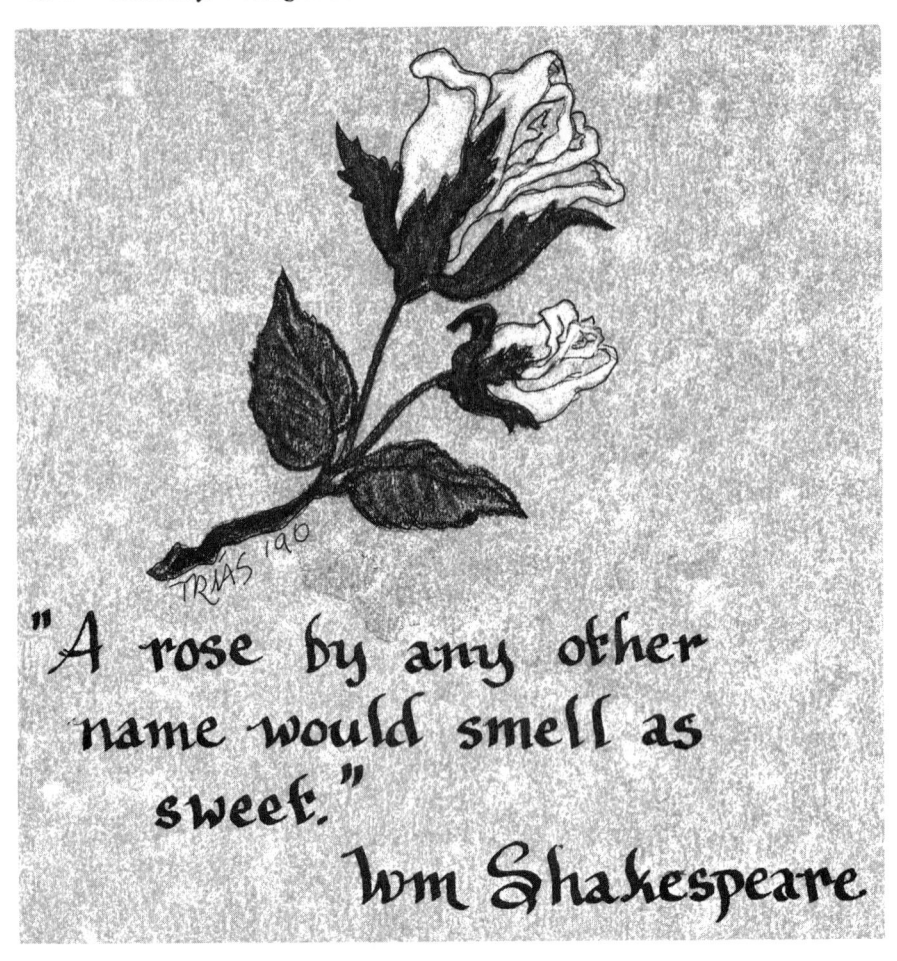

— Wm Shakespeare

    Define something by telling what it is not.
    Define something by telling a story.
8. Write a letter to one of your teachers; or
Write a letter to someone from the past; or
Write a letter to a politician
9. Respond to something that someone said in class.
10. Suggest ways the freshman orientation/pre-registration procedures could be improved.
11. Tell a story.
12. Ask questions.
13. Record some conversation that you overheard during the day.
14. Tape an advertisement from a newspaper or magazine into your journal. Explain why it's effective (or not).

15. Observe similarities between things: a telephone and a television; a dog and a pig; a flower and a person; snow and Jell-O. Stretch your imagination.
16. Remember something you used to love as a child (a Barbie doll, a favorite blanket, camping with your parents, a tree house). Describe it. Love it all over again.
17. Complain about writing with a computer.
18. Complain about keeping a journal.
19. Explain what the books you like reveal about yourself.
20. Describe an event that led you to a new insight.
21. Write about one of these experiences:

    becoming friends
    saying good-by
    a fight
    a brush with death
    an illness
    losing a false belief
    an incident while traveling
    moving to a new house

22. Explain how you deal with difference. Consider your encounters with people who differ from you (noticeable physical or psychological difference, difference of gender or race, cultural difference, class difference). Write about it. Note what you learn as a result of the writing.
23. Copy a favorite poem or song.
24. Write your own poem or song.
25. Answer these questions:

    Is it better to have one best friend or several friends?
    Where do you want to be in five years?
    Would you be willing to go back in time in a time machine?
    What college course are you most looking forward to taking?
    What do you consider to be the most serious hazard to your own health?
    What are the three most important unanswered questions?

26. List several disgusting images: the bloated, maggot-ridden body of a dead possum; the smell of a sewage treatment

plant; being hugged by a child with an actively running nose. Choose one of the images and describe it in detail.
27. Imagine yourself back in the period of the Wild West. Explain which of the usual characters you see yourself being. (That is, would you be the villain, barmaid, sheriff, saloon entertainer, cowboy, Indian, rodeo performer, or sidekick?)
28. Write a parody of Robert Frost's "The Road Not Taken" (in Chapter Nine). Or write a parody of some other poem you know. Or of a familiar song lyric. Or of a TV commercial. Or of this textbook.
29. Describe an event that changed your attitude about something.
30. Write your own obituary (as if you died today).
31. Write a meditation (as described in chapter 5).
32. Tell lies.
33. Record an awkward event in your life (an argument, a social blunder, an embarrassing moment), then explain why you behaved the way you did in that situation.
34. Explain how your parents' values have influenced your behavior.
35. React to this textbook (or to one chapter of it).
36. Finish a paragraph which begins "The thing that is really important to me right now is. . . ."
37. Ask yourself what you feel inadequate about, unsure of, afraid of. Explain why you shouldn't feel this way.

Appendix Two

More on the Writing Process

I
Additional Invention Techniques

In Chapter Three I suggested three methods for discovering ideas for an essay. Here are several more. Try out any that appeal to you. All of them have worked, at one time or another, for many different writers.

1. The Reporter's Formula

Like cubing, this technique uses questions, this time the six questions that newspaper reporters are trained to ask about any news story: Who? What? When? Where? Why? How? They are useful questions to ask whenever you are preparing to tell a story in a paper, and may be used sometimes for other writing situations as well. For example, asking these questions when analyzing a poem or explaining a scientific process may reveal some details you might otherwise overlook.

2. Questioning

Once you get used to using the cubing questions or the reporter's formula, you may want to strike out on your own and develop your own questions. Asking appropriate questions about a topic is probably the richest method for discovering what you know about a subject and what you still need to learn about it. Questions like these can get you started:

What do I know about the subject?
How did I learn it?
What is the order in which things happen?

197

How can it be illustrated?
What does it reveal?
What were the causes?
What were the consequences?
What sort of structure does it have?
Who needs it?

As you develop your questions about a specific subject, you'll need to move beyond these general questions. That is, your questions will need to become specific *to* your subject. Then, of course, you need to try to answer them. You'll find that your responses to some of your questions can become the central issues to write about in your paper.

This technique can also be used to extend invention throughout the drafting process. As you write your draft, keep on asking questions. If you don't want to stop the flow of your writing to answer them immediately, keep track of them for later reference. Note them in the margins if you're drafting by hand, or, if you're working at a computer, record them at the end of your document, or right in the text itself (perhaps using capital letters to distinguish them from the rest of the text). Of course you'll need to remember to erase these notes to yourself during revision.

3. Track-switching

Track-switching is a variation on looping. In looping you read over each five-minute free-writing to get an idea for starting the next loop. In track-switching each loop is marked by a deliberate change of direction. Start by making a statement about your subject and writing for five minutes. Now make a counter-statement—something that will take you in an opposite direction. Continue, starting each five-minute writing session with a statement that is as different as possible from the direction of the preceding writing.

4. Dialog

While free-writing and looping allow you to free associate in writing, letting your pen take you where it will, the dialog method is a more structured writing exercise. First, write a question about your subject. Answer it briefly, then let that answer lead you to a second question. Answer that question, ask a third, and so on, until you begin to develop some useful insights into the subject. It may help to give names to the two speakers in your dialog. Let them talk to one another. Let them develop personalities.

5. Blind Writing

This variation on free-writing is only possible with a computer. If you're not yet used to composing at the computer, this exercise might help you to get started. It's really quite simple. Just turn the brightness dial on the monitor all the way down, so that the screen goes blank. Now write, at the keyboard, as quickly as you can. Notice that, since you can't see what you're writing, you can't go back to make corrections. You just have to keep on writing. You'll also find that your hands won't get as tired as they do when you write with a pen, so you can keep up the free-writing for a longer period of time. When you're done, turn the monitor back on, edit your work just enough to make it readable, save it, print it out if you want, and try it again.

6. Brainstorming

Of course you will get a lot of ideas for writing by talking to other people. This happens all the time. Brainstorming is a technique to formalize that activity and make it work a little more efficiently. It can be done in groups of any size, but four to six people is probably an ideal size.

Here are the rules for formal brainstorming on a specific idea:

1. All the members of the group should say whatever comes to mind about the topic. *Quantity* is important.
2. Everyone should get a chance to speak.
3. Reach for the unconventional. Sometimes the strangest ideas will work to stimulate someone else's thinking.
4. Build on other people's ideas.
5. Never criticize another idea. Everyone must be nonjudgmental, in order to encourage the free flow of ideas. Save evaluation for later.
6. Keep a written list of the ideas that everyone suggests. (Don't forget to write your own ideas down too.)
7. As soon as possible after the brainstorming session, review the list, evaluating the value of the various ideas and developing your own plan for the assigned essay.

200 *Discovery: Writing to Learn*

7. Clustering

The purpose for clustering is to let you quickly see relationships among facts and ideas. Begin by writing your topic in the center of a piece of paper. Circle it.

Around it, also circled, write the major divisions or main ideas of the topic. Connect each of these with a line to the central circle. Then for each of these parts/ideas/divisions develop sub-classifications, or specific examples, or facts or ideas related to them. Keep on going, connecting the items with lines to show relationships.

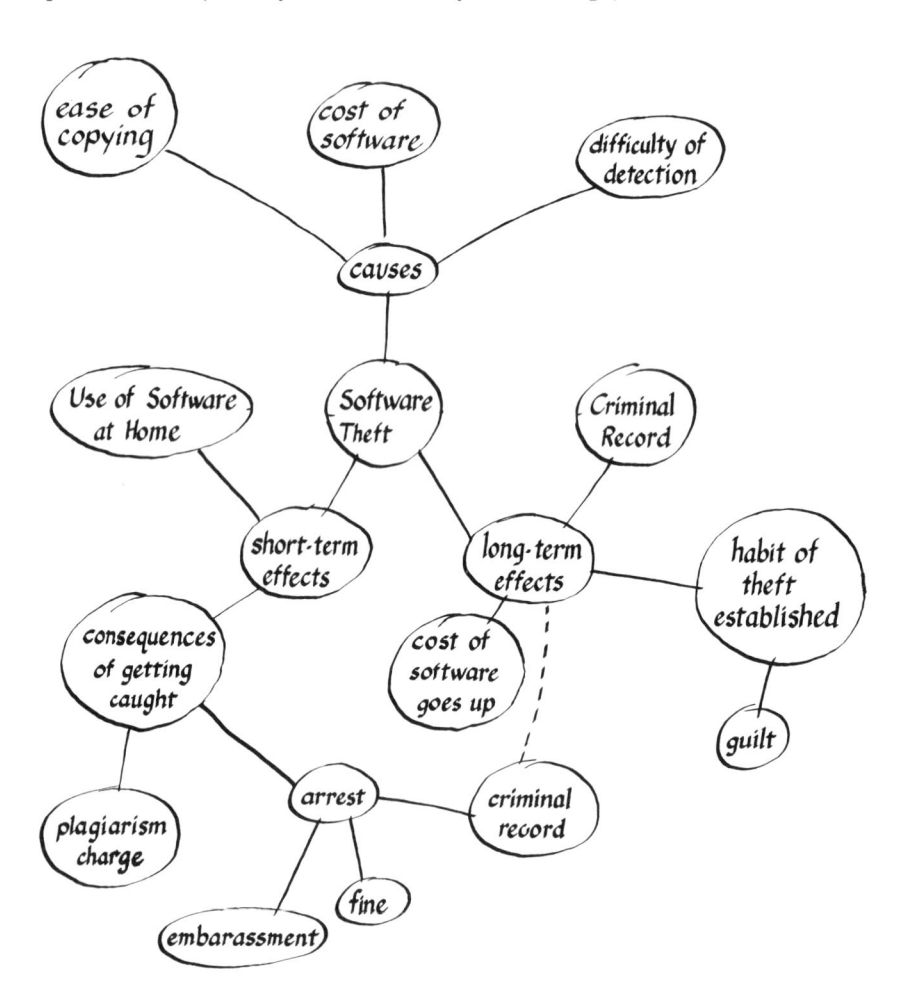

When you are done, you'll have a page that looks a bit like a spider's web (or maybe a tinker-toy assemblage). Examination of the page will reveal where your ideas are the richest and most detailed. You'll also have a pretty clear sense of how the paper can be organized.

8. Meditation

In Chapter Five you worked on a form of essay that I called a "meditation." The *act* of meditation can also be a useful invention technique. Initially you should use it when you are going to write about a particular object or place—something you can look at. With practice you can develop ways to apply the technique to writing about a variety of topics.

Close your eyes. No, wait. Finish reading this paragraph first. With your eyes closed, you are going to try to relax. Let the tension in your body drop away, into the earth. Clear your mind of any distracting worries, perhaps by repeating a comforting phrase or statement (the serenity prayer works well) or even a nonsense syllable.

When you are relaxed (but not asleep) open your eyes and look closely at the object you are going to write about. Focus your attention on it totally. Let the thoughts and feelings it evokes flow through you for three or four minutes. Then start writing.

9. Journal

As a final invention technique I have to list the journal you've been keeping. As I noted when I first described the journal in Chapter One, many writers use this method to generate ideas for their work. They record impressions, conversations, images, ideas, anything that strikes their fancy or that might someday be useful. If you've been careful about keeping your journal you may have recorded there some stories or ideas that may be useful in a paper. For instance, you may have written about a difficult decision you had to make which could become the basis for your essay on an ethical issue (in Chapter Nine).

And even if you don't already have something useful among your earlier journal entries, you can use it to gather your thoughts in preparation for a current paper assignment. Over a period of three or four days you can jot down the ideas that occur to you so that when you begin the paper in earnest you already have a collection of impressions to draw on.

II
Drafting

You may already be familiar with the idea of the "first draft," that thing that you're supposed to write before you write the version of the paper to turn in. And you're probably familiar with the usual ways of avoiding writing it (writing the paper out by hand, giving it to someone to type, and calling the two versions "first draft" and "final draft" is a favorite).

Of course that way of writing isn't exactly what I mean by the writing process, and while I promised that I wouldn't dictate what your personal process ought to be, I will let myself rule that the "first draft = final draft" method is not usually the most appropriate way to proceed. There are alternative ways to use the first draft, and it may help if we use different terms to describe it. This early version of your essay might be better called a "trial draft," a "discovery draft," or a "development draft." Seen this way, it can be an extension of the invention process, a way to continue your thinking.

The term "trial draft" emphasizes that this version of your paper is just a first attempt, a chance to try out things to see whether or not they work. Like a trial run in a race, it's just a way of getting started, of getting warmed up, of getting familiar with the territory. It does not necessarily represent your best work. (Indeed, racers deliberately don't do their best in the trial run; they save their best effort for later.) Nothing in the trial draft is permanent; any or all of it can be deleted or changed later on.

Accordingly, the trial draft should be written quickly. Let the ideas come, much as you did when you did free-writing. Only this time you aren't under the constraint of keeping the writing going non-stop. You are free to stop and think a bit before continuing. Or you might re-read what you've just written—perhaps the last paragraph, or perhaps just the last few lines on the computer screen (the " – " key on the numeric keypad will let you move backward quickly), or perhaps the whole draft from the beginning. That re-reading will probably trigger an awareness of where you need to go next. Remember, though, to keep moving. Don't worry about editing yet.

Calling the first draft a "discovery draft" reveals some other uses and techniques. The term "discovery" emphasizes the connection between drafting and invention. The draft is a place to learn more about your subject, to discover what you really want to say. This additional discovery happens as you work more deliberately to develop sentences and establish logical relationships among your ideas. As you begin to put the words together, new ideas and relationships will occur to you.

You will need, of course, to allow the discoveries to happen. You can't become so committed to a single direction for your draft that you block out new possibilities. You may find yourself following some digressions, just to see where they lead you. Who knows—a digression may give you an entirely new perspective, or even a new subject. The digression may actually become the paper. Or, if it remains a digression, you can always cut it out later.

In the discovery draft you must be careful not to worry about an introduction or thesis. After all, you don't know yet exactly what you will be writing, so it will be hard to introduce it. Perhaps the perfect introduction will occur to you in the middle of your drafting, or it may not get written till the end. The computer will let you easily return to the beginning to insert it, or you can just write it out where you are in the document and move it later.

Development: Calling the first draft a "development draft" also emphasizes the connection with invention, though it assumes that the basic ideas have already been revealed and now need to be developed. Details need to be added, examples explored, comparisons considered, and organization tried out.

A major force behind your development will be the way you organize your ideas. As you place one point in a logical relationship with another, or as you let one point lead to another, you'll find that new ideas emerge. You may find that you have three or four points to discuss in order (as this appendix discusses first invention, then drafting, then revision). Or you may need to spend part of your paper making a detailed, point by point comparison between two things. Or perhaps the need to define a term or concept will create a focus for your essay. Or the exploration of a problem will lead to the discussion of a solution.

One way to help you discover the appropriate organization (which in turn will let you discover what you need to say) is to keep your reader in mind. You are moving through a process of discovery, and when you are done you will be taking your reader through that process with you. What will the reader need to know? What will help him or her to understand? What will let your reader most easily understand your point?

Which leads to one more question: Do you know yet what your main point is going to be? If you don't, you don't need to panic, but you will, sometime during the drafting stage, need to discover it. You should be able to summarize, preferably in a single sentence, just exactly what your essay is about. And once you can do so, you should consider placing that sentence in your essay.

As I noted in Chapter Seven, placing this sentence somewhere near the beginning of an essay, as part of the introduction, is typical of much academic writing. Many teachers will expect to see it there. The term for this sentence is the THESIS, and it is governed by certain expectations:

> The thesis is usually contained in a single declarative sentence.
> A question does not usually serve as a thesis statement.
> The thesis usually appears in the introduction, though in some formats (such as an essay exploring a problem and proposing a solution) it is more appropriate at the end.
> The thesis must be a discussible assertion. A statement of a known fact (WIU is in Macomb, Illinois) will not serve as a thesis, since it does not need development in an essay.
> Even though it is a summary statement, the thesis should be as precise as possible in order to let the reader know what to expect.
> All of the discussion and development in the essay must follow logically from the thesis statement.

Of course not all essays will have this single sentence thesis statement. Certainly not all of the essays you have read in this text have had one, nor have all the papers you have written. An essay that presents a story of personal experience, for example, probably won't begin with a summary thesis. But a paper that reports information or argues toward a conclusion will generally need a thesis in order to help the reader along. And even if you don't include it, you should be able to state for yourself the main point of your paper.

III
Revision with a Self-evaluation of Writing

From time to time in the text I have made observations about revising as a part of the writing process. Here I want to develop a suggestion that I made briefly in Chapter Six: Part of your revision process should be an attempt to read your draft as if it had been written by someone else and you were seeing it for the first time. In other words, you need to play the role of your reader. Only by doing this role-playing will you be able to stand outside the writing process and see what your product looks like. It is usually easier to achieve this distance if you read from a printout rather than from the screen. It is also important to give yourself some time between the drafting and the re-reading. Get away from the paper for a while, and then come back to it. But do come back to it. Without this step, you are likely to be mislead by what you *think* your paper says. You won't be able to see what is really there on the page.

And what is actually on the page may surprise you. You may have forgotten to provide an essential detail, or to explain the significance of an event which, while obvious to you, will mystify your reader. On the other hand, you are also likely to be surprised and delighted by the occasional flashes of insight, the well-constructed sentences, the witty phrases, the things that work. Re-reading as a reader can sometimes be fun!

As you review the product of your writing process, it may be helpful to keep in mind a few analytical points. You can, first of all, use the same questions that you have been using as you read the papers by the members of your group. Alternatively, you can check your paper against the points about good writing that you've been keeping in your journal. Or the following summary may be useful:

What part of your essay do you like the best? Why?
Which part gave you the most trouble?
What do you want your reader to notice?
What do you hope your reader won't notice?
What was the most surprising thing you discovered by writing
    the essay?
What is your purpose in writing the essay? Why do you care?
    Why should the reader care?
What is the thesis of the essay?
How does the essay follow logically from the thesis?
What ways did you use to organize your ideas?
Who is the audience for the paper?
Will the first paragraph attract the reader's attention?
What features of the paper will keep the reader interested?
Have you provided specific details at every point?
Why are the things you have to say important?

Does the end of the paper leave the reader satisfied?
Are there mechanical errors which will interfere with the reader's enjoyment or understanding of the essay?
What revisions are needed to correct the problems that this self-evaluation has revealed?

I'll conclude with one more suggestion for revision. This one has a tendency to make people a little self-conscious, but if you can overcome that, you may find that it's well worth it. Here is it: Pick a time when it's fairly deserted in your residence hall or apartment. Lock your door. Unplug your phone. Then read your essay out loud to yourself. That's right. Out loud.

What you'll hear, and feel, is the coherence ("flow") of your sentences. If everything is cohering, you'll be able to read smoothly and evenly. But if a sentence is out of place, or written with awkward syntax, or lacking a logical transition, or built around an inappropriate word, you'll hear it. Quite likely you'll stumble, or your tongue will trip over the words. Make note of those places. Those are sentences that you need to fix.

We're finally to the last step in the process: Preparing to turn the paper in. Check it all one more time on the computer screen, comparing it to a printout of the essay. Use the Spell Check, if your haven't done so yet (or done so recently). Make sure that it is formatted the way you want it. Do you have a title? Is your name on the paper? Have you started paragraphs in the appropriate places? Have you double spaced the text?

Now check the printer to make sure that there is enough paper, and that the first sheet is in the right place in the machine. Remind yourself how to print a document (Chapter Two), and print it. And when you're done, *please* tear the pages apart carefully. Don't ruin the effect of the neatly typed paper with a big tear across the second page!

Appendix Three

Additional Writing Assignments

1. Did you ever have an argument with your parents, or another adult, in which they just couldn't understand what you were talking about? Describe the incident in detail, showing how you were using two different languages, or how you had two different sets of assumptions, or how you were working from incompatible sets of values.

2. Think about someone you had a conflict with lately. It can be a brother, sister, parent, roommate, classmate, anyone at all. For this assignment, you are to become that person and write about the conflict from his or her perspective. Be fair to the other person. After all, for this assignment you *are* that other person.

3. Explore the differences between expectations about college and the reality. What had you imagined that college would be like? Were you right? Where did the expectations come from? Why does reality differ? Which is better? Alternatively, you could consider your expectations about Christmas (or other appropriate holiday). Is it ever what you anticipated? Or how about a family excursion that turned out to be less fun than anticipated?

4. Write about a time when you were outcast from a group (a team, a group of friends, a clique, a club).

5. Take a look at the things you have and display in your room, either at home or at school. Think also about some of the things you don't own and display. Write an essay explaining how the things you own (or don't own) define you as a person.

Some questions you *might* think about: How and why are your belongings significant to you? What values do your possessions represent? What are a few of your most valued possessions and why are they more important than others? What don't you own that you wish you did? What kinds of things will you never own? What do your things "tell" others about you? Is there anything in your room you could get rid of?

6. Describe the worst place you ever spent the night, with a goal of capturing the atmosphere of the place. Use the specific details of your description to evoke a central feeling. You'll be most successful if you can create that feeling without ever having to name it.

7. Assume that you will be a parent. Will you enforce the same rules that your parents did? Why or why not? If there will be differences, what rules will you enforce?

8. Do you think you would like to raise your own children in the same kind of neighborhood you were raised in? Why or why not? Explain in as much detail as you can. (You will, of course, need to clarify what you mean by "neighborhood." And some writers may need to adapt the question to *"Did* you raise your children. . . ." or "Are you raising. . . .")

9. "Slice of Life." Visit a local gathering place such as the University Union, the doughnut and coffee shop on the Square, a pizza parlor, a church. Observe and describe the behavior of the inhabitants. Why do they behave this way?

10. People United to Support the Handicapped (PUSH) hosts regular "Awareness Days" during the school year. Participants have the opportunity to simulate different disabilities to gain insight into what it is like to be physically challenged. Activities include manipulating a wheelchair, experiencing diminished hearing or sight, and simulating learning disorders.

Participate in a PUSH Awareness Day and describe the new insights you gained into the challenges facing fellow students.

11. It was just a short time ago that you came to WIU and found yourself surrounded by strangers and faced with a new way of life. Slowly you began the process of becoming acquainted with the daily routines and with the new people. Now that some time has passed, many of those first weeks' concerns have been dealt with successfully, and many have proven groundless. Reaching this point has not been easy, and you are aware that some problems remain in your future; however, you have a greater degree of confidence in your ability to face them than when you arrived.

Your friend, who is still in high school, is a capable and talented person, but somewhat lacking in self-confidence. Your initial dread about college has frightened him/her, and now he/she isn't too sure about going to school next year. Since your friend has planned a career that will require a college degree, you don't want to be responsible for destroying that dream.

Write a letter to your friend. Be honest about the difficulties you have had and the doubts which remain, but try to emphasize your successes and to convey a feeling of hope and growing confidence.

Appendix Four

Guides for Groups

Part of your work in English 180 this semester involves learning, writing, and problem-solving in groups. This may be a familiar activity from high school; just as likely, though, it represents a new way of learning.

Group work (usually called "collaborative learning" or "cooperative learning" by education theorists) is based on the idea that people learn better when they are actively involved in the process. You can learn more by talking to one another than you can by listening to an instructor all the time. Not that you won't need to learn from your instructor some of the time—he or she will regularly provide information, explain assignments, review principles, and supplement this text. But you will also spend much of your time working together in groups.

In order for this group learning to succeed, everyone involved must agree from the beginning to cooperate. You must agree to work together, even if you don't become friends, or more importantly, even if you *do* become friends. You must agree to be fair to one another, neither too harsh nor too easy. You must agree to contribute your share to the group's work, which means, at minimum, coming to all class meetings and coming prepared.

You will be responsible for your group and to your group. You must be sure to prepare your share of any assignment if the group is to complete its work. And you must be present, or you'll put an extra burden on the other group members. Your absence may not be noticed in a class of twenty-two; it will be in a group of five. Your sense of identification with your group may even begin to extend out of the class. Don't discount the possibility of having your group meet after class to work on a assignment together.

The rest of this appendix offers a series of exercises and projects which your instructor may assign from time to time. These are supplements to the group projects that appear in the text.

1. *Introductions.* Since your group will be working closely all semester, it's important that you get to know one another. You'll need one another's addresses and phone numbers, as well as a sense of who each of you are. Introduce yourselves in the usual way, with the important factual information, then describe something you have in your room that reveals something about you to anyone who sees it. An alternative might be to interview and introduce a partner to the group or to the class.

2. One of the first tasks you'll have in this class will be to become comfortable with the computer and with the WordPerfect program. Chances are that one or more members of your group will have more computer experience that others. Working together will allow the novices to get immediate answers to their questions, as well as let the pros solidify the things they know by teaching them to someone else.

3. For a writing assignment that involves a choice of topics (such as the assignment in Chapter Four), discuss the various possibilities in your group and come to agreement about which of the choices you will all write about. If some members don't agree with the majority, help them to see how they can write on the chosen topic.

4. *Brainstorming.* Your group will provide a good opportunity to practice some invention techniques. For any paper assignment you can discuss the possibilities informally in the group, do a formal invention technique together (such as cubing), or practice brainstorming, as described in Appendix Two. The purpose here is to help one another get started, collect ideas, and discover the possibilities for writing.

5. *Sharing.* Read an early draft of a paper aloud to the members of the group. The goal here is simply to share your work with others, to communicate with them. The group members will listen attentively and thank you for your work. This is a chance for them to get to know more about you, and they will be a supportive audience. (In the process of reading your own paper, you are likely to hear some things that don't work, places where you were not clear enough, sentences where you stumble or get lost. These are things you should try to improve when you revise.)

Before long, you may be invited to read an essay to the whole class. After the experience with the small group, this should not be a difficult or troublesome experience. All the members of the class will know how to listen as a supportive audience.

Here's how to read aloud to a group:

1. Relax, make eye contact with people in the group, relax, make any necessary introductory remarks, relax, and begin reading.
2. Read slowly. Remember that your listeners are hearing this for the first time. If you go too fast, someone may ask you to slow down.
3. Read loudly enough for everyone to hear.
4. Pause briefly between paragraphs.
5. Concentrate on the meaning of your paper, rather than just reading words.
6. Relax and enjoy the attention.

6. *Feedback.* After everyone in the group has had a chance to read a piece of writing to the group, you can move toward providing feedback. Initially, this feedback will be descriptive, rather than judgmental. This nonjudgmental response will allow you to see how well you've communicated and what your audience has heard. It will also allow you to decide for yourself what changes you will need to make in order to communicate better. Obviously, this is best done with an early draft, rather than a finished essay.

Sayback: This is a technique developed by Sondra Perl and Elaine Avidon, who borrowed it from psychologist Carl Rogers. It simply asks the listener to actively process what she hears and repeat it (or "say it back") to the writer. The writer then has a chance to clarify what was really meant or intended, first for the person who responded, then in the paper itself during revision. The purpose is both to let the writer see where he is or isn't communicating effectively, and also to stimulate some new ideas as a result of the exchange.

For sayback to work, the writer/reader and the listener must try to be both fair and understanding. The listener must try to sum up what the writer is getting at, whether or not she agrees with it, or even likes it. The writer must accept the listener's response without getting defensive. She is, after all, merely explaining what she heard.

Pointing: After the writer has read the paper, each member of the group points out the best, strongest, or most memorable features. These may be a strong word or phrase, an especially effective sentence, a good descriptive passage, a strong characterization, a useful point of view, or an original metaphor. Everyone should try to be as specific as possible.

Analysis: Analysis of writing isn't limited to the study of literature. The same principles can be applied to essays written for class. Two analytical principles are particularly useful: analysis of structure and analysis of the writer-reader relationship. For both of these it will probably be necessary to read the text of the essay, rather than (or in addition to) having the writer read it aloud.

Structure: Analysis of structure involves looking at the parts of the essay and defining the relationship among them. Questions to ask include:

> Is there an introduction? How does it work to introduce the main subject of the paper? If there is not an introduction, what replaces it?
> What is the main point of the paper? How do the details develop and support the main point?
> What is the overall principle of organization? Are events narrated chronologically? Is a subject analyzed in its various parts? Is the essay built around a comparison? a question? a problem? a process?
> What does the writer do to let the reader move easily and logically from point to point?
> Is there a conclusion? Does it fit the paper you have just read? What new directions does the conclusion point toward?
> What would an outline of this essay look like?

Writer-Reader Relationship:

> Who is the intended audience for the essay? Who does the writer seem to be writing to? What assumptions are made about the reader?
> What kind of person does the writer seem to be? How does the writer suggest qualities of his/her personality, character, attitudes, or beliefs? Try to define the writer's tone of voice.
> How does the writer treat the reader? Is the attitude respectful, condescending, submissive, authoritarian, self-assured, disdainful, whatever?

Do mechanical errors suggest a lack of concern for the reader?

What is the implied relationship between the writer and the reader?

Reader Response: A piece of writing only comes to life and accomplishes a purpose when it is read and responded to. In other words, the reader is an essential part of the writing. The "Reader Response" technique is designed to let writers know how their words actually affect a variety of readers.

In "Pointing" readers responded by indicating the parts of an essay they liked, or responded to favorably. In "Reader Response" all responses are noted: good, bad, and neutral (perhaps the worst of all). Several pre-conditions have to be met before this technique can work. First of all, the participants have to trust one another. Some of the other techniques (like "pointing") should be tried first. Second, the person doing the responding needs to be both honest and kind: honest because a response of "I like it" at every point will do the writer no good; kind because any criticism can be hard for a writer to take. And if the writer gets offended, he won't be able to understand the response or make the necessary adjustments in his work. Third, the writer must be extraordinarily mature and accepting. Not all the responses will be what was expected. The writer must be willing to hear what the reader is saying and to learn from it. (Learning from readers is, after all, just another part of the discovery process.)

There are several ways to conduct a reader response session. The writer can read the draft aloud to a partner or to the whole group, pausing after every paragraph or two to let the listeners respond. Or the responders can read the draft themselves, explaining their responses as they go along. Alternatively, the responses can be recorded in writing. These responses are most effective if they are offered at several points during the process of reading, though they can also be recorded at the end, after the whole essay has been read. And you might consider presenting your written responses to an essay in a personal letter to the writer.

And what should those responses be? They need to be more substantial than "I like it," certainly, though the form of that sentence (an "I" statement, noting a reaction) is just right. Here are some questions that readers can use to form their responses:

How do you feel as you read this paragraph? Be as specific as possible.

What in the paragraph creates this feeling?

Do you understand everything?

Can you see (or hear, or smell, or taste, or feel) the things that the writer describes?

Can you share the experience fully with the writer? Where does this happen to you? Where doesn't it?

Are you irritated by anything? Or confused? Or impatient? Or bored?

On the other hand, are you excited by anything? Or moved? Or amused? Or convinced? Or frightened? Or caught up? Or entertained?

Are there sentences, or words, or phrases that make you stumble or get confused or stop to figure out what was meant?

What does the first paragraph lead you to expect about the rest of the paper?

What does each paragraph lead you to expect will come next?

Formal Analysis: This type of response is called "formal" here because it asks you to respond to a series of questions on a response form. In general, these questions will ask you to indicate what you liked best about the paper you read and what parts particularly need revision. Most writing teachers have their own favorite set of specific questions, and your teacher will give groups the appropriate forms to work with.

7. Work together to proofread one another's finished papers. You will have already experienced how distracting typographical errors can be to a reader. And you know how difficult it is to proofread your own work accurately. This situation provides a good opportunity for collaborative work, as you join forces to make everyone's paper as good as it can be.

8. Decide as a group which of the completed essays by group members will be read to the whole class.

9. Keep track of classwork, lecture notes, and assignments for one another. Group members can take responsibility for one another when someone is unavoidably absent. This is not merely kindness; it will assure that all the group members are prepared for the classwork you will be expected to do.

Appendix Five

Advanced WordPerfect Commands

In Chapter Two you learned some basic WordPerfect commands—the commands you need to open files, enter text, save, and print. As your skill increases using WordPerfect, you'll probably want to manipulate files in different ways. In this appendix Kris Jacobus, who wrote the Chapter Two instructions, has collected a number of additional WordPerfect functions. And if you're interested in learning even more, you should look up one of the many books about WordPerfect that are now available.

I. Copying Files

Besides the routine saving of files as you write and revise, you will often need to make copies of your work. Many times you will need to copy a file that you are working on in class onto a disk that you can take home with you. Perhaps you've put off copying files until you need to copy more than one file to another disk. The copy command sequences that follow will help with most of your copying needs. Remember, always back up your work!

TO COPY ONE FILE ONTO ANOTHER DISK:

1. Retrieve the file that you want to copy onto the screen.
2. Remove your disk from the bottom drive (B:) and replace it with the disk you want to save the file on.
3. Press the F10 key to save the file. If you have a file on the new disk with the same name as the one you are trying to save, a prompt "Replace [filename]? (Y/N)" will appear. If you want the file saved as it appears on the screen press

"Y"; if you want to keep both files, change the name at the bottom of the screen and press ENTER (this will save the new file under the new name and leave your original copy of the file under the old name).

TO COPY TWO OR MORE FILES ONTO ANOTHER DISK:

1. Open the directory of your source disk with the F5 key.
2. Remove the WordPerfect disk in the top drive (A:) and replace with the disk you want to copy the files onto.
3. With the arrow keys, highlight the first file that you want to copy. Press the STAR (Shift/number 8 key on the keyboard), and a star (*) will appear behind the file length number.
4. Place a star (*) in each file that you want to copy to the second disk.
5. Press the 8 ("Copy") key and the prompt "Copy marked files? (Y/N) N" will appear. Press the "Y" key.
6. After the prompt "Copy all marked files to _____," type A: and press ENTER. All marked files will be copied onto the disk in drive A: (top).

TO COPY ALL FILES FROM ONE DISK TO ANOTHER

Copying an entire disk is best accomplished by exiting from WordPerfect and using DOS.

1. Exit the WordPerfect by using the EXIT F7 key.
2. Place the disk which contains the files you want to copy in the top drive (A:).
3. Place the disk that you want to copy the file onto in the bottom drive (B:).
4. At the A prompt (A>) type: copy *.* b: and press ENTER.
5. All the files on the disk in the A: drive will be copied onto the disk in B:.

Moving Blocks of Text

The ability to move text from one place to another in a document is one of the most useful functions of a word processor. Instead of rewriting a block of text in its new location, you can move it by using the BLOCK/MOVE commands. WordPerfect allows this movement not only within a file, but between two different files as well. (This movement between files is useful when you write a longer paper and use different files for notes or invention exercises.) The same sequence of commands is used to move text within a file or between files.

TO MOVE BLOCKS OF TEXT

1. Place the cursor on the first space of the text you want to move. Press the ALT-F4 key and "Block on" flashes in the lower left corner of the screen.
2. Move the cursor to the last space of the text that you want to move. The block should be highlighted on the screen.
3. Press the MOVE (CTRL-F4) key to move the text.
4. Type 1 to erase the text from the original position in the document and write it into the new location. Type 2 to copy the text, leaving it in the original position and at the same time moving a copy of it to a new location.
5. Move the cursor to the place that you would like the block to appear (either in the original document or in a new file).
6. Again press the MOVE (CTRL-F4) key and, type 5 to retrieve the text at the cursor position.

III. Spell Check and Thesaurus

Nearly every writer makes errors in spelling when drafting papers. In fact, many writers consider themselves poor spellers. If you fall into either category, the Spell Check becomes essential to a good paper. The procedure takes only a few minutes, and you will be able to correct most misspelled words. Please be aware that the Spell Check recognizes only the spelling of the over 10,000 words in its dictionary. If you use a homonym (substitute "there" when "their" is correct) or misspell one word with the correct spelling of another word (type "horse" instead of "house") the Spell Check will not catch this error. Proofreading is still needed. Nonetheless, the Spell Check is a particularly valuable feature of WordPerfect. Take the time to use it before handing in each paper.

TO USE SPELL CHECK

1. With your document on the screen, replace the disk in drive B: with the Spell Check disk. Press the SPELL (CTRL-F2) key and the prompt "Check: 1 Word; 2 Page; 3 Document;

4 Change Dictionary; 5 Look Up; 6 Count" will appear on the bottom of the screen. Press the number 3 key to check the entire document for misspelled words.

2. When the Spell Check finds a questionable word it stops checking the document and highlights the word it cannot find in its dictionary. You will then have six options with any highlighted word:

1 Skip once: Ignore this one occurrence of the highlighted word.
2 Skip: Ignore the highlighted word for the rest of the spell check.
3 Add word: Add the highlighted word to the supplemental dictionary. You should add the word if you feel it is one you will use often *and* you are sure that the spelling is correct. The next time the Spell Check finds the word, it will recognize it as a correct spelling.
4 Edit: Correct the highlighted word using the standard editing keys. Press ENTER key to reactivate the checking process.
5 Look up: List additional words based on a word pattern similar to the one highlighted.
6 Phonetic: List additional words based on how the highlighted word sounds.

Alternate prompts will occur when certain kinds of words (or errors) appear in your document:

3 Ignore words containing numbers: Since most words don't contain any numbers, Spell Check will recognize any combination of numbers and letters as an error. This prompt lets you tell the program to ignore words containing numbers (for example, F4). This feature was used when checking the spelling in this appendix. Otherwise Spell Check would have stopped checking to indicate an error every time a function key was named.

5 Disable double word checking: Spell Check will highlight any occurrence of the same word repeated twice: "The manta ray can jump out of of the water...."

Options:

You can check the spelling of only a portion of the document by blocking text with the BLOCK (ALT-F4) key before pressing the SPELL (CTRL-F2) key.

You may choose to spell check only a word or a page instead of an entire document by choosing one of those options from the Spell menu.

The Speller function also allows you to perform a word count (option number 6 on the first Spell Check prompt).

THESAURUS

The Thesaurus becomes a valuable program if you need to substitute a word with the same meaning as the one you have used in a sentence. The Thesaurus also will list antonyms, words meaning the opposite of the word you have used. Be sure that the word you substitute means exactly what you believe it to mean; relying on the Thesaurus without checking the meaning can lead to some embarrassing errors! Dictionaries still serve a useful purpose. If you're not absolutely sure of the meaning of a word, look it up.

TO USE THE THESAURUS

1. Retrieve to the screen the document you want to use the Thesaurus with.
2. Replace your document disk with the Thesaurus disk.
3. Put the cursor on a word in the document that you want to look up. Press the THESAURUS (ALT-F1) key to activate the Thesaurus program.
4. If the word at the position of the cursor is not one of the 10,000 words in the Thesaurus, the prompt "Word:" will appear at the bottom of the screen. Enter a word that you would like to substitute.
5. If you find an acceptable substitute for the word which you looked up, press the letter of the word and the Thesaurus will replace the original word with the one you want to substitute.
6. If you do not find an acceptable substitute, you can sometimes find more choices. Type the letter of any nearly acceptable alternative that has a dot (•) beside it. The program will ask you if you want to insert that word in your text or look up the synonyms of that word. The Thesaurus will list alternatives for any word that has the dot beside it.

7. To move from column to column in the Thesaurus display, use the arrow keys.
8. To exit the Thesaurus, press the ENTER key.

IV. Deleting Text

Use Delete commands sparingly. Recovering deleted text is possible if you recover text soon after deleting it, but the best policy is to not delete unless you are absolutely sure you do not want the text.

TO DELETE TEXT

Any of the following keystrokes can be used to delete text and codes.

BACKSPACE	Delete text to the left.
DEL	Delete text at the cursor. Continue pressing to delete text to the right.
CTRL-BACKSPACE	Delete the word at the cursor. Continue pressing to delete words to the right of the cursor.
HOME, BACKSPACE	Delete from the cursor to the beginning of the current word. Press both again to delete words to the left of the cursor.
HOME, DEL	Delete from the cursor to the end of the current word. Press both again to delete words to the right of the cursor.
CTRL-END	Delete text from the cursor to the end of the line.
CTRL-PGDN	Delete from the cursor to the end of the page. You are asked to confirm this type of deletion.

Additional delete commands:

Press the BLOCK (ALT-F4) key to highlight a section of text, then press DEL or BACKSPACE to delete the block. You will be asked "Delete Block? (Y/N) N." Type Y to delete it or press any other key to leave the block. If you decide to leave the block, it remains highlighted.

The MOVE (CTRL-F4) key can be used to delete a sentence, paragraph, or page.

1. Place the cursor in the text to be deleted and press MOVE (CTRL-F4).
2. Type 1 for the current Sentence, 2 for the Paragraph, or 3 for the entire Page. The text will be highlighted.
3. Type 3 to delete the highlighted section.

RESTORING DELETED TEXT

If you accidentally delete text, you can restore it by pressing CANCEL (F1) and typing 1. This will bring back the last deletion you made. If you type 2, you can display the previous two deletions. Again, be careful. The program cannot restore any earlier deletions you made. It's best not to erase without being sure that's what you want to do.

V. Using Windows

WordPerfect allows you to view two texts on the screen at the same time. The second text appears in a "window." This window function can be very handy. You can set up your screen so that you can look at a rough draft at the same time that you are writing a final paper. Try the technique and imagine the possibilities.

TO SEE TWO FILES ON THE SCREEN AT THE SAME TIME (WINDOWS):

1. Retrieve one of the files that you want to work with by pressing F5, highlighting the file, and pressing the number 1 key to retrieve.
2. Press the CTRL-F3 (SCREEN) key.
3. Select number 1 on the menu displayed on the bottom of the screen: "0 Rewrite; 1 Window; 2 Line Draw; 3 Ctrl/Slt keys; 4 Colors; 5 Auto Rewrite: 0."
4. A prompt will appear: "# Lines in this Window: 24." Type in the number 12 and the screen will be split in half. (Since there are 24 lines on the screen, a 24-line window would leave no room for the other file!)
5. To move from the first window to the second, press the SHIFT-F3 (SWITCH) key. Now you can load another docu-

ment into this window, or use it to write a new document. When you press SHIFT-F3 again, the cursor will return to the original document.

6. To return to only one document on the screen, exit using the F7 key or press the CTRL-F3 key, press number 1 for Window, and set the number of lines in the window back to 24. (If you have written new material or have made changes, be sure to save the work in your screen before exiting.)

Windows provide an easy way to move blocks of text between files. Just put the source document in one window and the document you will move the block to in the other. You can now see not only where the block is lifted from, but also where you will place it, and all on the same screen!

VI. Miscellaneous Commands

UNDERLINE

To underline a word (or any number of words), press the F8 key. All text you type will be underlined until you turn the function off by pressing F8 again. (WordPerfect reminds you the underline function is activated by underlining the cursor position number in the status line at the bottom of the screen.)

BOLDFACE

To type a word (or words) in boldface, press the F6 key. Everything you type after pressing F6 will be boldfaced until you press F6 again. (The position number in the status line is boldfaced when this function is activated.)

CENTER A LINE

To place a word (or words) at the center of a line (as you should do with the title of your paper), press SHIFT-F6. The cursor will jump to the middle of the line. Type in the text and the line will center itself as you type.

JUSTIFY TEXT

WordPerfect will automatically "justify" your text. That means that spaces will be added to each line to make the text line up evenly on the right-hand side of the page. This function is useful to people who are preparing copy for publication and want it to look like a printed text. There will be times, however, when you want a jagged right margin (when, for instance, you want the text to looked typed).

To turn off the right justification, press CTRL-F8. An option menu will appear on the screen. Now press the number 3 key, then the Return key to return to your document. Turn off the justification just before printing.

VII. Space to record additional commands:

226   *Discovery: Writing to Learn*

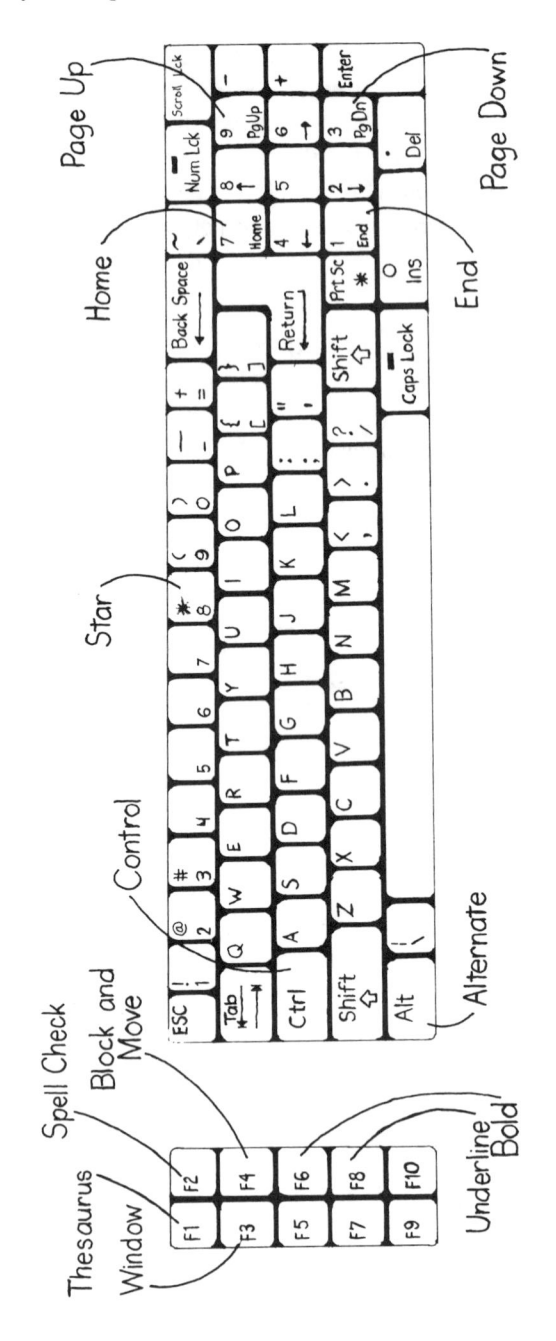

Appendix Six

Additional Readings

This appendix contains a varied collection of essays by both student writers and professionals. Your instructor may assign some of these essays from time to time, though I invite and encourage you to read them all. Each is preceded by a brief introductory comment.

   I. Bill Cosby, "Turn That Crap Down" **228**
  II. David Jackson, "Grate" **230**
 III. Alice Walker, "Brothers and Sisters" **231**
  IV. Russell Baker, "The Wonders of Writing on a Computer" **235**
   V. Faye Sudgen, "Table Talk" **238**
  VI. Jim Courter, "It's All in the Jeans" **240**
 VII. Nancy Mairs, "On Being a Cripple" **242**
VIII. Ebrima Jow, "The School Day" **255**
  IX. Diana Merideth, "Covering Campus Tragedy" **259**
   X. John Leonard, "Nausea in the Afternoon" **261**
  XI. Steve Fay, "The Drought Grapes" **263**
 XII. Robert Fulghum, "Mushrooms" **268**

I. Bill Cosby has become a household name for his weekly portrayal of Cliff Huxtable, as well as for his various commercial endorsements. He is also a prolific author, constructing essays out of the personal experience he once used in his stand-up comedy routines. "Turn That Crap Down" is from his book *Fatherhood.*

227

Turn That Crap Down
Bill Cosby

Nothing separates the generations more than music. By the time a child is eight or nine, he has developed a passion for his own music that is even stronger than his passions for procrastination and weird clothes. A father cannot even convince his kids that Bach was a pretty good composer by telling them that he made the cover of *Time* a few years ago. The kids would simply reply that he isn't much in *People.*

"Okay," says the father grimly, standing at his stereo, "I want you guys to forget that Madonna stuff for a few minutes and hear some Duke Ellington."

"Duke Ellington?" says his son. "Is he a relative of Prince?"

Yes, the kids will listen to neither the old masters nor the great popular music that Mom and Dad loved in their own youth, the modern classics like "The Flat Foot Floogie" and the immortal ballads like "Cement Mixer (Put-ti Put-ti)."

When I was a boy, Patti Page made a record called "That Doggie in the Window." It swept the country, but it wouldn't sell ten copies today because it couldn't be filmed for a video. A cocker spaniel scratching himself in a pet store window lacks the drama a video needs, unless the dog were also coming into heat and fifty dancing veterinarians were singing, "Go, you bitch!"

Today's parents grew up with the silly notion that music was meant to be heard, that one picture was superfluous to ten thousands words. We now have learned, of course, that music has to be seen, that the 1812 Overture is nothing unless you also see twenty regiments of Russian infantry. Duke Ellington was lucky to have done "Take the 'A' Train" when he did. If Duke were doing the song today, he would have to play it in the subway, with the lyrics being sung by a chorus of break-dancing conductors.

I doubt that any father has ever liked the music his children did. At the dawn of time, some caveman must have been sitting on a rock, contentedly whistling the song of a bird, until he was suddenly jarred by music coming from his son, grunting the

Excerpt from FATHERHOOD by Bill Cosby, copyright © 1986 by William H. Cosby, Jr. Used by permission of Doubleday, a division of Bantam, Doubleday, Dell Publishing Group, Inc.

sound of a sick monkey. And eons later, Mozart's father must have walked into the parlor one day when Mozart was playing Bach on the harpsichord.

"Turn that crap down," the father must have said.

And Mozart must have replied—in German, of course—"But, Dad, this stuff is fresh."

The older generation is simply incapable of ever appreciating the strange sounds that the young one calls music.

One day last year, my daughter, who is eighteen now, came to me and said, "Dad, can I have ten dollars?"

As a typical father, I knew that I would be giving her the money; and, as a typical father, I also knew that I would be making her squirm before I gave it.

"What do you want it for?" I said.

"I want to buy a new album."

"A new album by whom?"

"The Septic Tanks."

When I was a kid, singing groups were named after such things as birds: we had the Ravens, the Robins, and the Orioles. But only the Vultures or the Pigeon Droppings could be singing groups today. And the lyrics are even worse than the names: these groups are singing the stuff that sent Lenny Bruce to jail. What my wife and I have always fondly known as sex is just foreplay today. Against a background as romantic as the Battle of Guadalcanal, these singers describe oral things that you never heard from your dentist.

The grotesque violence of some of these rock videos reflects a philosophy that many kids seem to hold:

"Well, it's your fault that everything will be destroyed."

But the kids have it backward. If they don't like the idea of destruction, then why don't they show us nymphs and shepherds merrily dancing on the grass instead of a guy who looks as though he is being electrocuted by his guitar?

About an hour after I had given my daughter ten dollars for her music, she came home with an album, and for the next twenty minutes I heard:

> Slish-slish,
> Boom-boom,
> Slish-slish,
> Boom-boom.
> Grick, grack, greck
> And dreck.

During this performance, the dog wandered in, glanced at the stereo, and sat down to listen. The dog loves this kind of music; he likes to breathe to it. At last, after the melody had segued to a noise that sounded like eruptions of natural gas, some singing began; and this singing was perfectly matched to the quality of the instrumental that had preceded it:

> Oh, baby,
> Uhh-uhh, uhh-uhh.
> Come to my place
> And sit on my face.

II. "Grate" is a short story which was published in *Elements,* Western's student literary magazine. It describes a childhood experience from the point of view of the child, using the child's language and capturing the child's perceptions of things.

Grate

David Jackson

This's my school. It's all brick with pink doors. It's kinda girly with the doors like that, but it does have a thing that n'other school has. Principal Baldwin calls it a "grate."

It's over here by the fifth grade doors. It's the same size as the boys' bathroom only it's got three walls and no roof. The floor's all fulla holes, and it's metal. It's where the school keeps its leaves, see 'em all? There must be millions of 'em. They have leaves down there all the time, even in the spring and summer! See the door over in that wall down there? That's how all them teachers get in t' play in the leaves after all us kids are gone. I don't think it's very nice that they don't share, and let us play too.

I seen a dead mousey down there once. At least I think it was dead, 'cause when I dropped a rock on it, it didn't move. I figure this here metal part is made outta nickel 'cause it's the same color as a old nickel I got and about as tough. Me 'n' Bobby tried t' get down there once t' play. We jumped up and down on the

From Dave Jackson, "Grate," © 1989 by ELEMENTS. Reprinted by permission.

grate all recess one day but couldn't break through. First I thought this was jail, where they put bad kids. I haven't seen anybody in there yet, not even Peter Himen. I figured if Pete ain't been in there yet, it must not be jail. There's room to stand up, even Mr. Uther. He has trouble gettin' through doorways wifout hittin' his head.

If you stand on the grate and the curtains is open, you can see through the windas inta the teachers' classroom. They don't have desks like us. They got couches. All they do is practice smokin'. I asked 'em if they'd teach me how. They said, "It wasn't for little boys." I tried t' explain to 'em math isn't for little boys either, and they got kinda mad.

I like t' sit back here when the wind comes whippin' around and messes up my hair. I can feel it spinnin' round and round like a tornado. Every few weeks, it really stinks back here, and I go play on the playground. It may be the dead mousey or wet leaves, I don't know. If ya lay here and look up, the sky looks like it's on TV. The best part is it don't have commercials.

When I grow up I wanna be a teacher and smoke. I'll go t' their classroom and learn how t' smoke and yell a lot. I'll play in the teachers' leaves, and I'll let the kids come and play with me and invite my friends. Maybe I'll leave Pete down there. Ha Ha Ha Ha Ha HaHa. I'd say, "You've been very bad Peter Himen! I'm going to put you in jail, and I hope you'll learn your lesson young man!" See, I could teach. Nothin' to it.

III. "Brothers and Sisters," from *In Search of Our Mothers' Gardens,* is one of Alice Walker's stories of a southern childhood. It is a revealing study of the attitudes, rituals and expectations embodied in a culture.

Brothers and Sisters
Alice Walker

We lived on a farm in the South in the fifties, and my brothers, the four of them I knew (the fifth had left home when I

From Alice Walker, BROTHERS AND SISTERS, © 1967, 1971, 1975, 1983 by Alice Walker. Reprinted with permission of Harcourt Brace Jovanovich, Inc.

was three years old), were allowed to watch animals being mated. This was not unusual; nor was it considered unusual that my older sister and I were frowned upon if we even asked, innocently, what was going on. One of my brothers explained the mating one day, using words my father had given him: "The bull is getting a little something on his stick," he said. And he laughed. "What stick?" I wanted to know. "Where did he get it? How did he pick it up? Where did he put it?" All my brothers laughed.

I believe my mother's theory about raising a large family of five boys and three girls was that the father should teach the boys and the mother teach the girls the facts, as one says, of life. So my father went around talking about bulls getting something on their sticks and she went around saying girls did not need to know about such things. They were "womanish" (a very bad way to be in those days) if they asked.

The thing was, watching the matings filled my brothers with an aimless sort of lust, as dangerous as it was unintentional. They knew enough to know that cows, months after mating, produced calves, but they were not bright enough to make the same connection between women and their offspring.

Sometimes, when I think of my childhood, it seems to me a particularly hard one. But in reality, everything awful that happened to me didn't seem to happen to me at all, but to my older sister. Through some incredible power to negate my presence around people I did not like, which produced invisibility (as well as an ability to appear mentally vacant when I was nothing of the kind), I was spared the humiliation she was subjected to, though at the same time, I felt every bit of it. It was as if she suffered for my benefit, and I vowed early in my life that none of the things that made existence so miserable for her would happen to me.

The fact that she was not allowed at official matings did not mean she never saw any. While my brothers followed my father to the mating pens on the other side of the road near the barn, she stationed herself near the pigpen, or followed our many dogs until they were in a mating mood, or, failing to witness something there, she watched the chickens. On a farm it is impossible not to be conscious of sex, to wonder about it, to dream . . . but to whom was she to speak of her feelings? Not to my father, who thought all young women perverse. Not to my mother, who pretended all her children grew out of stumps she magically found in the forest. Not to me, who never found anything wrong with this lie.

When my sister menstruated she wore a thick packet of clean rags between her legs. It stuck out in front like a penis. The boys laughed at her as she served them at the table. Not knowing any better, and because our parents did not dream of actually discussing what was going on, she would giggle nervously at herself. I hated her for giggling, and it was at those times I would think of her as dim-witted. She never complained, but she began to have strange fainting fits whenever she had her period. Her head felt as if it were splitting, she said, and everything she ate came up again. And her cramps were so severe she could not stand. She was forced to spend several days of each month in bed.

My father expected all of his sons to have sex with women. "Like bulls," he said, "a man needs to get a little something on his stick." And so, on Saturday nights, into town they went, chasing the girls. My sister was rarely allowed into town alone, and if the dress she wore fit too snugly at the waist, or if her cleavage dipped too far below her collarbone, she was made to stay home.

"But why can't I go too," she would cry, her faced screwed up with the effort not to wail.

"They're boys, your brothers, that's why they can go."

Naturally, when she got the chance, she responded eagerly to boys. But when this was discovered she was whipped and locked up in her room.

I would go in and visit her.

"Straight Pine," she would say, "you don't know what it feels like to want to be loved by a man."

"And if this is what you get for feeling like it I never will," I said, with—I hoped—the right combination of sympathy and disgust.

"Men smell so good," she would whisper ecstatically. "And when they look into your eyes, you just melt."

Since they were so hard to catch, naturally she thought almost any of them terrific.

"Oh, that Alfred!" she would moon over some mediocre, square-headed boy, "he's so sweet!" And she would take his ugly picture out of her bosom and kiss it.

My father was always warning her not to come home if she ever found herself pregnant. My mother constantly reminded her that abortion was a sin. Later, although she never became pregnant, her period would not come for months at a time. The painful symptoms, however, never varied or ceased. She fell for the first man who loved her enough to beat her for looking at someone else, and when I was still in high school, she married him.

My fifth brother, the one I never knew, was said to be different from the rest. He had not liked matings. He would not watch them. He thought the cows should be given a choice. My father had disliked him because he was soft. My mother took up for him. "Jason is just tender-hearted," she would say in a way that made me know he was her favorite; "he takes after me." It was true that my mother cried about almost anything.

Who was this oldest brother? I wondered.

"Well," said my mother, "he was someone who always loved you. Of course he was a great big boy when you were born and out working on his own. He worked on a road gang building roads. Every morning before he left he would come in the room where you were and pick you up and give you the biggest kisses. He used to look at you and just smile. It's a pity you don't remember him."

I agreed.

At my father's funeral I finally "met" my oldest brother. He is tall and black with thick gray hair above a young-looking face. I watched my sister cry over my father until she blacked out from grief. I saw my brothers sobbing, reminding each other of what a great father he had been. My oldest brother and I did not shed a tear between us. When I left my father's grave he came up and introduced himself. "You don't ever have to walk alone," he said, and put his arms around me.

One out of five ain't too bad, I thought, snuggling up.

But I didn't discover until recently his true uniqueness: He is the only one of my brothers who assumes responsibility for all his children. The other four all fathered children during those Saturday-night chases of twenty years ago. Children—my nieces and nephews whom I will probably never know—they neither acknowledge as their own, provide for, or even see.

It was not until I became a student of women's liberation ideology that I could understand and forgive my father. I needed an ideology that would define his behavior in context. The black movement had given me an ideology that helped explain his colorism (he did fall in love with my mother partly because she was so light; he never denied it). Feminism helped explain his sexism. I was relieved to know his sexist behavior was not something uniquely his own, but, rather, an imitation of the behavior of the society around us.

All partisan movements add to the fullness of our understanding of society as a whole. They never detract; or, in any case, one must not allow them to do so. Experience adds to experience. "The more things the better," as O'Connor and Welty both have said, speaking, one of marriage, the other of Catholicism.

I desperately needed my father and brothers to give me male models I could respect, because white men (for example; being particularly handy in this sort of comparison)—whether in films or in person—offered man as dominator, as killer, and always as hypocrite.

My father failed because he copied the hypocrisy. And my brothers—except for one—never understood they must represent half the world to me, as I must represent the other half to them.

IV. Russell Baker is a humorist who writes regularly for magazines and newspapers. In this newspaper column Baker demonstrates one hazard of writing with a computer: the temptation to revise before any text has been produced.

The Wonders of Writing on a Computer
Russell Baker

The wonderful thing about writing with a computer instead of a typewriter or a lead pencil is that it's so easy to rewrite that you can make each sentence almost perfect before moving on to the next sentence.

An impressive aspect of using a computer to write with

One of the plusses about a computer on which to write

Happily, the computer is a marked improvement over both the typewriter and the lead pencil for purposes of literary composi-

Copyright © 1987 by The New York Times Company. Reprinted by permission.

tion, due to the ease with which rewriting can be effectuated, thus enabling

What a marked improvement the computer is for the writer over the typewriter and lead pencil

The typewriter and lead pencil were good enough in their day, but if Shakespeare had been able to access a computer with a good writing program

If writing friends scoff when you sit down at the computer and say, "The lead pencil was good enough for Shakespeare"

One of the drawbacks of having a computer on which to write is the ease and rapidity with which the writing can be done, thus leading to the inclusion of many superfluous terms like "lead pencil," when the single word "pencil" would be completely, entirely and utterly adequate.

The ease with which one can rewrite on a computer gives it an advantage over such writing instruments as the pencil and typewriter by enabling the writer to turn an awkward and graceless sentence into one that is practically perfect, although it

The writer's eternal quest for the practically perfect sentence may be ending at last, thanks to the computer's gift of editing ease and swiftness to those confronting awkward, formless, nasty, illiterate sentences such as

Man's quest is eternal, but what specifically is it that he quests, and why does he

Mankind's quest is

Man's and woman's quest

Mankind's and womankind's quest

Humanity's quest for the perfect writing device

Eternal has been humanity's quest

Eternal have been many of humanity's quests

From the earliest cave writing, eternal has been the quest for a device that will forever prevent writers from using the word "quest," particularly when modified by such adjectives as "eternal," "endless," "tireless" and

Many people are amazed at the ease

Many persons are amazed by the ease

Lots of people are astounded when they see the nearly perfect sentences I write since upgrading my writing instrumentation from pencil and typewriter to

Listen, folks, there's nothing to writing almost perfect sentences with ease and rapidity provided you've given up the old horse-and-buggy writing mentality that says Shakespeare couldn't have written those great plays if he had enjoyed the convenience of electronic compositional instrumentation.

Folks, have you ever realized that there's nothing to writing almost

Have you ever stopped to think, folks, that maybe Shakespeare could have written even better if

To be or not to be, that is the central focus of the inquiry.

In the intrapersonal relationship played out within the mind as to the relative merits of continuing to exist as opposed to not continuing to exist

Live or die, a choice as ancient as humanities' eternal quest, is a tough choice which has confounded mankind as well as womankind ever since the option of dreaming was first perceived as a potentially negating effect of the quiescence assumed to be obtainable through the latter course of action.

I'm sick and tired of Luddites saying pencils and typewriters are just as good as computers for writing nearly perfect sentences when they—the Luddites, that is—have never experienced the swiftness and ease of computer writing which makes it possible to compose almost perfect sentences in practically no time at

Folks, are you sick and tired of

Are you, dear reader

Good reader, are you

A lot of you nice folks out there are probably just as sick and tired as I am of hearing people say they are sick and tired of this and that and

Listen, people, I'm just as sick and tired as you are of having writers and TV commercial performers who oil me in cornpone politician prose addressed to "you nice folks out

A curious feature of computers, as opposed to pencils and typewriters, is that when you ought to be writing something more interesting than a nearly perfect sentence

Since it is easier to revise and edit with a computer than with a typewriter or pencil, this amazing machine makes it very hard to stop editing and revising long enough to write a readable sentence, much less an entire newspaper column.

V. In Chapter Five you worked on a meditation, exploring a place and examining the memories and ideas raised by that place. In

"Table Talk," Faye Sudgen performs the same action with a thing: a kitchen table. The essay first appeared in *Country Living* magazine.

Table Talk
Faye Sudgen

If one were to try to find the center, well, and hub of a country family's life, the humble kitchen table would certainly emerge as the focal point. Whereas other areas of the house and other pieces of furniture hold more honor, the plebeian kitchen table witnesses the gamut of country life and links the individual members of the family. It's the place where a family unites at breakfast to begin the day's activities, comes together again briefly at noon, and reunites at supper to share the day's adventures. Dining-room tables are formal and distinguished, but the kitchen table is simple and relaxed, welcoming the good home-cooked meals that come its way.

It is the perfect place for pork and beans, a prime-rib roast with all the trimmings, a TV dinner, or a pepperoni pizza. The kitchen table is not a snob.

However, the kitchen table is more than a congenial filling station. It is also the place where babies are dressed and changed, socks are sorted, clothes are mended, and gossip is swapped. It's the round table of discussion or a quiet corner for secrets. It's the perfect place to talk about the weather, the latest grain prices, or what happened at school today. A steaming cup of coffee or an amiable game of cards with friends can be truly savored only at the kitchen table. Here, family arguments are won and lost, advice is sought and counsel given, and tears are wiped away from children's eyes following physical and emotional cuts and bruises. Pictures are painted, bread is kneaded, and cakes are mixed. The kitchen table is a quiet haven in the morning before anyone else is up, and it is the perfect place to read the Bible, a new recipe, or the instructions and guarantee for the lawn mower. It's the place to browse through a magazine or the funnies in blissful in-

Reprinted by permission from the October 1988 issue of COUNTRY LIVING, © 1988 by the Hearst Corporation.

dolence or study diligently for your next algebra exam. You can use the kitchen table to shine your shoes or pot a dainty plant. You can welcome the sunrise here or burn the midnight oil. It is the place to face reality and pay the bills as well as a place to dream and build elaborate castles in the air.

My table is a warm golden brown. It is oak and has a pedestal base and four ladder-back chairs. With its two leaves it sits ten friends comfortably. An anniversary present from us to us, our table is frankly beautiful. It is the aristocrat of the many kitchen tables we have had in our sixteen years of marriage. The last was much like the others, a Formica-and-aluminum number held together since the 1960s with a lot of soldering. Its latest home had been a Goodwill store from which the impoverished like us furnished their homes. The table was hopelessly scratched and shook incessantly whenever people wrote on it or ate from it, which they did constantly. Still, it served heroically, and the good times it supported were never missing even though the table's screws were.

My parents' kitchen table for many years was an enamel-topped box with four straight wooden legs and a drawer for cutlery in the middle. One of my biggest thrills as a child was being able to see over the top of that table unassisted. Here, I learned to make bread, mixing it up in my mother's huge blue plastic tub. It is where I did my homework, cried over boyfriends, and learned to can fruit and vegetables. The table became a utility table and was finally relegated to some dark, dusty corner of our barn. Too bad. Sometimes I miss that old table and the experiences that went with it.

My mother-in-law's table is a dark, flared oak Queen Anne-style antique. It is always covered with oilcloth, except for special occasions, when it is dressed up with a beautiful pure-white linen cloth, a Norwegian heirloom. Every inning, period, and quarter of every game known to man (or so it seems to my long-suffering "Ma") has been discussed, mulled over, and dissected at that table. Religion and politics have been hotly debated there. Many family reunions have had their start in the kitchen around the table as the ladies—aunts, mothers, cousins, and grandmas—prepared the noon meal. My mother-in-law has cooked, sewn, embroidered, knitted, crocheted, quilted, played games, and washed the family's dishes all from the same spot at the foot of that old beautiful table.

Yet though kitchens and styles may differ, one thing remains constant: Be it beautiful or ugly, antique or brand new, pine or Plexiglas, the kitchen table has an undeniable, immovable place in our country hearts.

VI. Jim Courter's essay "It's All in the Jeans" originally appeared in the *Western Courier*. It is a meditation which finds its beginning in one of the chief cultural artifacts of our time.

It's All in the Jeans
Jim Courter

A friend of mine in high school—we were class of '65—used to beat a new pair of jeans against the side of his garage, against a gnarly old tree trunk in his back yard, or jump up and down and stomp them into the yard itself, between washings, over and over, before ever wearing them. He claimed to be beating the newness and stiffness out, and while that might have been true, knowing my friend, I knew that he was also trying to beat a certain look into them. Like all the guys, he wanted that rough-and-tumble look, and like most of the guys he didn't want to have to live rough and get tumbled to have it.

Then as now, image was everything, and of all the things that added to it—brains, hair, complexion—few were as important as jeans.

New jeans, for instance, carried a stigma, the same one that attached to new, spanking-white sneakers; they gave you the look of a kid who would make his mother proud, who helped out around the house and got homework done on time, a *nice* boy, and in the crowd we ran with that was the last thing you wanted to be.

What you did want to be was a tough guy, someone nobody would care to mess with. But since most of us were about as tough as a cocker spaniel pup, we had to settle for looking the part, and the key to that was faded, beat-up jeans. They were our

---

Reprinted from Jim Courter, "It's All in the Jeans," Western COURIER, October 6, 1989, © Western COURIER. Reprinted with permission.

badge of initiation, our attempt to convince people that we had paid our dues in the coin of experience. Of course scruffy jeans didn't make you tough, but without them, no matter how tough you were, you had a big credibility problem.

But it took forever to break in a new pair of jeans. They might have been cut from a circus tent and dyed in the Blue Nile under a blue moon for all our puny attempts at roughhousing could soften or fade them. We didn't have stone-washed jeans in those days, which was too bad; they would have saved my friend a lot of effort and his mom, who threatened to do to him what he did to his jeans, much pulling of hair and gnashing of teeth.

Now the big selling point to stone-washed jeans is that they are supposed to give you right off the rack that broken-in feel and appearance. In fact they look like they've been worked over by an avant-garde artist with a bottle of bleach. But the trick, as in high school, is to pretend. Even if your idea of adventure is a trip to a shopping mall in an outlying suburb, you can walk around in your stone-washed jeans like you just got back from hacking your way with a machete through an equatorial rain forest or doing battle as a soldier of fortune in some Third World guerrilla war. You don't have to spend months breaking in a new pair or go to the trouble my friend went to.

He usually got the effect he was after, though. By the time he put on his jeans for the first time they looked like he had trekked in them from Katmandu to Ulan Bator. All swagger and sneer, he'd haunt the hallways at school, thumbs hitched into his pockets, looking ready to pounce. It was an impressive show, and I used to hang around taking mental notes on style until he'd run me off, probably because I knew his secret.

Personally, I never tried very hard for the tough look. It seemed too much trouble, and I must have sensed that I couldn't pull it off, with my squeaky voice and sticks for arms. Besides, by the time I got my jeans to that well-worn state, my mom considered them beyond respectability and cut them up for rags. They'd disappear from my closet, in their place a brand new pair with the tags still on, blue as a bruise and stiff as tree bark. I never bothered complaining because I knew how much good it would do and the line she'd give me: "When I was your age I *had* to wear old clothes to school. You father works hard so that you don't have to, so that you can look *nice*."

They grew up during the Depression, see, and there was no end of hearing about all the hardships they had endured as kids—walking for miles through knee-deep snow to school, getting up at three A.M. to work at a job that paid a dollar a year. You know the stuff. They wanted me to know how easy I had it compared to them. And I suppose I did.

But as awed as I was by those stories, I couldn't help wondering when I heard them what I'd be able to tell any kids of mine to impress them with how easy they have it compared to me. How does this sound?

"Son, in my day, we didn't have stone-washed jeans. Talk about *hardship*."

VII. Nancy Mairs is a poet and essayist whose work explores issues of feminism, parenthood, handicaps, and writing. In "On Being a Cripple" she meditates on her illness, explores the issues, and reaches tentatively toward insight.

On Being a Cripple
Nancy Mairs

> *"To escape is nothing. Not to escape is nothing."*
> Louise Bogans

The other day I was thinking of writing an essay on being a cripple. I was thinking hard in one of the stalls of the women's room in my office building, as I was shoving my shirt into my jeans and tugging up my zipper. Preoccupied, I flushed, picked up my book bag, took my cane down from the hook, and unlatched the door. So many movements unbalanced me, and as I pulled the door open I fell over backwards, landing fully clothed on the toilet set with my legs splayed in front of me: the old beetle-on-its-back routine. Saturday afternoon, the building deserted, I was free to laugh aloud as I wriggled back to my feet, my voice bouncing off the yellowish tiles from all directions. Had anyone

From Nancy Mairs, PLAINTEXT. Copyright © 1986 by University of Arizona Press. Reprinted with permission.

been there with me, I'd have been still and faint and hot with chagrin. I decided that it was high time to write the essay.

First, the matter of semantics. I am a cripple. I choose this word to name me. I choose from among several possibilities, the most common of which are "handicapped" and "disabled." I made the choice a number of years ago, without thinking, unaware of my motives for doing so. Even now, I'm not sure what those motives are, but I recognize that they are complex and not entirely flattering. People—crippled or not—wince at the word "cripple," as they do not at "handicapped" or "disabled." Perhaps I want them to wince. I want them to see me as a tough customer, one to whom the fates/gods/viruses have not been kind, but who can face the brutal truth of her existence squarely. As a cripple, I swagger.

But, to be fair to myself, a certain amount of honesty underlies my choice. "Cripple" seems to me a clean word, straightforward and precise. It has an honorable history, having made its first appearance in the Lindisfarne Gospel in the tenth century. As a lover of words, I like the accuracy with which it describes my condition: I have lost the full use of my limbs. "Disabled," by contrast, suggests any incapacity, physical or mental. And I certainly don't like "handicapped," which implies that I have deliberately been put at a disadvantage, by whom I can't imagine (my God is not a Handicapper General), in order to equalize chances in the great race of life. These words seem to me to be moving away from my condition, to be widening the gap between word and reality. Most remote is the recently coined euphemism "differently abled," which partakes of the same semantic hopefulness that transformed countries from "undeveloped" to "underdeveloped," then to "less developed," and finally to "developing" nations. People have continued to starve in those countries during the shift. Some realities do not obey the dictates of language.

Mine is one of them. Whatever you call me, I remain crippled. But I don't care what you call me, so long as it isn't "differently abled," which strikes me as pure verbal garbage designed, by its ability to describe anyone, to describe no one. I subscribe to George Orwell's thesis that "the slovenliness of our language makes it easier for us to have foolish thoughts." And I refuse to participate in the degeneration of the language to the extent that I deny that I have lost anything in the course of this calamitous disease; I refuse to pretend that the only differences between you and me are the various ordinary ones that distinguish any one person from another. But call me "disabled" or "handicapped" if you like. I have long since grown accustomed to them; and if they are vague, at least they hint at the truth. Moreover, I use them myself. Society is no readier to accept crippledness than to accept death, war, sex, sweat, or wrinkles. I would never refer to another person as a cripple. It is the word I use to name only myself.

I haven't always been crippled, a fact for which I am soundly grateful. To be whole of limb is, I know from experience, infinitely more pleasant and useful than to be crippled; and if that knowledge leaves me open to bitterness at my loss, the physical soundness I once enjoyed (though I did not enjoy it half enough) is well worth the occasional stab of regret. Though never any good at sports, I was a normally active child and young adult. I climbed trees, played hopscotch, jumped rope, skated, swam, rode my bicycle, sailed. I despised team sports, spending some of the wretchedest afternoons of my life, sweaty and humiliated, behind a field-hockey stick and under a basketball hoop. I tramped alone for miles along the bridle paths that webbed the woods behind the house I grew up in. I swayed through countless dim hours in the arms of one man or another under the scattered shot of light from mirrored balls, and gyrated through countless more as Tab Hunter and Johnny Mathis gave way the Rolling Stones, Credence Clearwater Revival, Cream. I walked down the aisle. I pushed baby carriages, changed tires in the rain, marched for peace.

When I was twenty-eight I started to trip and drop things. What at first seemed my natural clumsiness soon became too pronounced to shrug off. I consulted a neurologist, who told me that I had a brain tumor. A battery of tests, increasingly disagreeable, revealed no tumor. About a year and a half later I developed a blurred spot in one eye. I had, at last, the episodes "disseminated in space and time" requisite for a diagnosis: multiple sclerosis. I have never been sorry for the doctor's initial misdiagnosis, however. For almost a week, until the negative results of the tests were in, I thought that I was going to die right away. Every day for the past nearly ten years, then, has been a kind of gift. I accept all gifts.

Multiple sclerosis is a chronic degenerative disease of the central nervous system, in which the myelin that sheathes the nerves is somehow eaten away and scar tissue forms in its place, interrupting the nerves' signals. During its course, which is unpredictable and uncontrollable, one may lose vision, hearing, speech, the ability to walk, control of bladder and/or bowels, strength in any or all extremities, sensitivity to touch, vibration, and/or pain, potency, coordination of movements—the list of possibilities is lengthy and, yes, horrifying. One may also lose one's sense of humor. That's the easiest to lose and the hardest to survive without.

In the past ten years, I have sustained some of these losses. Characteristic of MS are sudden attacks, called exacerbations, followed by remissions, and these I have not had. Instead, my disease has been slowly progressive. My left leg is now so weak that I walk with the aid of a brace and a cane; and for distances I use an Amigo, a variation on the electric wheelchair that looks rather like an electrified kiddie car. I no longer have much use of my left hand. Now my right side is weakening as well. I still have the blurred spot in my right eye. Overall, though, I've been lucky so far. My world has, of necessity, been circumscribed by my losses, but the terrain left me has been ample enough for me to continue many of the activities that absorb me: writing, teaching, raising children and cats and plants and snakes, reading, speaking publicly about MS and depression, even playing bridge with people patient and honorable enough to let me scatter cards every which way without sneaking a peek.

Lest I begin to sound like Pollyanna, however, let me say that I don't like having MS. I hate it. My life holds realities—harsh ones, some of them—that no right-minded human being ought to accept without grumbling. One of them is fatigue. I know of no one with MS who does not complain of bone-weariness; in a disease that presents an astonishing variety of symptoms, fatigue seems to be a common factor. I wake up in the morning feeling the way most people do at the end of a bad day, and I take it from there. As a result, I spend a lot of time *in extremis* and, impatient with limitation, I tend to ignore my fatigue until my body breaks down in some way and forces rest. Then I miss picnics, dinner parties, poetry readings, the brief visits of old friends from out of town. The offspring of a puritanical tradition of exceptional venerability, I cannot view these lapses without shame. My life often seems a series of small failures to do as I ought.

I lead, on the whole, an ordinary life, probably rather like the one I would have led had I not had MS. I am lucky that my predilections were already solitary, sedentary, and bookish—unlike the world-famous French cellist I have read about, or the young woman I talked with one long afternoon who wanted only to be a jockey. I had just begun graduate school when I found out something was wrong with me, and I have remained, interminably, a graduate student. Perhaps I would not have if I'd thought I had the stamina to return to a full-time job as a technical editor; but I've enjoyed my studies.

In addition to studying, I teach writing courses. I also teach medical students how to give neurological examinations. I pick up freelance editing jobs here and there. I have raised a foster son and sent him into the world, where he has made me two grandbabies, and I am still escorting my daughter and son through adolescence. I go to Mass every Saturday. I am a superb, if messy, cook. I am also an enthusiastic laundress, capable of sorting a hamper full of clothes into five subtly differentiated piles, but a terrible housekeeper. I can do italic writing and, in an emergency, bathe an oil-soaked cat. I play a fiendish game of Scrabble. When I have the time and the money, I like to sit on my front steps with my husband, drinking Amaretto and smoking a cigar, as we imagine our counterparts in Leningrad and make sure that the sun gets down once more behind the sharp childish scrawl of the Tucson Mountains.

This lively plenty has its bleak complement, of course, in all the things I can no longer do. I will never run again, except in dreams, and one day I may have to write that I will never walk again. I like to go camping, but I can't follow George and the children along the trails that wander out of a campsite through the desert or into the mountains. In fact, even on the level I've learned never to check the weather or try to hold a coherent conversation: I need all my attention for my wayward feet. Of late, I have begun to catch myself wondering how people can propel themselves without canes. With only one usable hand, I have to select my clothing with care not so much for style as for ease of ingress and egress, and even so, dressing can be laborious. I can no longer do fine stitchery, pick up babies, play the piano, braid my hair. I am immobilized by acute attacks of depression, which may or may not be physiologically related to MS but are certainly its logical concomitant.

These two elements, the plenty and the privation, are never pure, nor are the delight and wretchedness that accompany them. Almost every pickle that I get into as a result of my weakness and clumsiness—and I get into plenty—is funny as well as maddening and sometimes painful. I recall one May afternoon when a friend and I were going out for a drink after finishing up at school. As we were climbing into opposite sides of my car, chatting, I tripped and fell, flat and hard, onto the asphalt parking lot, my abrupt departure interrupting him in mid-sentence. "Where'd you go?" he called as he came around the back of the car to find me hauling myself up by the door frame. "Are you all right?" Yes, I told him, I was fine, just a bit rattly, and we drove off to find a shady patio and some beer. When I got home an hour or so later, my daughter greeted me with "What have you done to yourself?" I looked down. One elbow of my white turtleneck with the green froggies, one knee of my white trousers, one white kneesock were blood-soaked. We peeled off the clothes and inspected the damage, which was nasty enough but not alarming. That part wasn't funny: The abrasions took a long time to heal, and one got a little infected. Even so, when I think of my friend talking earnestly, suddenly, to the hot thin air while I dropped from his view as though through a trap door, I find the image as silly as something from a Marx Brothers movie.

I may find it easier than other cripples to amuse myself because I live propped by the acceptance and the assistance and, sometimes, the amusement of those around me. Grocery clerks tear my checks out of my checkbook for me, and sales clerks find chairs to put into dressing rooms when I want to try on clothes. The people I work with make sure I teach at times when I am least likely to be fatigued, in places I can get to, with the materials I need. My students, with one anonymous exception (in an end-of-the-semester evaluation), have been unperturbed by my disability. Some even like it. One was immensely cheered by the information that I paint my own fingernails; she decided, she told me, that if I could go to such trouble over fine details, she could keep on writing essays. I suppose I became some sort of bright-fingered muse. She wrote good essays, too.

The most important struts in the framework of my existence, of course, are my husband and children. Dismayingly few marriages survive the MS test, and why should they? Most twenty-two- and nineteen-year-olds, like George and me, can vow in clear conscience, after a childhood of chickenpox and summer colds, to keep one another in sickness and in health so long as they both shall live. Not many are equipped for catastrophe: the dismay, the depression, the extra work, the boredom that a degenerative disease can insinuate into a relationship. And our society, with its emphasis on fun and its association of fun with physical performance, offers little encouragement for a whole spouse to stay with a crippled partner. Children experience similar stresses when faced with a crippled parent, and they are more helpless, since parents and children can't usually get divorced. They hate, of course, to be different from their peers, and the child whose mother is tacking down the aisle of a school auditorium packed with proud parents like a Cape Cod dinghy in a stiff breeze jolly well stands out in a crowd. Deprived of legal divorce, the child can at least deny the mother's disability, even her existence, forgetting to tell her about recitals and PTA meetings, refusing to accompany her to stores or church or the movies, never inviting friends to the house. Many do.

But I've been limping along for ten years now, and so far George and the children are still at my left elbow, holding tight. Anne and Matthew vacuum floors and dust furniture and haul trash and rake up dog droppings and button my cuffs and bake lasagna and Toll House cookies with just enough grumbling so I know that they don't have brain fever. And far from hiding me, they're forever dragging me by racks of fancy clothes or through teeming school corridors, or welcoming gaggles of friends while I'm wandering through the house in Anne's filmy pink babydoll pajamas. George generally calls before he brings someone home, but he does just as many dumb thankless chores as the children. And they all yell at me, laugh at some of my jokes, write me funny letters when we're apart—in short, treat me as an ordinary human being for whom they have some use. I think they like me. Unless they're faking. . . .

Faking. There's the rub. Tugging at the fringes of my consciousness always is the terror that people are kind to me only because I'm a cripple. My mother almost shattered me once, with that instinct mothers have—blind, I think, in this case, but unerring nonetheless—for striking blows along the fault-lines of their children's hearts, by telling me, in an attack on my selfishness, "We all have to make allowances for you, of course, because of the way you are." From the distance of a couple of years, I have to admit that I haven't any idea just what she meant, and I'm not sure that she knew either. She was awfully angry. But at the time, as the words thudded home, I felt my worst fear, suddenly realized. I could bear being called selfish: I am. But I couldn't bear the corroboration that those around me were doing in fact what I'd always suspected them of doing, professing fondness while silently putting up with me because of the way I am. A cripple. I've been a little cracked ever since.

Along with this fear that people are secretly accepting shoddy goods comes a relentless pressure to please—to prove myself worth the burdens I impose, I guess, or to build a substantial account of goodwill against which I may write drafts in times of need. Part of the pressure arises from social expectations. In our society, anyone who deviates from the norm had better find some way to compensate. Like fat people, who are expected to be jolly, cripples must bear their lot meekly and cheerfully. A grumpy cripple isn't playing by the rules. And much of the pressure is self-generated. Early on I vowed that, if I had to have MS, by God I was going to do it well. This is a class act, ladies and gentlemen. No tears, no recriminations, no faint-heartedness.

One way and another, then, I wind up feeling like Tiny Tim, peering over the edge of the table at the Christmas goose, waving my crutch, piping down God's blessing on us all. Only sometimes I don't want to play Tiny Tim. I'd rather be Caliban, a most scurvy monster. Fortunately, at home no one much cares whether I'm a good cripple or a bad cripple as long as I make vichyssoise with fair regularity. One evening several years ago, Anne was reading at the dining room table while I cooked dinner. As I opened a can of tomatoes, the can slipped in my left hand and juice spattered me and the counter with bloody spots. Fatigued and infuriated, I bellowed, "I'm so sick of being crippled!" Anne glanced at me over the top of her book. "There now," she said, "do you feel better?" "Yes," I said, "yes, I do." She went back to her reading. I felt better. That's about all the attention my scurviness ever gets.

Because I hate being crippled, I sometimes hate myself for being a cripple. Over the years I have come to expect—even accept—attacks of violent self-loathing. Luckily, in general our society no longer connects deformity and disease directly with evil (though a charismatic once told me that I have MS because a devil is in me) and so I'm allowed to move largely at will, even among small children. But I'm not sure that this revision of attitude has been particulary helpful. Physical imperfection, even freed of moral disapprobation, still defies and violates the ideal, especially for women, whose confinement in their bodies as objects of desire is far from over. Each age, of course, has its ideal, and I doubt that ours is any better or worse than any other. Today's ideal woman, who lives on the glossy pages of dozens of magazines, seems to be between the ages of eighteen and twenty-five; her hair has body, her teeth flash white, her breath smells minty, her underarms are dry; she has a career but is still a fabulous cook, especially of meals that take less than twenty minutes to prepare; she does not ordinarily appear to have a husband or children, she is trim and deeply tanned; she jogs, swims, plays tennis, rides a bicycle, sails, but does not bowl; she travels widely, even to out-of-the-way places like Finland and Samoa, always in the company of the ideal man, who possesses a nearly identical set of characteristics. There are a few exceptions. Though usually white and often blonde, she may be black, Hispanic, Asian, or Native American, so long as she is usually sleek. She may be old, provided she is selling a laxative or is Lauren Bacall. If she is selling a detergent, she may be married and have a flock of strikingly messy children. But she is never a cripple.

Like many women I know, I have always had an uneasy relationship with my body. I was not a popular child, largely, I think now, because I was peculiar: intelligent, intense, moody, shy, given to unexpected actions and inexplicable notions and emotions. But as I entered adolescence, I believed myself unpopular because I was homely: my breasts too flat, my mouth too wide, my hips too narrow, my clothing never quite right in fit or style. I was not, in fact, particularly ugly, old photographs inform me, though I was well off the ideal; but I carried this sense of self-alienation with me into adulthood, where it regenerated in response to the depredations of MS. Even with my brace I walk with a limp so pronounced that, seeing myself on the videotape of a television program on the disabled, I couldn't believe that anything but an inchworm could make progress humping along like that. My shoulders droop and my pelvis thrusts forward as I try to balance myself upright, throwing my frame into a bony S. As a result of contractures, one shoulder is higher than the other and I carry one arm bent in front of me, the fingers curled into a claw.

My left arm and leg have wasted into pipe-stems, and I try always to keep them covered. When I think about how my body must look to others, especially to men, to whom I have been trained to display myself, I feel ludicrous, even loathsome.

At my age, however, I don't spend much time thinking about my appearance. The burning egocentricity of adolescence, which assures one that all the world is looking all the time, that passed, thank God, and I'm generally too caught up in what I'm doing to step back, as I used to, and watch myself as though upon a stage. I'm also too old to believe in the accuracy of self-image. I know that I'm not a hideous crone, that in fact, when I'm rested, well-dressed, and well made up, I look fine. The self-loathing I feel is neither physically nor intellectually substantial. What I hate is not me but a disease.

I am not a disease.

And a disease is not—at least singlehandedly—going to determine who I am, though at first it seemed to be going to. Adjusting to a chronic incurable illness, I have moved through a process similar to that outlined by Elizabeth Kubler-Ross in *On Death and Dying*. The major differences—and it is far more significant than most people recognize—is that I can't be sure of the outcome, as the terminally ill cancer patient can. Research studies indicate that, with proper medical care, I may achieve a "normal" life span. And in our society, with its vision of death as the ultimate evil, worse even than decrepitude, the response to such new is, "Oh well, at least you're not going to *die.*" Are there worse things than dying? I think that there may be.

I think of two women I know, both with MS, both enough older than I to have served me as models. One took to her bed several years ago and has been there ever since. Although she can sit in a high-backed wheelchair, because she is incontinent she refuses to go out at all, even though incontinence pants, which are readily available at any pharmacy, could protect her from embarrassment. Instead she stays at home and insists that her husband, a small quiet man, a retired civil servant, stay there with her except for a quick weekly foray to the supermarket. The other woman, whose illness was diagnosed when she was eighteen, a nursing student engaged to a young doctor, finished her training, married her doctor, accompanied him to Germany when he was in the service, bore three sons and a daughter, now grown and gone. When she can, she travels with her husband; she plays bridge, embroiders, swims regularly; she works, like me, as a symptomatic-patient instructor of medical students in neurology. Guess which woman I hope to be.

At the beginning, I thought about having MS almost incessantly. And because of the unpredictable course of the disease, my thoughts were always terrified. Each night I'd get into bed wondering whether I'd get out again the next morning, whether I'd be able to see, to speak, to hold a pen between my fingers. Knowing that the day might come when I'd be physically incapable of killing myself, I thought perhaps I ought to do so right away, while I still had the strength. Gradually I came to understand that the Nancy who might one day lie inert under a bedsheet, arms and legs paralyzed, unable to feed or bathe herself, unable to reach out for a gun, a bottle of pills, was not the Nancy I was at present, and that I could not presume to make decisions for that future Nancy, who might well not want in the least to die. Now the only provision I've made for the future Nancy is that when the time comes—and it is likely to come in the form of pneumonia, friend to the weak and the old—I am not to be treated with machines and medications. If she is unable to communicate by then, I hope she will be satisfied with these terms.

Thinking all the time about having MS grew tiresome and intrusive, especially in the large and tragic mode in which I was accustomed to considering my plight. Months and even years went by without catastrophe (at least without one related to MS), and really I was awfully busy, what with George and children and snakes and students and poems, and I hadn't the time, let alone the inclination, to devote myself to being a disease. Too, the richer my life became, the funnier it seemed, as though there were some connection between largess and laughter, and so my tragic stance began to waver until, even with the aid of a brace and a cane, I couldn't hold it for very long at a time.

After several years I was satisfied with my adjustment. I had suffered my grief and fury and terror, I thought, but now I was at ease with my lot. Then one summer day I set out with George and the children across the desert for a vacation in California. Part way to Yuma I became aware that my right leg felt funny. "I think I've had an exacerbation," I told George. "What shall we do?" he asked. "I think we'd better get the hell to California," I said, "because I don't know whether I'll ever make it again." So we went on to San Diego and then to Orange, up the

Pacific Coast Highway to Santa Cruz, across to Yosemite, down to Sequoia and Joshua Tree, and so back over the desert to home. It was a fine two-week trip, filled with friends and fair weather, and I wouldn't have missed it for the world, though I did in fact make it back to California two years later. Nor would there have been any point in missing it, since in MS, once the symptoms have appeared, the neurological damage has been done, and there's no way to predict or prevent that damage.

The incident spoiled my self-satisfaction, however. It renewed my grief and fury and terror, and I learned that one never finishes adjusting to MS. I don't know now why I thought one would. One does not, after all, finish adjusting to life, and MS is simply a fact of my life—not my favorite fact, of course—but as ordinary as my nose and my tropical fish and my yellow Mazda station wagon. It may at any time get worse, but no amount of worry or anticipation can prepare me for a new loss. My life is a lesson in losses. I learn one at a time.

And I had best be patient in the learning, since I'll have to do it like it or not. As any rock fan knows, you can't always get what you want. Particularly when you have MS. You can't, for example, get cured. In recent years researchers and the organizations that fund research have started to pay MS some attention even though it isn't fatal; perhaps they have begun to see that life is something other than a quantitative phenomenon, that one may be very much alive for a very long time in a life that isn't worth living. The researchers have made some progress toward understanding the mechanism of the disease: It may well be an autoimmune reaction triggered by a slow-acting virus. But they are nowhere near its prevention, control, or cure. And most of us want to be cured. Some, unable to accept incurability, grasp at one treatment after another, no matter how bizarre: megavitamin therapy, gluten-free diet, injections of cobra venom, hypothermal suits, lymphocytopharesis, hyperbaric chambers. Many treatments are probably harmless enough, but none are curative.

The absence of a cure often makes MS patients bitter toward their doctors. Doctors are, after all, the priests of modern society, the new shamans, whose business is to heal, and many an MS patient roves from one another, searching for the "good" doctor who will make him well. Doctors too think of themselves as healers, and for this reason many have trouble dealing with MS patients, whose disease in its intransigence defeats their aims and mocks their skills. Too few doctors, it is true, treat their patients as whole human beings, but the reverse is also true. I have always tried to be gentle with my doctors, who often have more at stake in terms of ego than I do. I may be frustrated, maddened, depressed by the incurability of my disease, but I am not diminished by it, and they are. When I push myself up from my seat in the waiting room and stumble toward them, I incarnate the limitations of their powers. The least I can do is refuse to press on their tenderest spots.

This gentleness is part of the reason that I'm not sorry to be a cripple. I didn't have it before. Perhaps I'd have developed it anyway—how could I know such a thing?—and I wish I had more of it, but I'm glad of what I have. It has opened and enriched my life enormously, this sense that my frailty and need must be mirrored in others, that in searching for and shaping a stable core in a life wrenched by change and loss, change and loss, I must recognize the same process, under individual conditions, in the lives around me. I do not deprecate such knowledge, however I've come by it.

All the same, if a cure were found, would I take it? In a minute. I may be a cripple, but I'm only occasionally a loony and never a saint. Anyway, in my brand of theology God doesn't give bonus points for a limp. I'd take a cure; I just don't need one. A friend who also has MS startled me once by asking, "Do you ever say to yourself, 'Why me, Lord?' " "No, Michael, I don't," I told him, "because whenever I try, the only response I can think of is 'Why not?' " If I could make a cosmic deal, who would I put in my place? What in my life would I give up in exchange for sound limbs and a thrilling rush of energy? No one. Nothing. I might as well do the job myself. Now that I'm getting the hang of it.

VIII. The next essay is by an international student at WIU. In this memory-based essay, Ebrima A. Jow describes an event from his childhood. Notice the information he provides in the beginning of the essay. Knowing that his readers will probably be unfamiliar with many aspects of his culture, he wisely provides the necessary background.

That background reveals some differences within Islamic culture. Like Christianity, Islam contains many groups, with widely varying beliefs and practices. In this story difference between practices in the village and those of the nearby town are at the heart of the conflict. Ebrima's experience reveals to Western readers that no single voice represents Islamic belief, any more than any Christian represents all of Christianity.

The School Day
Ebrima A. Jow

Islam is my religion and that of my people. The followers of this religion are called Muslims. As Muslims, we are supposed to learn the Kor'an (the Muslim Bible), which explains all about Islam, how we should act to one another, and how to offer prayers in worshipping God.

The Imam in our village, the priest who leads people in prayer, also happened to be the Kor'anic teacher. It has been a common belief among my people that Western education was detrimental to their religion; thus nobody sent his or her child to school. They would say that if a child goes to school he would easily be converted into another faith or at best, become a drunkard. From time to time, after the prayers on Fridays, the Imam would give a lengthy sermon to the villagers urging them never to send their children to school. The idea was to learn the Kor'an for worshipping God and farming as an occupation.

I do not believe in this. I had the desire to go to school but I dared not discuss it with my dad. Not that I could not have told him, but I was afraid he might say no to me. That would have been the end of my dream. I was not sure if my father shared the same belief with the villagers. Anyway, I told my mother about it and she thought it was a good idea. That was on a Saturday, and school was supposed to open on Monday. I said to myself, only two days to go, I'd better get prepared for Monday.

I woke up early that Monday, put on my gown, opened the door gently, and set on my way to school even without having a bath. It was a three mile walk to the next town and I made sure that nobody knew I was gone. It was still dark and the cold breeze was blowing from the ocean. I had shaved my hair only

Reprinted with permission of the author.

two days before, and could feel the cold morning air blowing over my head, making it tickle. I walked cautiously through the village looking back from time to time. Everybody was still asleep and the silence was only interrupted by the occasional barking of dogs, the croaking of frogs, and the fluttering of birds' wings. I was a bit scared but still determined to move on. It was not until I walked about hundred yards away from the village that I was really frightened. I could sense a real danger ahead of me. I suddenly stopped for a moment, looked behind, up, down, but could not see anything besides the thick bush on either side of the road. There was courage once more and I started to forge ahead.

As I was about to enter the town, I saw a man on a bicycle pedaling toward me. The day was getting clear now and I could see him well. It was Imam. Only God knows where he was coming from that early in the morning. He was a very huge pompous man, and had a protruding belly. I did not like his looks. I was sure he had something to tell me.

"Who are you? Where are you going at this time of the day?"

"I am going to school, Sir."

"What! Say it again," he groaned at me angrily. "You better turn back now or I'll get the hell of you!"

"But I want to go to school, Sir," I insisted.

You can now imagine what happened next. The "raps" and "taps" rained on my cheeks, like the intermittent flow of current. Imam was on top of me now doing whatever he felt pleased him. He was not satisfied yet; he rushed for a long cane at the other side of the road. By the time he raised his hand to strike me I had already dodged, leaving him to battle with his own weight. "'Pum" was the only sound to describe how he fell down; and there he lay on his back like a hippopotamus.

By 8:30 A.M. I was at the school gate. It was the first day of the Fall Semester. There was a lot of excitement. The street was full of people: children and parents, not to mention teachers and pupils at the school grounds. There was shouting, jumping, clapping, kissing, and shaking of hands all over the place. Teachers, friends and classmates were happy to meet again after a long break of five months.

The "ding-dong" of the bell soon called everybody to a line-up in front of a school building. One of the men in front of the assembly came forward and started reading from a book he held.

I could hear everybody say "Amen." That was the school master giving a prayer, I thought. About fifteen minutes later, the assembly dispersed at the end of a lengthy speech delivered by the master.

I had not yet entered the school grounds for all this time. I sat on a wooden log that was just by the gate, curious to know whatever was going on in the yard. I was afraid to go in, but at the same time did not want to stay out any longer. I had a fear that Imam or my father might come after me. As my mind was debating over this, I saw the school master coming toward me.

"You'd better get up! Haven't you heard the bell?"

"Ahh," I said, not knowing what he was saying. He stood over me for sometime not saying anything. I was almost dying of fear and confusion. What was he going to do? Am I to be beaten again? What is he thinking about? My heart was beating very fast this time. I almost regretted that I had come.

Finally, he asked me in my language what I was doing there. I told him exactly what I had come for and he was really happy about it. He then invited me to his office, and this made me myself again. I followed him through a big classroom and then to a small room just at the corner. This was the office. A big table in the center, heavily covered with dust, was sandwiched by an old bookshelf on one side and a rusty filing cabinet on the other. The floor was tiled with dust and the ceiling painted with spider webs. The only two chairs in the office both had broken legs and these were supported with stones. From the smell, it was an easy guess that this room had not been opened throughout the break.

"I am sorry," he said to me bending his head down. "The janitor has not yet cleaned this place. I will deal with him severely." He took out his handkerchief, cleaned his seat and handed it over to me to clean the chair he asked me to sit on.

"What is your name? Where do you live? What is your father's name? How old are you?"

"I am ten years old, Sir."

"What! Ten years! Wait a minute."

He got up from his chair and rushed to another room. Minutes later he came back with a short man, who he introduced as Mr. Sambou, his assistant.

"Are you sure you are ten years old?" asked Mr. Sambou.

"Yes, I am Sir."

"But why did you not come with your father?" the school master went on.

"I did not tell him about it, sir. I am afraid he was not going to allow it."

"Where do you come from?" Mr. Sambou intervened.

"From Bijilo, sir."

"Ah! I see," he was now talking to his boss. "This boy is right. Those people are against Western education and his father will never send him to school. Although he is over-aged, I think we should give him a chance."

"O.K.!" Master said to me. "You are now enrolled in the school. You can go with him and he will take you to your classroom."

I entered the class and found that I was the first to be there. Later I was joined by ten girls and twenty boys, all of whom came from the town. A young man came in and introduced himself as our teacher. He wrote our names down in his register and asked us to go home but to come on time the following day. I just cannot tell you how happy I was at that moment. It was just wonderful.

On my way home I met up with my friend, Ousman. He told me that Imam had reported me to my father and that I would likely be scolded on arrival. Ousman has not been to school and he is now a very poor farmer in the village. When I was coming to the States, he told me that if he had anything to regret in life it was the fact that he had not been to school.

Imam was giving his sermons again. Lots of people gathered around under the big mango tree that was not far from our house. I could observe how everybody was looking at me as I passed as if I had done something abominable. Imam looked at me and suddenly gave his back as if he did not want to set an eye on me. I do not know what he had told these people, but for sure it was not anything good about me. I suddenly had a feeling of deep guilt. I bent my head down and tried to suppress my feelings as I walked past.

When I arrived home I found my father seated in the parlor reading his Kor'an peacefully. I greeted him and to my surprise, he returned the greetings nicely and smiled at me.

"Sit down my son. Imam has told me everything about it— but I told him that he had no right to beat you up. I do not share with the villagers the belief they hold about Western education or going to school. I did not send you to school simply because I wanted you to help me on my farm, since I am alone. Now that you did it by yourself, it would be only fair that I give you all the support you need. As a matter of fact, I know of some men in this village who secretly drink alcohol, and they haven't gone to school either. I only hope that you will not disappoint me."

As my mind reflects on all the past memories of that great day, I feel proud that both my parents and I have nothing to regret.

IX. On July 25, 1989, two people were shot on the University of Washington campus. The next day the shooting was reported on the front page of the campus newspaper, *The Daily*. Inside, editor-in-chief Diana L. Meredith examined the ethical issues involved in reporting a violent crime. It was reprinted nationally in *U*.

Covering Campus Tragedy
Diana L. Meredith

This is my sixth attempt at writing this commentary.

Yesterday, several reporters, photographers and I dealt with many questions after two people were shot on campus.

I wanted to write a thoughtful essay on the dilemmas that a newspaper staff, especially this one, faces when covering a homicide. I can't seem to put my thoughts together cohesively, so I decided to subject my readers to something I swore I would never do: the stream-of-consciousness commentary.

The following is an approximation of everything that went through my mind yesterday.

Should I run a picture of the body? Should we run a picture at all? Where are my photographers? Oh, someone got recruited. Two guys have never met us *Daily* folk but offered to help us out. No, we're not going to run a picture of the body. I'm sorry you wasted a roll of film taking pictures of the body, but it's considered in poor taste to run things like that. Or is it poor taste? Won't it make the story more dramatic and compelling? This

---

From Diana L. Meredith, "Editor Questions Coverage Following Campus Tragedy," © 1989 by The DAILY, University of Washington. Reprinted with permission.

shooting really was a tragedy. Should the visual elements of the story try to sanitize that? Also, we compete with broadcast news, and they'll probably have rolling film showing everything.

Damn, there's another person on the phone wanting to know what happened. Everyone who knows someone who works here is calling to find out what's going on. The Seattle bureau of the Associated Press called here to find out the names of the victims.

How do you cover a homicide? I was at the scene, and I wanted to get the story, but I did not want to interfere or screw up the police work or hound witnesses who were probably already shaken up.

My reporters felt the same way. A broadcast reporter interrupted an interview that one of our reporters, Chris Welander, was conducting with a witness. The broadcast reporter wanted to interview this particular witness on camera. After the witness repeatedly refused to appear on camera, the reporter informed her that "this is a really big story."

This is a really big story. Yes, this is a really big story, and I must admit that I was relieved to have something to put on the front page. But as reporters we must not lose sight of what we deal with—tragedy, people's feelings and delicate situations that can get really messed up if reporters forget that they are there to observe, not interfere.

X. John Leonard wrote the following blast at daytime television in 1972, and you might ask yourself, as you read it, if things have changed much since then. While Leonard based the essay on his experience of watching three afternoon game shows (details of which he provides), he is able to imply a larger condemnation of the networks, the contestants, and the viewers. He does so with satire, allusions, and outrageous puns.

Nausea In The Afternoon

John Leonard

It has drizzled on you for a month; charity shrinks. You're trapped in New York City over a long summer weekend; hope doesn't spring, it autumns. You wander into a midtown Chinese bar for a pisco sour and the Mets game: faith moves bowels. And, naturally, it is raining even in Montreal; a washout with a French accent. But the bartender has taken so much trouble to achieve a pisco sour, and the color TV set is already warmed up, and although you've already done a column about daytime TV you were sick at the time and maybe you missed some nuances—so you watch:

a. *Three on a Match,* and/or *Let's Make a Deal*
b. *The Newlywed Game,* and/or suicide.

You don't remember which host afflicted which game show, for the same reason that you don't remember which urea derivative was responsible for which custom-compounded plastic. They all make the pisco sour.

Does anybody know what's going on on NBC and ABC while decent people are supposed to be eating lunch? Conscripts, refugees, miscreants, the flotsam of an affluent society are press-ganged into embarrassing themselves for half an hour in front of millions of analgesiacs. Bastards-of-ceremony whip them into giggledom. Dashboards and control panels elaborated unto gimcrackery swallow, spit, hiccough and vomit. Klaxons admonish. Categories—"Famous Bald Heads" is my personal favorite—flap like lapwings around the studio. Simpletons sigh, simper, seethe and savage one another. Never before have greed and speed conspired at such a stupefying tryst. Who wrote *Aunt Jemima's Cookbook?* I'm sorry, your thyme is upchuck.

Three on a Match is so complicated—their tic-tac-toe had to go into systems analysis to find out why it hates itself—that even the advertising agencies can't figure it out. Therefore there isn't

---

From THIS PEN FOR HIRE by John Leonard. Copyright © 1973 by John Leonard. Reprinted with permission of Doubleday, a division of Bantam, Doubleday, Dell Publishing Group, Inc.

any advertising, unless you count commercials for how NBC intended to cover the political conventions and why drunks shouldn't drive. It's like watching an Apollo lift-off, only with rubber bands. But it's a great mistake to switch channels. On ABC, they're making a deal. Some weirdo prowls up and down the aisles, waving hundred-dollar bills, asking members of the studio audience whether they've got a whale tooth or Linda Kasabian's autograph or Spanish fly. If they do have it, they can either keep the cash or opt for the unseen. The unseen—a Polaris submarine, Dean Martin's bladder, thirty-four years on the jungleboat at Disneyland, capital punishment—sits behind a curtain. Zowie.

Neither program is in a class with *The Newlywed Game,* ABC's midday answer to the Salem witch trials. To qualify as contestants you must be a recently married couple within pogo-sticking distance of Los Angeles; otherwise, skyjack a lapwing. A bunch of men troop onto the stage and guess how their wives would respond to such questions as, "Last night, your hugging and kissing were (1) heavyweight, (2) middleweight, (3) lightweight." I'm serious. I'm always serious. This was a real question. Then of course the wives appear and prove their husbands dunderheads. The sexes are reversed for the next round of hugger-muggering. Cute enough to make your teeth ache.

I wish Karl Marx were alive to watch *The Newlywed Game.* I wish Sigmund Freud were alive to do the same thing. I wish the two of them were newlywed, living at Malibu on a rented surfboard, so they qualified for the program. I'd like to see the Hegelian dialectic interpreted as a sex act, Hamlet pedaling his Oedipal cycle all the way to the United Fruit Company, workers risible, *Das Kapital mit Traumdeutung.* Hell, I'd like to see Simone de Beauvoir and Jean-Paul Sartre glaring at each other because they blew their big chance at free dining-room furniture. Id Kant happen, *Herren,* you will say. But it does, every weekday at 2 p.m., and the days get weaker by the minute.

XI. Steve Fay includes natural history among his professional interests, and that interest is evident in "The Drought Grapes." Drawing on entries from Steve's journal, this autobiographical essay is centered (like your meditation) in a particular place.

The Drought Grapes
Steve Fay

This soft, mid-September morning, there seems to be more moisture in the air than in all the days of July and August. The heavy dew, dripping off of the awning over the back door, has formed a damp circle on the cement porch. Shadows from the nearby trees still recline across the yard, but the row of oaks along the ravine a quarter-mile west already catches the full flare of the sun. This is the first morning in several days that I have stopped to notice such things; I am happy. I am going to visit the farm today.

You might think that everyone who lives on a farm visits it every time they are at home, but that is not always so. Farmers who raise livestock generally do; as the old country blues song goes, "You got to milk 'em in the morning and feed 'em, milk 'em in the evening, too." Most livestock require some kind of daily chores, and that goes double or triple for a dairy herd. Today, however, many farmers have stopped raising livestock altogether and have specialized in grain crops, such as corn and soybeans.

Grain farming requires a very busy spring and fall, but with modern farming methods, just a few trips over the field to cultivate or spray are all that is required during the growing season. There is enough time on weekends for driving by fields or examining ears, pods, or weed problems, so that many farmers have time to employ their intellects and skills off the farm, full- or part-time. In the slack weeks, they may come home in the evening from their other jobs, put their feet up and watch television, just like many a town resident, with days passing between the times when they actually walk the land.

Then, there are also farmers like me, who no one would call "real farmers," who may plant, but rarely harvest, who let every thing go wild. Having no real farm chores to drive them, they, too, may miss opportunities to visit their farms when their obligatory off-farm jobs or other involvements get the better of their weekly calendars.

Reprinted with permission of the author.

In addition to this loss among grain farmers of a daily ritualistic communion with their land, there are other practices which were common among farmers prior to 1950, but which now exist mainly as examples of what might be called the folklore of rural life. In some parts of the country, even the stereotypical farm vegetable garden falls into this category. In his 1973 book, *Country Matters* (NY: Dial), outdoor writer Vance Bourjaily describes a region of Iowa:

> I know a number of farm families around here, and hardly any of them raise much of their own food. Either it isn't economic or it isn't fun. The great repository of gardening and preserving knowledge is in the very small towns, rather than on farms. In these towns of under a thousand live the jam and pickle makers, the tomato canners, the adherents of special varieties of pole beans and cabbages. . . . In these towns live the retired farmers and their wives, and here, too, the sons and daughters who were raised on the farm and who miss it, but who now work in the larger town nearby as carpenters and nurses, master mechanics and elementary school teachers. (35-6)

Bourjaily does not find much evidence of this gardening passion among city dwellers, even those with rural roots. He dismisses the latter as persons who were ambitious for high wages, who probably had a revulsion for country life that helped to fuel their escape from the farm. He overlooked the times in the past, and times he might have anticipated in the future, when a short move to a town of 1000 would not bring the farmer's son or daughter within commuting distance of any employment at all. He also overlooked the farmer's grandchildren who may have had little to say in their parents' decision to move.

Aside from these oversights, Bourjaily does demonstrate one simple principle: living with the loss of some aspect of one's inherited way of life, whether it be the garden on the old home farm or something else, can lead to a fuller assessment of the value of that aspect and may also lead to attempts to preserve it either mentally or through some form of limited practice, such as a backyard garden.

In my own case, I was the grandson of farmers and the child of townfolk from a village of about 150 people. And when my father's grain elevator construction and repair business dried up, and when he followed a job offer to the Chicago area, there was little anyone in the family could say to the contrary. We moved.

I was five at the time, old enough to have stored up some vivid memories of small town life and visits to my grandparents' farm. Somehow the move walled off these memories, protecting them like bubbles of air locked away in the oldest chambers of a nautilus's shell. Perhaps just as importantly, the way back to those memories was constantly reinforced, by annual visits to west-central Illinois, by my mother's farm stories, and by the general statements and attitudes voiced by parents who did not live in the "Rat Race" entirely by choice. There was an old saying applied to me frequently during my childhood: "You can take the boy out of the country, but you can't take the country out of the boy." Never forgetting where I learned to pick wild blackberries, to fish in a pond, and to milk a cow, I grew up believing I was this maxim incarnate.

Of course, I adapted to the suburbs and lost my rural drawl early, when I learned to spell. It is also noteworthy that I never developed some of the skills, habits, and tastes of my country cousins, but I never, ever, put down roots in the city either. Something about my family moving between four different neighborhoods, sending me to five different schools during my childhood, may have had more than a little to do with that. Also, the influence of my parents' own demonstrated desires to escape the city on weekends as frequently as possible should not be underestimated. But more than these reasons, I believe it was a conscious wish to retain my rural identity that helped me to hold on to my dream of returning to the country for nearly thirty years, until at last it was possible.

There is something else though, something unconscious, something organic that drove me. Ethologists, who study both the learned and inherited aspects of behavior in animals, speak of a factor called a "habitat imprint." For example, young field mice in their first days of life store away key impressions of the habitat in which they were born and reared. When they reach maturity and must strike out on their own and find mates, they look for another meadow which conforms to this internal picture of home. If all the meadows are full to capacity with other field mice, then a few individuals may have to settle for some marginal area unlike their habitat imprints. These less fortunate mice live out lives of heightened stress, suffer from various maladies, and are not as likely to parent as many offspring.

Surely, humans are less mechanical than mice, have the will and ability to reason out their responses to their local environment, yes, of course. But how do I account for the feeling that a great weight is being lifted off my chest every time I come back west of Joliet? And how do I explain a decidedly physical exhilaration which I have always felt whenever I have been near the Mississippi or Illinois rivers? It was only a few years ago, while studying an Illinois map, that I discovered to my complete surprise that my old home town of Basco was no more than ten mile as the crow flies from the Mississippi. Had I inhaled the stream's chemical label years ago, like some Pacific salmon fry, and always retained the ability to sort this marker out of the gusty corn wind of my region? Who can say?

What about maladies or failures of reproduction? I do not know whether a tendency to be overweight fits in this model. What I do know is that well in advance of our marriage, when I realized that we would probably live for a time in the Chicago area where Pam was already employed, I said plainly to her that I never wanted to raise children in or near the city. And despite our not being able to extricate ourselves from that metropolitan area for twelve long years, we still delayed all plans for having children.

Looking back, I am struck by the gravity of the implication that this compulsion to go back to my home country might have greatly changed the sort of life that my wife might have wished to have had. Of course, neither of us ever expected to become trapped near Chicago as long as that, and the country dream was something that she grew to make her own to such an extent that, at one point when I had virtually given up hope, she retained the dream for me.

So, now we have been here a few short years and financial considerations are the chief questions clouding our plans to raise a family. I do not walk these forty acres of pasture and wooded ravines every day, as I imagined I would. In fact, this summer's drought drove me indoors for much of several weeks. I, however, am far more likely to walk the land in the fall, winter, and spring, when portly men can travel far with ease.

Today, I go to inspect the pond which is down at least five feet below the spill-pipe; the atmosphere above the olive-colored water buzzes with the same electric clatter of dragonfly wings that I heard at my grandfather's pond thirty-two years ago. Frogs and turtles raise their periscope eyes and heads to warily track my path along the water's edge. At a nearby fencerow, I pick two depauperate bunches of wild grapes; their concentrated tartness, more sour than alum, will be relished by anything wild trying to prepare for winter. Truly, any child of mine must relish all these things.

I, however, grew up in two worlds, and I know now that my value for the first was gained through contrast with the second, whether this was due to a conscious idea of preserving a rural identity, or some deep biological stress from being out of my element, or both of these aspects playing complementary roles. To value the country the same way I do, I know that my child must be exposed to rural experiences early in life, as was I. But, I suspect, it may also be necessary for that child to have some urban experience, or life, showing that what is common and good in the country cannot be taken for granted.

This last point raises the possibility that I might have to deal with a child who moves to the city and stays. I believe that this would not be as difficult for me to accept as you might think; you see, I was not repulsed by the city so much as I rejected it as "home." I learned to place a high value upon it as a center for the arts, as a place where cultures and nationalities meet, and as the home of some of my friends. Moreover, it might be impossible for my own child to understand me without spending some length of time in a large metropolitan area. Or to put it another way, the child of two worlds may have to expose his children to those same two worlds, if they are ever to share his values of either.

It may then be that the child of mine who travels furthest, on his or her infrequent visits home, will be first to hunker down and pick up a handful of this sticky tan soil and the last to tire of listening to the story of how the German immigrant farmers, settling the Military Tract, spurned the prairies and cut their fields out of the wooded hills that reminded them of home. This will be the child in whom the beliefs and values of the father and mother live on. This will be the child who will understand what it means for wild grapes to come through a drought.

XII. Robert Fulghum achieved popularity recently with his essay "Everything I Need to Know I Learned in Kindergarten" (also the title of his best-selling book). His essays attempt to find uncommon significance in common things, such as a childhood encounter with mushrooms.

Mushrooms
Robert Fulghum

The first time was at Aunt Violet's apartment on Embassy Row in Washington, D.C., the summer I turned thirteen. I had come by train all the way from Waco, Texas, to visit the Big City on the Potomac. Aunt Violet was a hard-core social climber, a lovable snob, an aspiring gourmet—and she thought my mother was a twit. All of which endeared Aunt Violet to me. Aunt Violet and I got along just fine. Until the night of the Big Dinner.

The lineup included a senator, a couple of generals, and assorted foreigners with their assorted ladies. A very large deal, indeed, for a kid from Waco who had been upholstered for the occasion by Aunt Violet with a striped seersucker suit and a bow tie. Tres chic! Glorious me!

Anyhow. Having asked if I could help with dinner, I was handed a paper bag and told to wash the contents and slice them salad thin. What was in the bag was mushrooms. Frilly-edged, mottled-brown, diseased-looking creepy things.

Now I had seen mushrooms and knew where they grew. In dark slimy places in the cow barn and the chicken yard at home. Once some grew out of a pair of tennis shoes I left in my gym locker over the summer. And fungus I knew because I had it between my toes from wearing the same tennis shoes every day for a year. But it had never occurred to me to handle mushrooms, much less wash and slice and eat them. (My father told me Washington was a strange and wicked place, and now I understood what he meant.) So I quietly put the whole bag down the trash chute, thinking it was a joke on the country-boy-come-to-the-city.

From EVERYTHING I NEED TO KNOW I LEARNED IN KINDERGARTEN by Robert Fulghum. Copyright © 1986, 1988 by Robert L. Fulghum. Reprinted by permission of Villiard Books/Random House.

Guess they must have been some mushrooms, considering how old Aunty Voilet carried on when she found out. To this day I'm convinced that's why she left me out of her will when she died. I had no class. I confess that I still regard mushrooms and mushroom eaters with a great deal of suspicion. Oh, I've acquired the necessary veneer of pretentious sophistication all right—enough to eat the things when invited out to eat and to keep my opinions to myself, so I'm cool and all. But I still don't understand about mushrooms and mushrooms eaters—not entirely, anyhow.

In fact, there's a whole lot of things I don't understand about entirely—some large, some small. I keep a list, and the list gets longer and longer as I get older and older. For example, here's a few mysteries I added this year:

Why are grocery carts made with one wheel that has a mind of its own and runs cock-eyed to the other three?
Why do so many people close their eyes when they brush their teeth?
Why do people believe that pushing an elevator button several times will make the car come quicker?
Why can't we just spell it "orderves" and get it over with?
Why do people drop a letter in the mailbox and then open the lid again to see if it really went down?
Why are there zebras?
Why do people put milk cartons back into the fridge with just a tiny bit of milk left in the bottom?
Why aren't there any traditional Halloween carols?
Why does every tree seem to have one old stubborn leaf that just won't let go?
Is the recent marketing of cologne for dogs a sign of anything?

I know. Those aren't what you'd call industrial strength mysteries. All the big-ticket things I don't understand are at the beginning of the list, and have been for a long time. Things like electricity and how homing pigeons do what they do and why you can't get to the end of rainbows. And even further up toward the beginning of the list of things I don't understand are the real big ones. Like why people laugh and what art is really for and why

God doesn't fix some things or finish the job. And at the top of the list is why is there life, anyway, and how come I have to die?

Which brings me back to the subject of mushrooms. They were in this salad I was served for New Year's dinner, and I got to wondering about mushrooms again. So I got the encyclopedia out and read up on them a little. Fungi they are—the fruiting body, the sporophore of fungi. The dark underworld of living things—part of death, disease, decay, rot. Things that make their way in the world by feeding upon decaying matter. Yeast, smuts, mildews, molds, mushrooms—maybe one hundred thousand different kinds, maybe more, nobody knows for sure.

They're everywhere. In the soil, the air, in lakes, seas, river, rain, in food and clothing, inside you and me and everybody else—doing their thing. Without fungi there's not the loaf of bread or the jug of wine or even thou. Bread, wine, cheese, beer, good company, rare steaks, fine cigars—all moldy. The fungi, says the big book, "are responsible for the disintegration of organic matter and the release into the soil or atmosphere of the carbon, oxygen, nitrogen, and phosphorus that would forever be locked up in dead plants and animals and all people as well." Fungi—midwives between death and life and death and life again and again and yet again.

There is a terrible and wondrous truth working here. Namely, that all things live only if something else is cleared out of the path to make way. No death; no life. No exceptions. Things must come and go. People. Years. Ideas. Everything. The wheel turns, and the old is cleared away as fodder for the new.

And I picked at the mushrooms in that New Year's salad and ate them with respect if not enthusiasm. Wondering at what is going and coming. Quietly awed into silence by what I understand but cannot tell. Borne by grace downstream where I see but cannot say.

And so let's begin:

Bruce Leland

Index

"About Ethics," 158–169
Academic Writing, 111–147
Active Reading, 157
Ambiguity, 61–80
Ambiguity, 63–66, 107
Analysis of Writing 214–215, 216
Audience, 58, 77–78, 109, 133–137, 150–152, 214–215
"August 28th—A Meditation," 68–70

Baker, Russell, 235–237
Bambara, Toni Cade, 178–185
"Begin at the Beginning," 18–25
"Blackie's Death," 44–47
Blind Writing, 199
Blocks, 218–219, 222–223
Boldface, 224
Booting, 18
Brainstorming, 199, 212
"Brothers and Sisters," 231–235

Centering a Line, 224
Charters, Brian, 3
"Christmas Vacation," 51–58
"Church Going," 66–68
Clemons, Rick, 128–132
Clustering, 200–201
Collaborative Learning, 211
Composition of Place, 62
Computer, 9–27, 217–226
Computer Keyboard, 24, 226
Copying Files, 217–218
Cording, Sue, 68–70
Cosby, Bill, 228–230
Courter, Jim, 6–7, 240–242
"Covering Campus Tragedy," 259–260
Crouse, Darby, 120–123
Cubing, 38
Cursor, 180

"Darwin's Delay," 138–143
Deleting Text, 20, 25, 222–223
Details, 77
Development Draft, 203

Dialog, 198–199
Digression, 79–80, 149–150
Directory (Disk), 23, 25
Discovery Draft, 202–203
Disk Directory, 23, 25
Diversity, 81–110
Donley, Gregory Alan, 48–50
Drafting, 188, 202–204
"Drought Grapes, The," 263–267

Eberle, Judy, 124–127
Education Resources Information, 129–130
ERIC, 129–130
Error, 144–147
Essay Exams, 149–153
Ethics, 155–189
Etter, Dave, 144
Exiting a File, 23
Experience (Writing About), 41–60

Fay, Steve, 263–267
Feedback, 213–216
Finding a Topic, 119
"Fishes and Pike," 171
"Flora Rutherford: Postcard," 144
"Form and Content," 3
Formal Analysis, 216
"Forty-One Phone Book Names," 82–83
Free-Writing, 37
Frost, Robert, 176
Fulghum, Robert, 268–270
Function Keys, 19, 25

Gould, Stephen Jay, 138–143
Government Documents, 129–130
Grammar, 144–147
"Grate," 230–231
"Gravedigger: Elmer Ruiz," 99–103
Groups, 77–78, 136–137, 211–216
"Gutenberg Was Through," 10–16

Habib, Siraj, 105–107
Hallwas, John, 172–175

271

Harlan, Mary, 82–83
"Heinz's Dilemma," 170–171
Heroes, 172–175, 185–186
"Holiday Shoplifting Carries Big Pricetag," 115–118

"I'm Used to It," 85–89
Illinet, 128, 130–132
Information (Writing About), 111–147
Insert Key, 18–19
Insert Text, 19, 25
Internal Colloquy, 62
Interview, 31, 83–85
Invention, 36–39, 197–201
"It Doesn't Only Happen in America," 105–107
"It's All in the Jeans," 240–242

Jackson, David, 230–231
Jacobus, Kris, 18–25, 217–226
Journal, 5–7, 26, 34–35, 82, 108, 143, 193–196, 201
Jow, Ebrima, 255–259
Justifying Text, 224–225

Keyboard, 24, 226

Larkin, Philip, 65, 66–68
Leonard, John, 261–262
"Lesson, The," 178–185
Library, 128–132
Library Computer System, 128, 130–132
Library of Congress System, 129
Linewrap, 19
Listing, 37–38, 113
Looping, 37
Lopez, Rose, 114–115
LSC (Library Computer System), 128, 130–132

Mairs, Nancy, 242–254
Manon, Carshon, 44–47
"Mason, The: Carl Murray Bates," 89–94
Mayhew, Henry, 85–89
Mechanics, 144–147
Meditation, 61–80, 201
Meditation,
 Composition of Place, 62
 Internal Colloquy, 62
 Resolution, 63
Memory, 47
Merideth, Diana, 259–260
Moving Cursor, 22
Moving Text, 137, 218–219
Murray, Toss, 33–34
"Mushrooms," 268–270

Narrative, 107
"Nausea in the Afternoon," 261–262
Norton, Kay, 115–118

"On Being a Cripple," 242–254
"Once More to the Lake," 70–76
Ong, Walter, 134
Opening a File, 19–20
"Opening the Tap," 6–7
Organization, 79–80, 135–137

Peer Editing, 136–137
Plagiarism, 187
Pointing, 213–214
Previewing (Reading), 156
Prewriting, 36–39, 188, 197–201
Printing a File, 22, 25
Process, x, 29–39, 197–206
"Process of Writing, A," 33–34
"Promoting Hispanic Culture," 114–115
Prompt, 18
Proofreading, 146–147
Purpose, 59–60, 118–119

Questioning, 197–206

Reader, 58, 77–78, 109, 133–137, 146–147, 150–152, 214–215
Reader Response to Writing, 215–216
Reading, 156–157
Reading Aloud, 206, 212–213
"Reasons for Attendance," 65
Recursiveness in Writing, 188–189
Reporter's Formula, 197
Resolution, 63
Responding to Writing, 213–216
Restoring Text, 223
"Return of the Hero, The," 172–175
Reviewing (Reading), 157
Revision, 79–80, 108–110, 204–206
"Road Not Taken, The," 176

Saving a File, 20–21, 25
Saving to Another Disk, 21
Sayback, 213
"School Day, The," 255–259
Self-Analysis of Writing, 204–206
Sinclair, Upton, 171
Singer, Peter, 158–169
Spell Check, 219–221
Status Line, 18
Stewart, Donald, 62
Sudgen, Faye, 238–240
"Survivors," 171

"Table Talk," 238–240
"Telephone Operator: Heather Lamb," 94–99

Template, 19
Terkel, Studs, 89–103
"Theatre at its Best," 120–123
Thesaurus, 221–222
Thesis, 136, 151, 204
"To Spank or Not to Spank," 124–127
Toth, Susan Allen, 51–58
Tracking-Switching, 198
Trail Draft, 202
"Turn That Crap Down," 228–230
Typeover, 19

Underlining, 224

Values, 155–189
Villaneuva, Yolanda, 4
"Visit From My Grandfather, A," 48–50

"Western Illinois University Library, The," 128–132
Walker, Alice, 231–235
"What's Important," 4
White, E.B., 70–76
Windows, 223–224
"Wonders of Writing on a Computer, The," 235–237
Word Processing, 9–27
WordPerfect, 17, 18–25, 217–226
WordPerfect,
　Blocks, 218–219, 222–223
　Boldface, 224
　Booting, 18
　Centering, 224
　Copying Files, 217–218

Cursor, 18
Deleting Text, 20, 25, 222–223
Directory, 23, 25
Exiting, 23, 25
Function Keys, 19, 25
Help, 19, 25
Insert Key, 18–19
Insert Text, 19, 25
Justifying, 224–225
Keyboard, 24, 226
Linewrap, 19
Moving Cursor, 22, 25
Moving Text, 137, 218–219
Opening a File, 19–20
Printing a File, 22, 25
Prompt, 18
Restoring Text, 223
Saving a File, 20–21, 25
Saving to Another Disk, 21
Spell Check, 219–221
Status Line, 18
Template, 19
Thesaurus, 221–222
Typeover, 19
Underline, 224
Windows, 223–224
Working, 89–103
Writing Process, x, 29–39, 197–206
Writing to Learn, 29–30
Writing with a Computer, 25–26

Zinsser, William, 10–16